ROUTLEDGE LIBRARY EDITIONS:
THE INDUSTRIAL REVOLUTION

Volume 7

ECONOMIC ARITHMETIC

T0271826

ECONOMIC ARITHMETIC

A Guide to the Statistical Sources of
English Commerce, Industry,
and Finance
1700–1850

STANLEY H. PALMER

Routledge
Taylor & Francis Group

LONDON AND NEW YORK

First published in 1977 by Garland Publishing, Inc.

This edition first published in 2017
by Routledge
2 Park Square, Milton Park, Abingdon, Oxon OX14 4RN

and by Routledge
711 Third Avenue, New York, NY 10017

Routledge is an imprint of the Taylor & Francis Group, an informa business

© 1977 Stanley H. Palmer

British Library Cataloguing in Publication Data
A catalogue record for this book is available from the British Library

ISBN: 978-1-138-63291-2 (Set)
ISBN: 978-1-315-16309-3 (Set) (ebk)
ISBN: 978-1-138-70762-7 (Volume 7) (hbk)
ISBN: 978-1-138-70764-1 (Volume 7) (pbk)
ISBN: 978-1-315-20136-8 (Volume 7) (ebk)

Publisher's Note
The publisher has gone to great lengths to ensure the quality of this reprint but points out that some imperfections in the original copies may be apparent.

Disclaimer
The publisher has made every effort to trace copyright holders and would welcome correspondence from those they have been unable to trace.

Britannia Claiming the Wealth of the World

From J. Savary des Bruslons, *Universal Dictionary of Trade and Commerce*,
tr. M. Postlethwayt, 1751-55

Economic Arithmetic

A Guide to the
Statistical Sources of English
Commerce, Industry, and Finance
1700-1850

Stanley H. Palmer

Garland Publishing, Inc., New York & London

1977

Library of Congress Cataloging in Publication Data

Palmer, Stanley H
   Economic arithmetic.

   (Garland reference library of social science ;
v. 26)
   Bibliography: p.
   Includes index.
   1. England--Statistics--History--Sources--
Bibliography. 2. England--Economic conditions--
1760-1860--Sources--Bibliography. I. Title.
Z7554.G7P34 [HC254.5]   016.33'09'41   76-42890
ISBN 0-8240-9946-X

Printed in the United States of America

The materials, therefore, had to be collected and arranged by degrees, and to be drawn from original sources; and in this manner, the data sought for became the nucleus which has gradually expanded into the substance and capacity of a considerable volume. Of the incompleteness, the multifold imperfections of such a work, especially in its first edition; the tendency to error; the innumerable gaps and blanks that remain to be filled up, no one can be so well aware, probably, as its author. An unequal acquisition of statistical details is the inevitable result of all such undertakings. It will not, we admit, be difficult to point out these deficiencies, and critics may suggest abundant omissions and emendations, in this volume. However, as there must be some limit to the accumulative process and some cessation from the collector's toil, it has now become necessary to bring it to a close, and to commit it to the indulgence of the public.

—R. Taylor, *Statistics of Coal* (1848),
preface, p. iii

And here I may be permitted to observe, that, though I possessed the greatest elegance of stile, to which I make no pretension, the nature of the work presents but few opportunities, of which our most brilliant writers could avail themselves to display the captivating graces of their composition. If I have merely put proper words in proper places, I seek no further embellishments, content with humble praise, if it shall be allowed me, of having given the compressed commercial substance of many thousands of books, official papers, and accounts, and having collected a great thesaurus of solid materials, out of which a skilful architect may, with comparative ease, erect a very magnificent edifice.

—D. Macpherson, *Annals of Commerce* (4 v., 1805), I,
preface, p. xvii

Contents

Frontispiece (Britannia Claiming the Wealth of the World)

CONTENTS

Tables

Foreword

Economic history has always been the most quantitative branch of history, reflecting the interests and profiting from the techniques and concepts of economics. This emphasis on numerical data and their manipulation has increased markedly in recent years as a new generation of economic historians, trained as economists, has attacked old problems with new methods and posed questions unanswerable before. The so-called new economic history has thus enhanced more than ever the importance of numerical information, and it is no coincidence that recent years have seen the appearance of important compendia of historical statistics, in particular the revised edition of the *Historical Statistics of the United States* and Mitchell and Deane's *Abstract of British Historical Statistics.*

The essay that follows is a contribution to the swelling stream of quantitative historiography. It deals with that aspect of the sources that we know least and need most help with: the numerical data of the period that antedates the appearance of official statistical bureaus and systematic publication. In this regard, students of British history are more richly furnished than those of most other nations, for characteristically British reasons. It was not that the British government of the eighteenth century, like the cameralist regimes of central Europe, was especially curious about the performance of the economy; the one area where it made an effort to inform itself and keep records was that of tax revenues. It was the intellectual curiosity and personal initiative of private citizens—some of them, to be sure, employed in government service—that led to the collection and preservation of some of our most valuable series. Much of this initiative, moreover, was the direct outgrowth of the relative political freedom that Britain enjoyed: this was a nation whose precocious parliamentary development encouraged legislative curiosity and public debate, which in turn put a premium on supporting evidence. The contrast is particularly striking with France, where an inefficient monarchy feared the embarrassment and withdrawal of confidence that might ensue from a publication of facts and a debate on their meaning. Whereas those Frenchmen who sought to learn and analyze the facts were discouraged, to the point of personal disgrace, and their books were published, if at all, abroad, the British developed a school of "political arithmeticians" who invented the questions and methods of economic statistics for future generations and anticipated the techniques of national accounting.

In view of the potential value of these early statistical materials, Stanley Palmer's critical guide to the sources is specially welcome. We are all grateful for the remarkable collection of data provided in Mitchell and Deane; but these data are necessarily selective, hence incomplete, and they have already been processed. This makes them easier to work with, but only up to a point. Insofar as these early series are themselves the product of considerable manipulation, the historian who wants to work with them would be well advised to consult the original sources for information on their character, significance, and limitations. Here the Palmer bibliography will prove invaluable, not only for materials extracted by Mitchell and Deane, but for much other data as well.

The Palmer essay is based on materials available in the Harvard libraries, including the remarkable Kress collection of early writings in economics. This local focus necessarily limits its coverage: there is no doubt that an extensive survey of materials in British libraries, for example, would turn up other data. Given the richness of the Harvard collections, however, it is reasonable to assume that such increments of information would be largely peripheral—witness the extent to which Palmer's coverage goes beyond that of Mitchell and Deane. While *Economic Arithmetic* is a particularly valuable tool for those working or able to work in the Boston area, its value is considerably enhanced by a massive microfilming project, now partially completed, of the Goldsmiths'-Kress Library of Economic Literature. Now the scholar, whether he reads printed materials at Harvard or reels of microfilm on his own campus, will be able, with Palmer's guide at his elbow, to extract desired statistical data from the rich quarries of the Kress collection.

David S. Landes

Preface

Economic Arithmetic was born, almost a decade ago, in a graduate seminar at Harvard. In the years since 1967, it has survived childhood, passed through an occasionally irksome adolescence, and at length matured into adulthood, or, at any rate, into this final form. It is hoped that the present work will serve as a useful handbook to the sources of English economic statistics from 1700 to 1850. By consulting the following pages, scholars will be able to determine whether a desired statistical series exists in published form, and, if so, where *precisely* in a particular source it may be found. In their own research future writers should be spared some of the time-consuming, and often tedious, detective work which has produced this guide.

The utility of the book was originally limited to scholars working in the shadow of great rare book libraries: principally, the Kress Library at Harvard and the Goldsmiths' Library at the University of London. Since 1972, however, a major microform publication project has increased considerably the value of *Economic Arithmetic*. Research Publications, Inc.* is photographing a complete set of the holdings of the Kress and Goldsmiths' Libraries. This herculean undertaking—succinctly titled, the Goldsmiths'-Kress Library of Economic Literature will be complete in three Segments. "Segment 1: Printed Books through 1800," which is now available, incorporates approximately 30,000 works on about 1,500 reels of microfilm. Work on "Segment 2: Printed Books 1801-1850" will begin in 1976. "Segment 3: Serials and Periodicals through 1850" will follow. For easy reference, the complete set will include a multi-volume printed, hardbound *Consolidated Guide*, arranged in a year/subject/alphabetical format; for each title there will also be a

---

*12 Lunar Drive, New Haven, Connecticut 06525.

PREFACE

standard catalogue card. It is no exaggeration to say that the photographic reproduction of these two rare book libraries constitutes a revolution in economic historiography. Scholars in the last quarter of the twentieth century, freed from the necessity of visiting Boston or London, will be able to conduct significant primary research in any number of places around the globe.

Economic Arithmetic has been a solitary project, but along the way a number of people have given me advice, help, and encouragement. David Landes of the History Department at Harvard presided at the beginning and is present at the conclusion. Kenneth Carpenter, Curator of the Kress Library of Business and Economics, has pointed out references, answered questions, and guided me through the holdings on more occasions than I care to remember. Marion McClintock, his assistant, responded to my demands for printed materials with patience and promptitude. In Arlington, Toni Bost, who typed the manuscript, uncomplainingly did as I told her. From the beginning, my parents have been constant in their encouragement and support. Finally, my South African wife, Bettie, by her help in proofreading and indexing, and in many less tangible ways, has enabled me to complete the great trek.

University of Texas at Arlington   *Stanley H. Palmer*
March, 1976

Economic Arithmetic

"To declaim on commerce is as needless as haranguing learnedly on the bene-fit of air, rain, and sunshine," pronounced an historian of commerce in the middle of the eighteenth century. So rhapsodic was Malachy Postlethwayt on the benefits of trade that he presented a full-page drawing of a sceptred Britannia who, surrounded by kneeling and admiring peoples, both received and dispensed the wealth of the world. Below the picture is the legend:

O' Britain chosen Port of Trade
May Lux'ry ne'er thy Sons invade;
Wherever neighb'ring States contend,
'Tis thine to be the gen'ral Friend.

What is 't who rules in other Lands?
On Trade alone thy Glory stands.
That Benefit is unconfin'd,
Diffusing Good among Mankind.

That first gave Lustre to thy Regions,
And scatter'd Plenty o'er thy Plains:
'Tis that alone thy Wealth Supplies.
And draws all Europe's envious Eyes.

Be Commerce then thy sole Design:
Keep that, and all the World is thine.[1]

Postlethwayt's book appeared on the eve of England's great century of politi-cal and economic development: by the middle of the next century England would be indisputably the world's supreme commercial and industrial nation.[2] As the nation grew in wealth and power, Englishmen turned to the painstaking recording of the statistics of expansion.

[1]The picture is reproduced as the frontispiece to the present work. Jacques Savary des Bruslons, *The Universal Dictionary of Trade and Commerce,* translated from the French with large additions and improvements by Malachy Postlethwayt (2 v., London, 1751-55), I, frontis., 542. The lines are from Gay's poem, "To His Native Country," v. 2, fable 8, reprinted on the frontispiece. *Hereafter, for all books and pamphlets, place of publication is London unless otherwise specified.*

[2]See Paul Mantoux, *The Industrial Revolution in the Eighteenth Century,* tr. by M. Vernon (1928); Phyllis Deane, *The First Industrial Revolution* (Cambridge, 1965); Phyllis Deane and W. A. Cole, *British Economic Growth, 1688-1959* (Cambridge, 1962; 2nd ed., 1967); and David S. Landes, *The Unbound Prometheus* (Cambridge, 1969), ch. 2.

The two main sources for commercial statistics are the Ledgers of the Custom House for the period 1696-1780 and the Reports on the State of the Navigation, Commerce and Revenue of Great Britain from 1772 onwards.[3] The Ledgers list data for the total import and export trade of a country or region with England but, unfortunately, do not break down those figures into particular commodities. This may be explained because the government before the end of the eighteenth century was interested more in the balance of trade with a region than in the direction and amount of flow of selected commodities. On the other hand, the Ledgers do have the virtue of recording the amount of trade passing through London and the outports: hence, the relative importance of London is constantly being measured. In 1772, with the start of the Trade and Navigation Accounts, important changes were made in statistical recording. Some geographical detail is lost: British overseas possessions lose their individuality and are grouped regionally (e.g., American figures after 1783 are no longer by state but by nation). Also, unfortunately, there are no longer separate returns for London and the outports. These losses, however, are far outweighed by the gain of the new classification of commodities, so that trends in the trade of goods to different parts of the world are now possible to follow.[4]

Access to the sources of trade statistics before 1801 has been difficult for historians. Either the data were not in printed form, or, if so, were scattered. The best printed government sources in the eighteenth century for economic data are the *Journals of the House of Commons* (43 v., 1699-1800). Until 1801 the tables are scattered in the text, but from 1801 to 1834 (volumes 57 to 89) each volume contains thick appendices of scores of tables.[5]

[3]The Ledgers for 1696-97 and 1716-76 are in the London Custom House, with copies from 1696 to 1780 at the Public Record Office (reference: Customs 2, 3). The volumes for 1704-05, 1711-12, and 1726-27 are missing. The Trade and Navigation Accounts appear in the annual Finance Accounts of the *Parliamentary Papers* of the House of Commons, 1801-53. From 1854 to 1920 they are in the Annual Statement of Trade in the *Parliamentary Papers*. The accounts from 1772 to 1800 are not comprehensively printed in the *Journals of the House of Commons*, but much scattered data exists. For the years before 1801 E.B. Schumpeter, *English Overseas Trade Statistics, 1696-1808* (Oxford, 1960) is the best source to be consulted. Hereafter, this work is cited simply as 'Schumpeter.'

[4]See T.S. Ashton's introduction, in Schumpeter, 1-2.

[5]There are innumerable subject headings: wool and woolens, linen, silk, cotton, copper, tin, coal, etc. Commerce or trade is rendered as "Imports and Exports." Banking has such headings as "Country Bankers," "Bank of England," "Bullion," and "Bankruptcy." For finance, the headings are "Consolidated Fund," "Revenue," and "National Debt." There is no heading for Prices.

There are two indexes, one for 1801-20; the other, for 1821-37.[6] Especially rich for economic data are the volumes for 1801-20. After 1820 many of the economic statistics were printed instead in the Sessional Papers of Parliament, also known as the *Parliamentary Papers*.

The *Parliamentary Papers* are the basic nineteenth-century government source for economic data, as the *Journals* were for the eighteenth century. Each printed paper has a number, each year has from a dozen to six dozen volumes, and there is a convenient subject index for 1801-52. While the *Journals* average roughly one volume a year, the *Parliamentary Papers* are much more valuable. In the eighteenth century the annual output was small, with the period 1775-1800 averaging three volumes a year; this level of output, however, was a great increase over the period 1731-74 which produced four volumes. The nineteenth century witnessed the real explosion of output, with the annual average for 1801-29 being sixteen volumes and for 1830-50, forty-one volumes. In a thirty year period, from 1800 to 1830, the annual output had increased over thirteen times.[7]

G. N. Clark[8] was the first modern writer to make an assault on the mass of trade statistics. In 1938, in a "Catalogue of Statistical Materials," a long appendix in his handbook, he set forth a long and impressive bibliography of contemporary statistics in the form of a chart which ran for fifty-three pages.[9] The chart ranges from 1696 to 1782, specifying the commodity traded, whether by value or quantity, whether import or export, from which place to which, the dates covered, the document reference and date of the return, and remarks. This pioneering work was invaluable. But there were problems. The chart was arranged chronologically, not topically, and the types of measurement varied between quantity and value, so that the reader who was interested in a particular industry or commodity was left with much homework.

These 'problems' were probably the impetus for Elizabeth Boody Schumpeter, widow of the great economist, Joseph Schumpeter, to set about transcribing the entire Custom House Ledgers (1696-1780) and the Trade and Navigation Accounts (1772-1808). Her final product, published at the urging of T. S. Ashton, was the monumental *English Overseas Trade Statistics, 1696-1808* (1960).

[6]The index for 1801-20 was published in 1825, with a preface by the demographer, John Rickman.

[7]The count includes annual index volumes but excludes the two or three volumes each year dealing with reports or petitions and the votes and proceedings in Parliament.

[8]George Norman Clark (1890-   ) was a Fellow of All Souls College, Oxford (1931-43) at the time of writing his *Guide*. He has been Regius Professor of Modern History at Trinity College, Cambridge (1943-47) and Provost of Oriel College, Oxford (1947-57). He was knighted in 1953. Among his many other books are *The Seventeenth Century* (Oxford, 1929; 2nd ed., 1947), *The Later Stuarts, 1660-1714* (Oxford, 1934; 2nd ed., 1955; being v. 10 in the *Oxford History of England*, of which Clark was general editor), *The Wealth of England from 1496 to 1760* (1946), *Early Modern Europe from about 1450 to about 1720* (1957), and *War and Society in the Seventeenth Century* (Cambridge, 1958).

[9]G. N. Clark, *Guide to English Commercial Statistics, 1696-1782* (1938), 153-206. Hereafter, this work is cited simply as 'Clark.'

Entirely tabular in presentation, the work sets out data by subject, within each topic chronologically, and by value or quantity. The result is a comprehensive systematic work of reference indispensible to researchers. Historians, for the first time, could follow the trends in the trade of specific commodities. As Ashton advertised in his preface for fellow historians: "Freed from the burden of transcription and calculation, which bore heavily on their predecessors, they should be able to bring fresh minds" to interpreting the data.[10] For all its excellence, though, Mrs. Schumpeter's work did have a few shortcomings. It ended in 1808, hardly a logical cut-off, as the Industrial Revolution was then moving into high gear. It contained only trade statistics—important, to be sure—but lacked output, wages, price and other data. Lastly, by basing her book solely on the Ledgers and Trade and Navigation Accounts, Schumpeter did not use the multiplicity of sources which Clark had mentioned.

Following Schumpeter's work, Brian Mitchell and Phyllis Deane of the Department of Applied Economics at Cambridge collaborated to publish a volume of numerous statistical series[11] made possible by Schumpeter's arduous transcriptions but to which they added some improvements. Mitchell and Deane presented trade series considerably beyond 1808, indeed, up to 1959, and furnished data on wages and output as well. The greater breadth of this handbook is indicated by its sections on Population, Vital Statistics, and the Labor Force.[12]

'Mitchell and Deane,' like 'Schumpeter,' are now household words to economic historians. Why, then, another book on the subject? First, it is useful to show the comparability of parts of Mitchell and Deane's data with Schumpeter's. Secondly, there are many commercial and industrial statistics not printed in Schumpeter's work which are missing in Mitchell and Deane as well. Perhaps most importantly, neither Schumpeter nor Mitchell and Deane mention the many contemporary books and pamphlets which printed tables of statistics. The data in the government sources and in books and pamphlets may be compared for accuracy with the data given by Schumpeter and Mitchell and Deane. They may also fill gaps in the series provided in Clark, Schumpeter, and Mitchell and Deane.

(b) Purposes and Procedures

The purpose of this essay is to point out the contemporary awakening to and development of statistical recording of England's expansion to world supremacy. Based on the library resources of Harvard University, the essay traces topically from 1700 to 1850 the private and public chronicling of the details and dimensions of the economic revolution which transformed England.

[10] T. S. Ashton, in Schumpeter, 14.

[11] B. R. Mitchell, with the collaboration of P. Deane, *Abstract of British Historical Statistics* (Cambridge, 1962).

[12] A supplement, *Second Abstract of British Historical Statistics*, by B. R. Mitchell and H. G. Jones (Cambridge, 1971), carries many of the series through 1965.

In a work of this scope, selection is inevitable, and I have chosen to concentrate on commerce and industry, deliberately avoiding agriculture and national income.[13]

This essay is, in some ways, like a tour. There are different kinds of tours, and this one is meant to be a short but comprehensive visit to a dozen regions. It is not a long and critical sojourn in a few areas: there are too many monuments in each area. Let it be understood at the outset that it is a shortcoming—this quick visit—of which the author is aware. But the journey cannot be a whirlwind tour simply because of the vast resources in the Kress Library at Harvard.

A word on methodology. First, the author checked references in G. N. Clark's *Guide to English Commercial Statistics*, in Mitchell and Deane's *Abstract of British Historical Statistics*, in Deane and Cole's *British Economic Growth, 1688-1959*, and in other secondary literature. Then the procedure consisted, quite simply, of perusing Judith Williams' bibliography,[14] R. D. Collison Black's recent work,[15] J. R. McCulloch's *Literature of Political Economy*,[16]

[13]On agriculture, see William Marshall, *The Review and Abstract of the County Reports to the Board of Agriculture, from the Several Agricultural Departments of England* (5 v., New York, 1818); James Edwin Thorold Rogers, *A History of Agriculture and Prices in England, from the Year after the Oxford Parliament (1259) to the Commencement of the Continental War (1793)* (7 v., Oxford, 1866-1902); Rowland E. Prothero, Baron Ernle, *English Farming, Past and Present* (6th ed., 1961); Christabel S. Orwin and E. H. Whetham, *A History of British Agriculture, 1846-1914* (1964); Jonathan David Chambers and Gordon E. Mingay, *The Agricultural Revolution, 1750-1880* (1966); Herbert P. Finberg, ed., *The Agrarian History of England and Wales* (4 v., Cambridge, 1967); Eric Kerridge, *The Agricultural Revolution* (1967); John M. Stratton, *Agricultural Records, A.D. 220-1968* (1969). Mitchell and Deane, *Abstract of British Historical Statistics* (Cambridge, 1962), ch. 3, "Agriculture," has eleven statistical series. Hereafter, this work is cited as 'Mitchell and Deane.'

On national income, consult the researches and estimates of Phyllis Deane: "The Implications of the Early National Income Estimates for the Measurement of Long-Term Economic Growth in the United Kingdom," *Economic Development and Cultural Change*, IV (1955), 3-38; "Contemporary Estimates of the National Income in the First Half of the Nineteenth Century," *Economic History Review*, 2nd ser., VIII (1956), 339-54; and "The Industrial Revolution and Economic Growth: the Evidence of the Early British National Income Estimates," *Economic Development and Cultural Change*, V (1957), 159-74. See also Phyllis Deane and W. A. Cole, *British Economic Growth, 1688-1959* (2nd ed., Cambridge, 1967), ch. 5. Hereafter, this work is cited as 'Deane and Cole.'

[14]J. B. Williams, *A Guide to the Printed Materials for English Social and Economic History, 1750-1850* (2 v., New York, 1926).

[15]R. D. Collison Black, *A Catalogue of Pamphlets on Economic Subjects published between 1750 and 1900 and now housed in Irish Libraries* (New York, 1969). Three-fifths of the book's 632 pages deal with works published through 1850.

[16]John Ramsay McCulloch, *The Literature of Political Economy: a classi-*

and the four-volume *Catalogue* of the Kress Library.[17] Hundreds of books
which the catalogue noted as having tables were then called out: without
this notation, my task would have been impossible. Indeed, the absence of
such a notation in the Goldsmiths' Library's *Catalogue*[18] deterred me from
using that bibliography. This methodological deficiency is not significant,
thanks to a general overlap in English economic history holdings at Kress.
The journals of the London Statistical Society and the Society for the Encouragement of Commerce, Arts, and Manufactures were checked. Further, with
the help of indexes, all the pertinent volumes of the *Journals of the House
of Commons* and the *Parliamentary Papers* were scoured.

(c) Pitfalls in the Statistics

The trade statistics are loaded with landmines for the unwary. One of the
dangers is geographical. Until 1707 Scotland was treated as a foreign country in the statistics, but after that date exports from Scotland to England
which were thence exported were counted as English exports, not Scottish or
British. Beginning in 1761 Scotland's trade figures were listed separately;
this was continued in the Trade and Navigation Accounts after 1772. Ireland
until 1814 was treated as a foreign country; in that year the first summary
table for the United Kingdom appeared. A government paper in 1830 issued
trade statistics for the United Kingdom back to 1798.[19] A recurring problem
in all the figures is the fickleness of the measurement: one must always
watch to see if the statistic refers to England, England and Wales, Britain,
or the United Kingdom.[20]

Within the statistics themselves there are, first of all, errors of commission. The calendar one is not serious, so long as records are consistent.[21]
But deliberately false entries and entries which are figments of the imagina-

*fied catalogue of select publications in the different departments of that
science, with historical, critical, and biographical notices* (1845). Useful
for its index and organization, but most of all for McCulloch's opinions.

[17]Kress Library of Business and Economics, *Catalogue Covering Material
Published through 1776* (Boston, 1940); *Catalogue, 1777-1817* (Boston, 1957);
Catalogue, 1818-1848 (Boston, 1964); *Supplement, 1473-1848* (Boston, 1967).

[18]University of London Library, *Catalogue of the Goldsmiths' Library of
Economic Literature*, v. 1, compiled by Margaret Canney and David Knott, introduction by J. H. P. Pafford (Cambridge, 1970). Covering books published
through 1800, it is arranged by subject within each year, but does not have
an index. Unlike the Kress catalogue and Black's bibliography, there is no
indication of tables in the collations. The second volume of the *Catalogue*,
covering the period 1801-1850, was published in 1975. The third volume
will catalogue the library's manuscripts and periodicals, and will provide
an index to the completed set.

[19]See British *Parliamentary Papers 1830-31* (20), X, 263-67, the return
being dated April 5, 1830. Hereafter cited as *P.P.*

[20]Ashton, in Schumpeter, 9.

[21]T. S. Ashton, *Economic Fluctuations in England, 1700-1800* (Oxford, 1959),

tion do pose real problems.[22] Not until 1773 was there an official standard
for the measurement of cargo; a law in that year required weighing for customs to be done according to the length and breadth of the ship. But this
only induced merchants to have ships built deep to avoid 'full' taxation.
Not until 1855 was the criterion of "cubic feet" required, replacing an 1836
law which had made it optional.[23] The problem is further complicated by the
lack of any required registry of ships before 1786; Lloyds' voluntary marine
insurance did not begin until 1764. Another error built into the statistics—
in this case, of imports—concerns prize goods. In the Ledgers before 1772,
there were neither totals of prize goods nor separate listings; prize articles
were aggregated with import figures of the same type. Only from 1772 were the
totals of prize goods, now appearing without differentiation by commodity,
separated from the import register. This distinction is important for the
seizure of booty from enemies could be enormous in war years. Thus, in 1757,
1779, and 1781 prize goods caused the entire rise of total imports in those
years over the ones before! In 1794 they accounted for one-third of the increase in import totals over the 1793 figures.[24]

More significant are the errors of omission. Smuggling—by definition ex-
cluded from the records—was in the eighteenth century a lucrative, glamorous
livelihood but one, unfortunately, which causes a gap in our knowledge of
eighteenth-century trade. A contemporary estimated that it comprised one-
fourth of all trade, and a recent researcher has confirmed that it did form
a considerable proportion. In its greatest era (pre-1745 and 1775-83) smuggling may have amounted to one-fifth of all trade, although it was concen-
trated in tea, tobacco, and sugar imports.[25]

31-32, has pointed out that various subjects began their fiscal years at
different times. Thus, Government finance started its year at Michaelmas
until 1787 when it changed to January 5; figures for Scottish linens stamped
for sale began on November 1, annually; annual data for broad-cloth woolens
in the West Riding of Yorkshire started on March 13, while narrow-cloth ones
began on January 21. Excise figures started on June 25 until 1752 when they
changed to July 6. It was in 1752 that the Protestant monarchy changed from
the Julian to the Gregorian calendar, losing eleven days in September.

[22]Thomas S. Willan, *The English Coasting Trade, 1660-1750* (Manchester,
1938), 220, has noted suspicious uniformities in vessels registered in various
ports for 1709-51. J. H. Andrews, "Two Problems in the Interpretation of the
Port Books," *Economic History Review*, 2nd ser., IX (1956), 119-22, has ana-
lyzed the kinds of legitimate trade deliberately omitted from the records
and the way landing places were recorded. For a contemporary study, see "The
Report of the Committee appointed to Enquire into the Frauds and Abuses in the
Customs, to the Prejudice of Trade, and Diminution of the Revenue (1733)," in
House of Commons' Committees, I, 601-54. For defects of the trade statistics
generally, see Clark, 33-42, 52-56.

[23]Mitchell and Deane, 215.

[24]Ashton, in Schumpeter, 8.

[25]The contemporary is quoted in Clark, 34. See W. A. Cole, "Trends in
Eighteenth-Century Smuggling," *Economic History Review*, 2nd ser., X (1958),
395-410, and A. Rive, "A Short History of Tobacco Smuggling," *Economic His-*

A second omission was the failure of the Customs Office before 1772 to distinguish re-exports from imports, making it extremely hard for historians to determine whether variations in the volume of imports are due to changes in consumption, production, or the re-export trade. The rise of the textile industries, in any case, would have reduced the dimensions of this problem, since items for re-export as a percentage of imports fell from 30 per cent in 1800 to 10 per cent by 1840.[26]

A third omission in the official records before 1772 is the non-differentiation of types and origins of imports. Fourthly, there is the problem of the non-recording of declared or current value prices of exports and imports. This omission was made possible by the removal in the early eighteenth century of export duties, first on woolens (the main article of export) in 1700, then on all manufactured articles in 1721.[27] "From the time these outward duties were taken off," comments a writer in 1704, "the merchants have made their entries at pleasure."[28] Generally, the merchants overvalued their exports to deceive other exporters into believing the market would soon be glutted.

In the place of declared were 'official' valuations. Instead of determining the values of exports by mulitplying current prices by quantity, the Customs Commissioners in 1696 instructed the first Inspector-General of the Customs, William Culliford, to draw up a price series for all articles based on the price levels of 1696. Culliford did so, and the price base for computation of value remained virtually unchanged until 1870 when official values were no longer recorded. Culliford did make some adjustments to follow price changes until 1702,[29] but his successors Charles Davenant (1703-14) and Henry Martin (1714-21) made no alterations. Indeed, both Davenant and Martin were negligent also in following specific instructions to register Scottish trade at the Customs House, since, as we have seen, no data were recorded until 1761. It was not that Martin was unaware of the shortcomings in the trade figures. In an important memorandum of 1718,[30] he demonstrated that the value figures were deficient as a measure of trade due to the numbers of invisible imports and exports, smuggling, and the overvaluation of exports.[31] But he

tory, I (1929), 554-69. For contemporary views, see the first, second, and third reports of the "Committee on Illicit Practices used in Defrauding the Revenue (1783-84)," *House of Commons' Committees*, XI, 227-302.

[26]Deane and Cole, 31-32, 44.

[27]By statutes 11 Will. III, c. 20 and 8 Geo. I, c. 15, respectively.
[28]Charles Davenant, quoted in Clark, 15.

[29]David Macpherson, *Annals of Commerce* (4 v., 1805), III, 340, was mistaken when he said the price values did not change at all after 1696. See A. Maizels' short introduction to "Overseas Trade," in Maurice G. Kendall, ed., *The Sources and Nature of the Statistics of the United Kingdom* (1952), 21; see also Clark, 10 n. 4.

[30]C.O. 390/12 ff. 15-43 (Public Record Office, London), reprinted in Clark, App. 3, pp. 62-69.

[31]John Oxenford, Inspector-General (1722-58), in a memorandum attributed to him,"Essay towards finding the Balance of our Whole Trade annually from Christmas of 1698 to Christmas of 1719" deducts 2 per cent from the figures

sharply pointed out, as historians have since, that the constant price evaluation meant that the official valuation was a useful index of trends in the *volume* of trade. This conclusion leaves unresolved the question of why, if the value of the figures is in terms of quantity, the unit of measure should have remained in sterling. In any case, Inspector-General Martin adhered to the status quo, being "partly actuated by a desire to save himself trouble,"[32] as his office had only six clerks (an increase of only two over the original staff of four in 1694). Export valuations were not investigated seriously until the 1790's, while import and re-export values remained purely constant and 'official' until 1854 when declared values were added.[33]

The first recording of declared values of exports came in 1799, due to the work of Thomas Irving. Inspector-General since 1786 and the most able one since Martin, Irving was required to carry out the Convoy Act of 1798 which imposed new duties on exports and for the first time required merchants to declare the values of certain classes of goods. From this necessity, he proceeded to construct the real or declared values of exports from 1796 to 1798 and eventually continued the values to 1805.[34]

Contemporary writers began to record the declared with the official values. Henry Beeke (1751-1837), professor of modern history at Oxford and later Dean of Bristol, in his pioneering statistical treatise on the income tax calculates the real value figures for exports for 1798-99.[35] Patrick Colquhoun, the famous writer on both police and economic development,[36] writing in 1814, gives the real values for the exports for 1805-11. McCulloch in 1836 gives both declared and official values for exports from 1799 to 1836.[37] By 1832 most writers include both sets of valuation statistics.[38]

to deflate the export valuations (in C.O. 390/14, reprinted in Clark, App. 4, pp. 69-79).

[32]The opinion is by Clark, 23.

[33]For modern work computing the real values of imports and re-exports from 1796 to 1853, see Albert H. Imlah, *Economic Elements in the Pax Britannica* (Cambridge, Mass., 1958), 37-38; see also Mitchell and Deane, 282-84.

[34]The statute is 38 George III, c. 76. Irving's "epitaph of the old statistical system" (in Clark's phrase, 32) may be read in *The State of the Navigation, Revenue, and Commerce of the British Empire* (1790).

[35]Beeke, *Observations on the Produce of the Income Tax* (1800), 100-05.

[36]Colquhoun (1745-1820), a Scottish businessman, founded the Glasgow Chamber of Commerce in 1783, wrote on the cotton industry from 1785 to 1789, and evaluated the national income in *A Treatise on the Wealth, Power, and Resources of the British Empire* (1814; 2nd ed., 1815). He is equally famous as a London police magistrate from 1792 to 1818; his classic *Treatise on the Police of the Metropolis* (1796) went through seven editions by 1806. Another work, *A Treatise on the Commerce and Police of the River Thames* (1800), was written at the urging of West Indian merchants alarmed at the scale of dockside thefts.

[37]Colquhoun, *Treatise on the Wealth . . . of the British Empire* (2nd ed. 1815), 99; John R. McCulloch, *A Dictionary, Practical, Theoretical, and Historical, of Commerce and Commercial Navigation* (3rd ed., 1837), 672.

[38]E.g., John Marshall, statistician of the 1830's, in his *Digest of all the Accounts relating to . . . the United Kingdom* (1833), Part 3, pp. 56-62,

(d) Sources for Commercial Statistics

Because of the paucity of government documents, the earliest eighteenth-century sources of import and export data are incomplete and concentrate on a few nations. Inspector-General of Customs, Sir Charles Davenant, published data on trade in woolens, linen, silk, and lead to France for 1662-63, 1668-69, and 1699-1702. An anonymous pamphlet of 1713 presents similar data for 1674.[39] An early parliamentary source has trade figures (all goods specified by quantity) with France from London and England (total) for 1668-69.[40] Another parliamentary source has data for trade between France and England from 1714 to 1787.[41]

On trade with Holland, Davenant provides figures for national totals for 1699-1705, with details for selected articles for 1668-69 and 1703. For tin exports to Holland he has figures for 1662-63, 1668-69, and 1700-09.[42] Eighteenth-century statistics of trade with Portugal exist for 1703-87.[43]

120a-120d, 121-23, and Thomas Hopkins, *Great Britain for the Last Forty Years* (1834), 156-57.

[39]Charles Davenant, "A Report to the Honourable the Commissioners for putting in Execution the Act, intituled an Act for the taking, examining, and stating the Publick Accounts of the Kingdom" (1711), in *The Political and Commercial Works of that Celebrated Writer, Charles Davenant,* collected and revised by Sir Charles Whitworth (5 v., 1771), V, 353-60. The 1674 statistics are in *Some Further Observations on the Treaty of Navigation and Commerce, between Great-Britain and France* (1713), a pamphlet sometimes attributed to Defoe. The table also appears in two other editions of *Some Further Observations* (both 1713) and in *A Letter to the Honourable A———r M———re* (1714). For the seventeenth century, see Ralph Davis' "English Foreign Trade, 1660-1700," *Economic History Review,* 2nd ser., VII (1954), 150-66, and "Merchant Shipping in the Economy of the late 17th Century," *Economic History Review,* 2nd ser., IX (1956), 59-73. For earlier periods, see Lawrence Stone's "State Control in Sixteenth-Century England," *Economic History Review,* XVII (1947), 103-20, and "Elizabethan Overseas Trade," *Economic History Review,* 2nd ser., II (1949), 30-58.

[40]*Journals of the House of Commons,* volume 17, pp. 394-97, 423-24, for London and England, respectively. This reference would hereafter be cited as follows: *J.H.C. 17,* 394-97, 423-24.

[41]Parliamentary *Accounts and Papers 1787* (425-27), XIX. Hereafter abbreviated as *A. & P.*

[42]Charles Davenant, "A Second Report to the Honourable the Commissioners for putting in Execution the Act . . . " (1711) in *The Political and Commercial Works of . . . Charles Davenant* (5 v., 1771), V, 403-12, 414-16, 421. The selected articles are linen, silk and flax imports from Holland, and woolen, lead and brass exports from England.

[43]*A. & P. 1787* (429-30), XIX. Exports and imports, official value, specifying each article from 1772.

10

Sources for the trade with the East Indies and China in the eighteenth century are numerous, but the premier work is David Macpherson's *History of the European Commerce with India*.[44] West Indian trade records exist for 1760-1816, annually.[45] Numerous sources chart the trade between Great Britain and Ireland from 1700 to 1836.[46]

Printed government sources for national totals of trade with more than a few isolated nations do not appear until 1787, when a series for 1773-85 was published.[47] The next long series was not printed until 1797.[48] Although Davenant had published data on trade with France and Holland in the early eighteenth century (see footnotes 39 and 42), he made no synthesis of comprehensive trade figures. The first Inspector-General to do this was Henry

[44]Macpherson has numerous statistical appendices, the most impressive being an annual record, from 1710 to 1810, of the ships sailed and bullion and merchandize exported (*History of . . . Commerce with India* [1812], App. 7, pp. 419-20). There are other figures for the tonnage of shipping between London and India.(1793-1807), the prime cost of the Company's exports of woolens (1781-1810), and many others. John McGregor, *Commercial Statistics* (4 v., 1847-48), IV, 404-10, has decennial averages for trade, 1680-1811, and annual export figures, 1708-1811, from England to India and China by the East India Company, differentiating merchandize from bullion. See *J.H.C. 21*, 555, for the re-exports by the Company of their articles from London to all countries (not differentiated), 1720-27, by value. *J.H.C. 62*, 467, lists the exports of British manufactures to China by the East India Company from 1773 to 1805, using invoice value in pounds sterling. For bullion imports and exports in Britain and by the East India Company, see the very incomplete series from 1700 to 1819 in the tables in *Cursory Observations on some parts of the evidence before the Committees of both Houses of Parliament, on the expediency of resuming cash payments at the Bank of England*, (1819), App. 8-10, pp. 138-41.

[45]*J.H.C. 72*, 747-48. Official value only.

[46]Sir Charles Whitworth, *State of the Trade* (1776), Part 2, pp. 19-20, has trade figures between England and Ireland from 1697 to 1773. James Corry, in William Playfair's *Political and Commercial Atlas* (1786), Plate 40, graphs the trade totals between England and Ireland from 1700 to 1760. For data on 1750-83, see John Baker Holroyd, 1st Earl of Sheffield, *Observations on the Manufactures, Trade, and Present State of Ireland* (1785), App. 4, p. 284; for 1760-82, see David Macpherson, *Annals of Commerce* (4 v., 1805), IV, 59-61. For 1801-25, see *P.P. 1842* (305), XXXVIII, 447-54; for 1805-29, see Henry James, *State of the Nation* (1835), 96; for 1814-23, see John Powell, *Statistical Illustrations of the British Empire* (3rd ed., 1827), 53; and for 1801-36, see George R. Porter, *Progress of the Nation* (3 v., 1836-43), II (1838), 80-81, 84. In the trade ledgers Ireland ceases to be treated as a foreign country in 1825, being considered coasting traffic after that date. See Porter, *Progress of the Nation*, II (1838), 85, for the number and tonnage of vessels clearing British ports for Ireland from 1801 to 1837.

[47]*A. & P. 1787* (425, 428, 434), XIX.

[48]Trade statistics for 1777-96 are in "Lords Committee of Secrecy, relating to the Bank (1797)," reprinted in *P.P. 1810* (17), III, 368.

11

Martin who, in his "Essay towards finding the Balance of our whole Trade Annually from Christmas of 1698 to Christmas of 1719," provided data for trade with two dozen countries or places. This valuable document was not printed until 1938.[49] Because the official authorities were slow to collect and make public trade figures, private individuals often beat the government into print. The greatest of these writers were Whitworth, Chalmers, and Anderson.

The most useful publication on trade since Davenant's *Reports* of 1711 and 1712 is Sir Charles Whitworth's *State of the Trade of Great Britain* (1776).[50] The work sets out annual import and export statistics from 1697 to 1773 (official valuations), to and from twenty foreign countries, Ireland, the thirteen British North American colonies, and the West Indian "plantations." The work is in two parts, part one being annual totals, within which are differentiations by regions; part two, regional totals, within which are differentiations by years. George Chalmers, one of the greatest successors to Whitworth, had this to say about the book:

> Of the several works which the public owe to the
> attentive diligence of the late Sir Charles
> Whitworth, none can be of more importance
> to the Peer or the Commoner, to the mer-
> chant or mechanic, than *The State of the
> Trade of England,* since it is a transcript
> of the *Ledger of the Inspector General.* . . .
> It was of the greatest use to the compiler
> of these sheets; and he never looks into
> it, but he feels what he owes to the mem-
> ory of a person who employed his leisure in
> collecting details, which contain more real
> information than a hundred volumes of
> declamation.[51]

[49]In C.O. 390/14, reproduced in Clark, App. 4, pp. 69-149. The data appear in seventeen tables of a comprehensiveness and appearance unique to their historical period. The essay was at first attributed by Clark in 1938 to an assistant clerk named John Oxenford and dated 1723, but an earlier copy of the manuscript since discovered in a London bookshop, bears the date 1719 and the handwriting is not Oxenford's. Ashton, in Schumpeter, 3, attributes the essay to Inspector-General Martin. Martin authored another memorandum on the trade figures for 1696-1714 (in C.O. 390/12, reprinted in Clark, App. 3, pp. 62-69).

[50]Full title: *The State of the Trade of Great Britain in its Imports and Exports, progressively from the Year 1697: also of the Trade to each particular Country, during the above period, distinguishing each year* (1776). The copy in the Public Record Office, B. T. 6/185, has manuscript continuation for certain countries to 1801 (Clark, 153).

[51]George Chalmers, *An Estimate of the Comparative Strength of Britain* (1782), 35 n. *d.*

Whitworth (1714?-1778), younger brother of Charles, Baron Whitworth, lived most of his life in politics. His father had been an M.P. since 1732, and Charles took over his father's seat in 1747. A great lover of Parliament and the English artistocracy, he wrote several books about them.[52] He was active in the Society for the Encouragement of Arts, Manufactures and Commerce, of which he was a vice-president for twenty-three years, beginning in 1755. In 1768 he was chosen as chairman of the Committee for Ways and Means, a post he filled until his death in 1778. From the 1760's he was especially interested in parliamentary income and expenditure, authoring several books on these subjects.[53]

In the preface to the *State of the Trade* (1776) Whitworth tells us that he wrote the work to confront the pessimists with a statistical "Corrective of the gloomy Prophecies of those who are constantly alarming us with the visionary Dangers of a general Depopulation, a stagnation of Trade, and an approaching Loss of Credit."[54] Further, Whitworth quoted the Abbé Raynal[55] that it was "a mistaken notion almost to the present Times" that war, not commerce, was the font of prosperity. As Raynal observed, in war winner and loser alike exchange blood and death, while

> by Commerce, the conquering People must, of
> Necessity, introduce Industry into a Country,
> which they would not have conquered had Industry
> been there; which they would not keep, if, by
> keeping it, Industry were not established in it.[56]

[52]In 1764 he published *The Succession of Parliaments from the Restoration to 1761*; in 1765, *A List of the Nobility and Judges*. From 1758 to 1788 Whitworth was Lieutenant-Governor of Gravesend and Tillbury Fort, and, from its embodiment in 1759, was a Major in a Battalion of the West Kent Militia. He was knighted in 1768. His son, Charles, was envoy-extraordinary to Russia (1786-1800), Ambassador to France (1800-03), and Lord Lieutenant of Ireland (1813-17).

[53]See *A Collection of the Supplies and Ways and Means from the Revolution to the Present Time* (1764; 2nd ed., 1765), a revised edition (1778) of Timothy Cunningham's *History of Customs, Aids, Subsidies, & c. of England*, and a collection of *Scarce Tracts on Trade and Commerce* (1778). Whitworth also collected and published the *Political and Commercial Works of that Celebrated Writer, Charles Davenant* (5 v., 1771).

[54]*State of the Trade* (1776), preface, 4.

[55]Guillaume Thomas François Raynal, (1713-96), *Histoire Philosophique et Politique des Établissements, et du Commerce, des Européens dans les deux Indes* (10 v., Amsterdam, 1770), VII, 269. Numerous later editions were published. The Pope banned the work in 1774 and the Paris *parlement* in 1781 burned it and exiled the author. Raynal was permitted back in France in 1784, but not into Paris until 1790. The young Napoleon is said to have read the *Histoire Philosophique* when Raynal lived in Marseilles.

[56]From Raynal, *Histoire Philosophique* (1770), VII, 310, quoted in Whitworth, *State of the Trade* (1776), preface, 1, 4.

This attitude, which would be common in the future, is reminiscent of Malachy Postlethwayt's: the European nations must begin to follow England's pacific example in commerce if they are effectively to challenge her strength.

Whitworth's book, despite (or because of) its pioneering importance, has several defects. As a transcription of the Custom House Ledgers, it shows the import and export totals in one region but does not trace the movements of specific commodities. Not the least important reason for this statistical deficiency was the fear that foreigners might make improper use of knowledge of the movements of commodities. Another problem is the misleading title; the statistics are all for England, although Scottish figures were available after 1761. By far the greatest error, however, lies in his handling of the data for coin and bullion exports. For 1697-1764 Whitworth includes bullion with the export data, quite improperly, as coin pays for imports and drains wealth from rather than brings it into the country. As an example, for 1731-35 his inclusion of bullion incorrectly inflates the export statistics by 25 per cent, and gives the illusion of greater prosperity than actually existed. Furthermore, Whitworth lacks consistency. Because the 1765-73 export figures, unaccountably, *exclude* coin and bullion, the unwary reader, looking at the earlier data, is apt to deduce mistakenly a greater decline in exports than actually occurred. Unfortunately, Chalmers and Anderson unknowingly perpetuated Whitworth's original error.[57]

George Chalmers (1742-1825), a Scot, was chief clerk of the Committee of the Privy Council for Trade and Foreign Plantations (later called simply, the Board of Trade) for half his life, from 1786 until his death. His *Estimate of the Comparative Strength of Britain* (1782) provides national trade totals at intervals from 1663 to 1757; each of the editions has a continuous series from 1760 until the year before its publication.[58] Complete data from 1760 through 1811 appear in an Edinburgh, 1812 edition with a new title, *An Historical View of the Domestic Economy of Great Britain and Ireland* (1812). The second edition (1786) of the *Estimate*, using data in the Trade Office, was substantially different from the first; later editions were only slight alterations of the second.

Chalmers—like the other great Scottish statisticians, David Macpherson and William Playfair—was a man with two dispositions. In economic statistics he was calm, judicious, and trustworthy. He combined enormous research with deft organization and a style which successfully interwove text and figures. In political affairs, though, Chalmers could be a righteous, emotional, dogmatic harpy. The Americans were treacherous rebels,[59] the French revo-

[57]This paragraph is based on Clark, 30-31, and Ashton, in Schumpeter, 7.

[58]Second ed., 1786; 3rd ed., 1794; 4th ed., 1802; 5th ed., 1804; 6th ed., 1810; and 7th ed., Edinburgh 1812, mentioned above.

[59]After studies at Aberdeen and Edinburgh (law), Chalmers emigrated to America in 1763 where he set up a law practice in Baltimore. On the outbreak of the war, which he considered treasonous, he returned to London in 1775. To expose the fallacies of the rebels he penned the *Political Annals of the Present United Colonies* (1780) and *An Introduction to the History of the Revolt of the Colonies* (1782).

14

lutionaries were iniquitous demons,[60] the anti-slavery Evangelicals were
fools.[61] From 1794 he freely called those whose opinions differed with his,
"Jacobins." One feels that a major reason why Chalmers (as well as Macpherson
and Playfair) became increasingly involved with the antiquities of his native
Scotland[62] was to escape from the 'evils' of his own revolutionary age. Economic arithmetic was a form of reassurance, too. As early as 1782, in the
preface to the original edition of the *Estimate*, Chalmers sought to reassure
his countrymen that Dr. Price's grumblings and the defeat in America[63] were
not true reflections of the state of England. For Chalmers, the truth lay in
trade figures which proved a continuous progress. It is perhaps ironic that
this emotional and dogmatic man was, in his economic research, lucid and entirely reliable. To quote his biographer, who explores both sides of his character:
"One may confidently trust and make use of the facts which he sets forth."[64]

The motives for Adam Anderson (1692?-1765), a Scot and a clerk of forty
years' standing in the South Sea House, to write his two-volume work on commerce[65] were again a combination of disinterestedness and national self-esteem.
In his dedication he generously saw the progress of world trade as reflecting
"equal Honour on this Age and Nation," but added that it was only a matter of
time before we should "compleat our Superiority over the rest of the Commercial

[60]See the preface to the *Estimate of the Comparative Strength of Great
Britain* (1794 ed.) and Grace Cockroft, *The Public Life of George Chalmers*
(New York, 1939), ch. 5.

[61]Cockroft, *Public Life*, 144-45, 170, 183.

[62]His most famous work was a history of Scotland entitled *Caledonia* (3 v.,
1807-24).

[63]Richard Price, in his *Essay on the Population of England from the Revolution to the Present Time* (1780), had convinced many Englishmen that their
population and commerce were steadily declining. The British defeat at York-
town occurred on October 19, 1781.

[64]Cockroft, *Public Life*, 214. For a complete list of his forty-seven works,
see Cockroft, *Public Life*, 216-20; see also *The Dictionary of National Biography* (22 v., Oxford, 1885-1901; 1963-64 reprint), III, 1355. Hereafter
abbreviated as *D.N.B.*; all references are to the 1963-64 reprint of the original edition.

[65]*An Historical and Chronological Deduction of the Origin of Commerce from
the earliest accounts to the present time, containing an History of the great
Commercial Interests of the British Empire. To which is prefixed an Intro-
duction exhibiting a View of the ancient and modern State of Europe; of the
Importance of our Colonies, and of the Commerce, Shipping, Manufactures,
Fisheries, &c., of Great Britain and Ireland, and their Influence on the Land-
ed Interest, with an Appendix containing the Modern Politico-Commercial Geo-
graphy of the several Countries of Europe* (2 v., 1764; 2nd ed., 4 v., 1787-89).
The second edition is identical to the first through volume three, page 345.
The remainder of volume three and volume four were revised by W. Coombe. All
references are to the second edition, hereafter cited as Anderson, *Origin of
Commerce*.

World."[66] The work was substantial enough for Macpherson,[67] a reliable historian of commerce, to use the trade data, although the parts before 1492 he thought less trustworthy. One statistical problem with Anderson's work is that its data—on trade, prices, finance, and currency—are scattered rather than tabular. This flaw was corrected when an obscure compiler, William Coombe (1741-1823), in the second edition furnished tabular annual trade statistics for 1700-87.[68] Coombe, not Anderson, must be credited with the tables in Anderson's book.

The data in the works of Clarke and McArthur (see Tables 1 and 2 below) were peripheral to their books; neither writer pretended to be an historian of commerce.[69]

The most proficient historian of commerce before McCulloch and Porter was David Macpherson. A Scot and friend of Chalmers, Macpherson (1746-1816) was the son of an Edinburgh clothier. He became a land surveyor and made some money on real estate ventures in America and England, so that by 1790 he had retired to London to live the life of a man of letters. Unfortunately, his financial position became precarious, and he took the post of deputy-keeper of the Public Record Office. With Chalmers' interest and help, he authored a book on *Geographical Illustrations of Scottish History* (1796). In 1795 Chalmers, increasingly interested in Scottish antiquities, had passed on to Macpherson a publisher's request for a history of commerce. With Chalmers' help Macpherson, working in the public records and his own personal library, produced ten years later his monumental four-volume *Annals of Commerce*.[70] The set, though it relied on Anderson's work for volume two and part of volume three (the period 1492-1760), involved original research by Macpherson for

[66]Dedication to the Society for the Encouragement of Arts, Manufactures, and Commerce, in volume one of the first edition (1764).

[67]David Macpherson, *Annals of Commerce*, I, pp. iii-vi.

[68]Anderson, *Origin of Commerce*, IV, 692-94; see note 65.

[69]John McArthur (1755-1840) entered the navy in 1778 and, after 1791, was Secretary to Admiral Lord Hood, for whom he created a system of marine ship signals. He authored a gentleman's manual on fencing (1781), a work on naval courts-martial (1792), a study of Ossian's poems (1806), and, with J. S. Clarke, a *Life of Nelson* (2 v., 1809). He also produced *Financial and Political Facts of the Eighteenth Century and the Present Century; with comparative estimates of the revenue, expenditure, debts, manufactures, and commerce of Great Britain* (3rd ed., 1801).

The data in the Reverend Thomas B. Clarke's *A Survey of the Strength and Opulence of Great Britain* (1801)—note the title — appear accurate until 1772 when his figures would seem to be British, though he calls them English.

Note that both authors are taking a pleasant inventory of the wartime strength of England one year before the interlude of the Peace of Amiens.

[70]See Macpherson to Chalmers, July 25, 1795, in Andrew Wyntoun, "The Orygynale Cronykil of Scotland," ed. David Laing (3 v., Edinburgh, 1872-79), III (1879), in *The Historians of Scotland* (10 v., Edinburgh, 1872-80), IX (1879), App. 3, pp. xxxix-xlii. Macpherson acknowledged Chalmers' generosity and aid "which could alone make it proper for me to engage in a work rather

the period before 1492 and from 1760 to 1801. Macpherson's work substantially replaced Anderson's work in value, for Macpherson had the use of documents "which have been generally withheld from preceding writers" and was, furthermore, skeptical in his use of documents. For instance, unlike Whitworth and Chalmers, he includes Scottish data for the first time and avoids Whitworth's error over bullion exports. The format of the work is chronological, with a miscellany of data within each year, but at the end of each annual section from 1764 to 1800 he provides, "in the perspicuous and comprehensive form of tables," national trade figures with some two dozen places in the world.[71]

The thirty years after the termination of the Napoleonic Wars were important decades for the extension of statistical methods and presentation. The pre-eminent statisticians were John Powell, J. R. McCulloch, John Marshall, and G. R. Porter.

Little is known about John Powell, to whom is attributed a remarkable statistical compendium, *Statistical Illustrations of the Territorial Extent and Population; Commerce, Taxation, Consumption, Insolvency, Pauperism and Crime of the British Empire* (1825; 3rd ed., 1827). Though Powell did not actually compile the data, he supervised the project which resulted in the book.[72] He was a member of a group of London artisans who formed an "Association" in 1817 to study economic distress. It was this Association which sponsored the publication of *Statistical Illustrations*; by 1827, they were calling themselves the London Statistical Society. The purpose of the statistical work was to investigate the nature, extent, and causes of the "privation and misery endured by the productive classes of society." One way to do this, wrote Powell, was to assemble tables of data, even if it were in the face of

> the prevailing and inveterate dislike to
> an assemblage of figures. But it must be
> obvious, that the operations and resources
> of Great Britain are of a magnitude, too
> vast, to be brought within the power of
> human comprehension, without the aid of
> figures, however repulsive they may appear;
> and being properly applied, they lead to
> just conclusions with precision and accuracy.[73]

out of my line of study" (p. xli). Because of his access to the numerous official sources, Macpherson hoped for a final work of "a decided preference" to existing books on the history of commerce.

[71]Macpherson, *Annals of Commerce* (4 v., 1805), III, 409 ff; IV, *passim*. The phrase about tables is from Anderson, *Origin of Commerce*, I, preface, p. xi.

[72]John Powell, *The Causes of the Present Crisis Explained. First part of an analytical exposition of the erroneous principles and ruinous consequences of the commercial system of Great Britain, illustrative of its influence on the physical, social, and moral condition of the people* (1825), preface, p. viii. *Statistical Illustrations of the British Empire* also appeared as articles in *The Pamphleteer*, XXV (1825), 183-216; XXVI (1826), 353-68.

[73]Powell, *Causes of the Present Crisis Explained* (1825), preface, p. v.

17

Despite the radical opinions of the compilers, the figures are as reliable as they are painstakingly researched.

John Ramsay McCulloch (1789-1864)—again, a Scot—published the results of twenty years' research, his *Dictionary of Commerce*,[74] in 1832. It made available for the first time many economic statistics and immediately became the definitive economic gazeteer. In the wake of publishing his *Principles of Political Economy* (1825), *An Essay on the Circumstances which Determine the Rate of Wages and the Condition of the Labouring Classes* (Edinburgh, 1826), and an edition of Adam Smith's works (1828), McCulloch accepted in 1828 the unendowed chair of political economy at the new London University. Later, in 1832, for financial reasons, he resigned it. He revised his *Dictionary*[75] and published, with the aid of specialists from the Society for the Diffusion of Useful Knowledge, a statistical treatment of the British Empire in 1837.[76] Three years after his appointment as Comptroller of the Stationery Office (a fitting post), McCulloch published his compendious *Dictionary . . . of the Various Countries . . . in the World* (1841).[77] His final work was the pioneering critical bibliography, *The Literature of Political Economy* (1845). Though no pathbreaker in economic theory (he rigidly followed Smith and Ricardo), McCulloch was, with Porter, the pre-eminent statistical lexicographer. He remained a sturdy Scot and a lifelong Whig, writing for *The Scotsman* and contributing seventy-eight articles on liberal economics to the *Edinburgh Review* between 1818 and 1837. At his death in 1864 his library numbered roughly 10,000 volumes.[78]

John Marshall (1783-1841), unlike McCulloch or Porter, is a virtual unknown. He was for many years a supernumerary, or, in the words of the *Gentleman's Magazine*, "always a sort of hanger-on at the Home Office."[79] He dabbled in

This work is an essay complementing the tables in *Statistical Illustrations*. Herbert Somerton Foxwell, collector of the nucleus of the Kress Library, thought *Causes* "a very remarkable tract, which . . . gives its author claim to rank among the founders of the English Socialist school." The essay appeared both separately and in *The Pamphleteer*, XXVI (1826), 481-524.

[74]*A Dictionary, Practical, Theoretical, and Historical, of Commerce and Commercial Navigation* (1832). Hereafter cited simply as *Dictionary*.

[75]Numerous up-dated editions and reprints were published. Between 1832 and 1882, at least nineteen were issued in London; and in Philadelphia, between 1840 and 1852, at least seven.

[76]*A Statistical Account of the British Empire: Exhibiting its extent, physical capacities, population, industry, and civil and religious institutions* (2 v., 1837). Later editions: 2nd, 1839; 3rd, 1847; 4th, 1854.

[77]*A Dictionary, Geographical, Statistical, and Historical of the Various Countries, Places, and principal Natural Objects in the World* (2 v., 1841-42; 2nd ed., 1851). Many later editions were published.

[78]See Hugh G. Reid's biographical notice of McCulloch which was privately printed in 1865 and republished in the 1869 and later editions of McCulloch's *Dictionary*.

[79]*The Gentleman's Magazine*, new ser., XV (1841), Part 1, p. 549.

electoral and population studies from 1830 to 1832, and in the later 1830's in factory inspection. He is known, when he is at all, for his statistical *Digest* of 1833.[80] Marshall says in the preface that he was led to research the book after witnessing the economic downturns of 1815, 1817, and 1819, "to endeavour to inform myself of the causes which had led to the counteraction of the usual results to all honourable enterprise." The data he collected from six hundred parliamentary volumes, "at no inconsiderable expense of means, and great sacrifice of time and labour." He then arranged them in tables, for "the absence of all method, uniformity, and connexion in the Accounts, rendered it exceedingly perplexing and unsatisfactory to refer to them." Marshall saw his tables as quite useful for the future, for it is "an inalienable axiom, that legislation can only be beneficial in proportion as it is based on indubitable facts."[81]

Unfortunately, though, Marshall's work is the most confusing of all the comprehensive statisticians. Because it is in three parts with separate pagination its ease of reference is diminished. The presentation of the tables is unsettling because of differing sizes of columns and of print, often within one table. The data themselves are in places questionable, as for example, in the exports of cotton manufactures and of brass and copper, where the British figures are 5 per cent greater than those for the United Kingdom. Similar incongruities, on the order of 10 per cent, exist for the statistics of silk and iron and steel exports. In the case of coals, the difference is 400 per cent![82] For these reasons, Marshall is not recommended as a reliable source.

With George Richardson Porter (1792-1852) we are again on firm statistical ground. The son of a well-to-do London merchant, Porter himself was less successful in business, for he failed as a sugar broker. Turning to the study of economics and statistics, he had to his publishing credit a recent article on life insurance when Lord Auckland asked him in 1832 to assemble economic statistics for the Board of Trade. Porter proceeded to examine all of the parliamentary papers from 1820 to 1831. His "two principal objects," he wrote in the preface to the first edition of the annual government document which came to be known as *Porter's Tables*, were "the greatest attainable accuracy" and the coverage of "every point of Statistical information within reach." Porter observed,

> It cannot be requisite to point out the
> advantages that must result to the Govern-

[80]*Digest of all the Accounts relating to the Population, Productions, Revenues, Financial Operations, Manufactures, Shipping, Colonies, Commerce, &c., &c., of the United Kingdom of Great Britain and Ireland, diffused through more than 600 volumes of journals, reports, and papers presented to Parliament during the last thirty-five years* (1833). Reprinted in 1834.

[81]Marshall, *Digest* (1833), introduction, 3-4. Following Joseph Hume's motion, some 3,000 copies of the *Digest* were distributed among Members of Parliament.

[82]Marshall, *Digest* (1833), Part 3, pp. 62-65, 81. McCulloch did not think the *Digest* important enough to include in his *Literature of Political Economy* (1845).

> ment and Legislature of every country from
> the possession of accurate information upon
> all those points of national interest which
> are comprehended under the name of Statistics.
> That the Members of both Houses of
> Parliament are fully aware of these advan-
> tages is evident from the extent of the Returns
> called for during every Session. Those printed
> during twelve years [1820-31]. . . occupy . . .
> 304 bulky folio volumes; while the Sessional
> Papers of the past year [1832] extend to 48
> volumes. .....Unfortunately, however, their
> bulk, and the miscellaneous mode of their
> arrangement, are such as must deter from their
> examination most of those persons who are other-
> wise engaged in the performance of active duties,
> but who could therefore best profit from the study;
> and documents, which have been collected at a
> considerable expense of money and labour, are
> thus, in a great degree, unproductive of the
> benefits which they might be found capable of
> affording.
> In order to place the contents of the
> following compilation in a form calculated to
> impart the greatest amount of useful information
> with the smallest degree of labour, a tabular
> arrangement has been adopted, and the Statements
> are brought together in such a manner as to admit
> of comparison being readily made between similar
> matters occurring in the different years embraced
> by the compilation.[83]

The document, comprising data on all manner of economic and social subjects, was in two parts: part 1, 235 tables in 264 pages (with index); part 2, 147 tables in 146 pages (with index). The first publication of its kind, *Porter's Tables* had by 1850 gone through eighteen editions.

Porter was active in organizing the Statistical Society of London in 1834. In 1840, he became senior member of the railway department at the Board of Trade, and, in 1841, joint secretary of the Board. A commercial publisher brought out his three-volume *Progress of the Nation* (1836-43), an extended statistical essay on all aspects of English life for which he could locate data. The title tells the story: Englishmen in the present generation have "made the greatest advances in civilisation that can be found recorded in the annals of mankind."[84] Statistics for Porter (as for Whitworth, Chalmers, and

---

[83]*Porter's Tables No. 1* [hereafter cited as *P.T. 1*], *P.P. 1833*, XLI, preface, pp. iii-v.
[84]Porter, *Progress*, I (1836), 1.

Colquhoun before him) were proof of English pre-eminence in the world. The work itself, as described by the *Athenaeum*, was "without the sagacity or philosophy of Adam Smith, or the wide-spread information of Mr. McCulloch," but possessed "excellences of its own such as future writers on similar subjects may well be proud to gather even at secondhand."[85] Especially outstanding was Porter's skillful interweaving of text and tables to produce cogent arguments. In the twenty years before his death in 1852 Porter was rivalled only by McCulloch for recognition as the leading statistician of his time.

All the leading statisticians, though working on many other subjects, too, compiled figures on the imports and exports of Great Britain. The major sources for this most general of the commercial categories appear in TABLES 1 and 2 below.

Certain data pertinent to the above tables but difficult to present there must be mentioned. First, for imports and exports, some sources give data, especially for the early eighteenth century, only at given points in time. Thus, two sources have figures for national trade totals at eight decennial points from 1700 to 1770.[86] Other sources provide fuller decennial or quinquennial data. Chalmers has annual figures for 1700-02, 1720-22, 1740-42, 1750-52, 1760-62, and 1770-72 (in each year, to several places), while Anderson has statistics for 1701 and quinquennially from 1705 to 1760.[87] Thirdly, there are the statistics in the form of three-, five-, or seven-year averages. Chalmers has three-year averages for 1700-02, 1713-15, 1726-28, 1736-38, 1739-41, 1749-51, and 1755-57. Marshall has eleven sets of averages for trade with fifteen countries from 1698 to 1792. McCulloch has averages for trade with two dozen places for 1698-1701, 1749-55, 1784-92, and 1816-22.[88]

Secondly, for imports, there is a table in Schumpeter of quinquennial averages of the total imports from twenty-one places for 1701-1800. There is also, in a parliamentary source, a table of imports for 1785-1802, annually, *excluding* wheat or other grain imports and *excluding* East Indian and Chinese imports.[89]

Thirdly, for re-exports, Schumpeter lists the quantities of coffee, tea, rum, sugar, tobacco and cotton wool re-exported annually from 1700 to 1808. Powell's *Statistical Illustrations* (1827) has a series of re-exports of thirty articles (official value) from 1814 to 1822. McCulloch has similar data for numerous articles of re-export (quantities only) for 1832-35.[90]

Fourthly, for exports, Schumpeter has tables for the quantity and value of the principal textile exports *excluding* woolens, 1697-1807, annually, and of the principal non-textile exports, annually for 1697-1771, 1775, and 1780.[91]

[85]Quoted in *The Gentleman's Magazine*, new ser., XXXVIII (1852), Part 2, p. 429.

[86]*J.H.C. 47*, 356; Powell, *Statistical Illustrations*, 47.

[87]Chalmers, *Estimate* (1782), 61-75; Anderson, *Origin of Commerce*, IV (1789), 30-43.

[88]Chalmers, *Estimate* (1782), table facing 37; Marshall, *Digest* (1833), Part 3, pp. 71-75; McCulloch, *Dictionary* (3rd ed., 1837), 671.

[89]Schumpeter, Table VI, p. 18 [hereafter cited simply as VI, 18]; *J.H.C. 58*, 801.

[90]Schumpeter, XVIII, 60-62; Powell, *Statistical Illustrations* (1827), 40-41; McCulloch, *Dictionary* (1837), 673-77.

[91]Schumpeter, X-XI, 29-34; VII-VIII, 19-24, respectively.

Table 1

TOTAL IMPORTS OF GREAT BRITAIN

Primary Sources

Government Documents	*Books and Pamphlets*

Government Documents

1774-1785: *A.& P. 1787* (428, 432-37) XIX. *a*

1777-1796: *Rep. 1796-97* (134), XIX, App. 8, p. 165; reprinted in "Lords' Committee of Secrecy, rel. to the Bank (1797)," *P.P. 1810* (17), III, 368; reprinted in *P.T. 6, P.P. 1837-38* [137], XLVII, No. 161, p. 175. *b*

1780-1790: *J.H.C. 47,* 356.

1783-1845: "S.C. (Secret) on Commercial Distress," *P.P. 1847-48* (395), VIII Part I, 465.

1784-1801: *J.H.C. 57,* 954. *b*

1785-1802: *J.H.C. 58,* 800. *b*

1792-1816: *J.H.C. 72,* 745; also in *P.P. 1817* (113), XIV, 243.

1796-1845: *P.P. 1846* (360), XLIV, 21. *c*

1798-1829: *P.P. 1830-31* (20), X, 265.

1799-1805: *J.H.C. 61,* 775. *b*

1801-1846: *P.P. 1847-48* (38), LVIII, 443. *d*

1805-1811: *P.P. 1812* (202), X, 60; also in *J.H.C. 67,* 760-66. *e,f*

Books and Pamphlets

1697-1773: Whitworth, *State of the Trade* (1776), Part I, pp. 1-79. *a,i*

1697-1799: Clarke, *Survey of . . . Great Britain* (1801), 14-16. *i*

1697-1800: McArthur, *Financial and Political Facts* (1801), 318-20. *i*

1699-1719: Martin, "Essay" (1719), in Clark, *Guide* (1938), App. 4, pp. 69-79. *a,i*

1700-1787: Anderson, *Origin of Commerce* (4 v., 1787-89), IV (1789), 692-94. *i*

1760-1780: Chalmers, *Estimate* (1782), table facing 37; reprinted in Anderson, *Origin of Commerce* (4 v., 1787-89), IV (1789), facing 322. *j,k*

1760-1792: Chalmers, *Estimate* (1794), table facing 207. *j,k*

1760-1797: McCulloch, *Dictionary* (2 v., 1854), I, 711.

1760-1800: Chalmers, *Estimate* (1802), table facing 234. *j,k*

1760-1800: Wheatley, *Essay on the Theory of Money* (1807), table facing 158. *j,l*

Table 1
(continued)

Government	*Books and Pamphlets*

Government

1820-1831: *P.T. 1, P.P. 1833*, XLI, 48.
    g

1822-1850: *P.P. 1851* (140), XXXI, 172.
    d

1827-1834: *P.T. 4, P.P. 1836*, XLVI,
No. 77, pp. 83-356. *a,d,h*

1831-1840: *P.P. 1842* [375], XXXIX,
1-118, 180-381. *a,d,h*

1841-1850: *P.P. 1854-55* [1987], LII,
1-174. *a,d,h*

Books and Pamphlets

1760-1809: Chalmers, *Considerations
on Commerce, Bullion and Coin*
(1811), App. 1, p. 213 ff. *j,k*

1760-1811: Chalmers, *Historical View
of the Domestic Economy* (1812),
table facing 315. *j,k*

1760-1834: Taylor, *Catechism of
Foreign Exchanges* (1835), appendix,
pp. 121-25.

1764-1800: Macpherson, *Annals of
Commerce* (4 v., 1805), III, 409
ff.; IV, *passim. a,j*

1771-1823: Powell, *Statistical
Illustrations* (1825), 47-49. *b*

1773-1795: Vansittart, *Inquiry into
State of the Finances* (1796),
appendix, Table 6.

1777-1796: Allardyce, *Address to
. . . the Bank of England* (3rd ed.,
1798), App. 40, p. 64. *b*

1777-1796: Wheatley, *Essay on the
Theory of Money* (1807), table
facing 246. *b*

1777-1800: Eden, *Eight Letters on
the Peace* (1802), 49-50. *b*

1779-1798: Beeke, *Observations on
the Income Tax* (1800), 101.

1785-1798: Rose, *Brief Examination*
(5th ed., 1799), App. 1, facing
p.78.

Table 1
(continued)

Government Documents
Books and Pamphlets

1793-1828: Marshall, *Digest* (1833),
Part 3, pp. 71-75. *a,h*

1798-1829: Taylor, "Currency" (1844),
appendix, p. 84, in Taylor,
Currency (1845).

1798-1852: McCulloch, *Dictionary*
(2 v., 1854), I, 711. *d*

1799-1836: McCulloch, *Dictionary*
(1837), 672.

1801-1836: Porter, *Progress* (3 v.,
1836-43), II (1838), 98. *d*

1801-1849: Porter, *Progress* (1851),
356. *d*

1814-1822: Powell, *Statistical
Illustrations* (1825), 37-39. *a,h*

1814-1831: Marshall, *Digest* (1833),
Part 3, pp. 56-61. *a,h*

Secondary Works

1697-1850+: Mitchell and Deane, 279-83. *m*

1700-1800: Schumpeter, IV, 16. *i*

24

Table 1
(continued)

By official value for Great Britain unless otherwise indicated.
All references to the *Journals of The House of Commons* [*J.H.C.*] are to the
pages in the appendix of the volume.

a
From each of two dozen countries or
places.

b
Differentiating whether from "East
Indies and China" or "all other."

c
From all parts of the world except
Ireland.

d
For United Kingdom, not Great
Britain.

e
Differentiating from six regions
of the world.

f
For declared value as well as
official value.

g
For both the United Kingdom and
Great Britain.

h
Specifying dozens of articles.

i
For England and Wales.

j
Differentiating England and
Scotland.

k
Imports may be calculated from the
exports and "balance of trade"
which Chalmers sets forth.

l
"By Mr. Chalmers."

m
1697-1791, for England and Wales;
1772-1804, Great Britain;
1796-1853, United Kingdom.

She also has a table for the destinations (eighteen places) of all English
exports, official values only, for 1701-1800.[92] Finally, there are two interesting parliamentary sources, whose publication was prompted by the abolition of the Corn Laws, which compare the figures of British exports (declared value) with the wheat import figures (by quantity, in quarters) of
those "countries from which the chief supplies of wheat have been obtained"
from 1828 to 1848.[93]

The printed trade returns by the middle 1830's become regular and systematic for individual industries. TABLES 3 and 4, based on the fourth edition

[92]Schumpeter, V, 17.
[93]For eight countries from 1828 to 1844, see *P.P. 1846* (360), XLIV, 24;
for thirty-three places from 1839 to 1848, see *P.P. 1849* (588), L, 407-26.

Table 2

TOTAL EXPORTS OF GREAT BRITAIN

Primary Sources

Government Documents	*Books and Pamphlets*
1774-1785: *A.& P. 1787* (428, 432-37), XIX. *a*	1697-1773: Whitworth, *State of the Trade* (1776), Part 1, pp. 1-79. *a,m*
1777-1796: *Rep. 1796-97* (134), XIX, App. 8, p. 165; reprinted in "Lords' Committee of Secrecy, rel. to the Bank (1797)," *P.P. 1810* (17), III, 368; reprinted in *P.T. 6, P.P. 1837-38* [137], XLVII, No. 161, p. 175. *b*	1697-1799: Clarke, *Survey of . . . Great Britain* (1801), 14-16. *m*
	1697-1800: McArthur, *Financial and Political Facts* (1801), 318-20, *m*
1780-1790: *J.H.C. 47,* 356.	1699-1719: Martin, "Essay" (1719), in Clark, *Guide* (1938), App. 4, pp. 69-79. *a,m*
1783-1845: "S.C. (Secret) on Commercial Distress," *P.P. 1847-48* (395), VIII Part 1, 465. *c*	1700-1787: Anderson, *Origin of Commerce* (4 v., 1787-89), IV (1789), 692-94. *m*
1784-1801: *J.H.C. 57,* 954. *b*	
1785-1802: *J.H.C. 58,* 800. *b*	1760-1780: Chalmers, *Estimate* (1782), table facing 37; reprinted in Anderson, *Origin of Commerce* (4 v., 1787-89), IV (1789), facing 322. *n*
1792-1816: *J.H.C. 72,* 745; also in *P.P. 1817* (113), XIV, 243. *b*	
1796-1845: *P.P. 1846* (360), XLIV, 21. *d*	1760-1792: Chalmers, *Estimate* (1794), table facing 207. *n*
1798-1829: *P.P. 1830-31* (20), X, 264-65. *b,e*	1760-1797: McCulloch, *Dictionary* (2 v., 1854), I, 711. *b*
1798-1845: "S.C. (Secret) on Commercial Distress," *P.P. 1847-48* (395), VIII Part 1, 466. *e*	1760-1800: Chalmers, *Estimate* (1802), table facing 234. *n*
1799-1805: *J.H.C. 61,* 775. *b,e*	1760-1800: Wheatley, *Essay on the Theory of Money* (1807), table facing 158. *n,o*

Table 2
(continued)

Government Documents	*Books and Pamphlets*
1801-1846: *P.P. 1847-48* (38), LVIII, 443. *b,f*	1760-1809: Chalmers, *Considerations on Commerce, Bullion and Coin* (1811), App. 1, p. 213 ff. *n*
1805-1811: *J.H.C. 67,* 760-66. *b,e,g*	
1805-1846: *P.P. 1847-48* (38), LVIII, 443. *e,f*	1760-1811: Chalmers, *Historical View of the Domestic Economy* (1812), table facing 315. *n*
1820-1831: *P.T. 1, P.P. 1833,* XLI, 48. *a,b,e,h*	1760-1834: Taylor, *Catechism of Foreign Exchanges* (1835), appendix, pp. 121-25.
1822-1850: *P.P. 1851* (140), XXXI, 172. *b,e,f*	1764-1800: Macpherson, *Annals of Commerce* (4 v., 1805), III, 409 ff.; IV, *passim. a,n*
1827-1834: *P.T. 4, P.P. 1836,* XLVI, No. 77, pp. 83-356. *a,f,i,j,k*	
1827-1843: *P.T. 13, P.P. 1845* [621], XLVIII, No. 105, pp. 116-17. *a,f,l*	1770-1774: Porter, *Progress* (3 v., 1836-43), II (1838), 103.
1831-1840: *P.P. 1842* [375], XXXIX, 1-381. *a,b,e,f,i,j*	1771-1823: Powell, *Statistical Illustrations* (1825), 48.
1841-1850: *P.P. 1854-55* [1987], LII, 1-505. *a,b,e,f,i,j*	1773-1795: Vansittart, *Inquiry into State of the Finances* (1796), appendix, Table 6.
	1777-1796: Allardyce, *Address to . . . the Bank of England* (3rd ed., 1798), App. 40, p. 64. *b*
	1777-1796: Wheatley, *Essay on the Theory of Money* (1807), facing 246. *b*
	1777-1800: Eden, *Eight Letters on the Peace* (1802), 51. *b*
	1779-1798: Beeke, *Observations on the Income Tax* (1800), 71. *l,p*

Table 2
(continued)

Government Documents   *Books and Pamphlets*

1784-1791: Porter, *Progress* (3 v.,
1836-43), II (1838), 103.

1785-1798: Rose, *Brief Examination*
(5th ed., 1799), App. 1, facing
p. 78. *b*

1787-1798: Beeke, *Observations on
the Income Tax* (1800), 65. *b*

1793-1828: Marshall, *Digest* (1833),
Part 3, pp. 71-75, *a,i*

1798-1822: Powell, *Statistical
Illustrations* (1825), 36. *l*

1798-1829: Taylor,"Currency "
(1844), appendix, p. 84, in Taylor,
Currency (1845). *b,e*

1798-1852: McCulloch, *Dictionary*
(2 v., 1854), I, 711. *b,f,l*

1799-1836: McCulloch, *Dictionary*
(1837), 672. *b,e*

1800-1811: Chalmers, *Historical View
of the Domestic Economy* (1812),
table facing 315. *n*

1801-1836: Porter, *Progress* (3 v.,
1836-43), II (1838), 98. *e,f*

1801-1849: Porter, *Progress* (1851),
356. *b,e,f*

1805-1831: Marshall, *Digest* (1833),
Part 3, pp. 62-63, 81. *i*

Table 2
(continued)

Government Documents

Books and Pamphlets

1805-1836: Porter, *Progress* (3 v.,
1836-43), II (1838), 102. *f,g,l*

1805-1849: Porter, *Progress* (1851),
359-60. *g,l*

1814-1822: Powell, *Statistical
Illustrations* (1825), 42-45. *d,e,i*

1814-1831: Marshall, *Digest* (1833),
Part 3, pp. 64-65, 81. *i,l*

1817-1822: Powell, *Statistical
Illustrations* (1825), 32-33. *a,e*

1827-1836: Porter, *Progress* (3 v.,
1836-43), II (1838), 104-09. *a,f,i,
j,l*

1827-1849: Porter, *Progress* (1851),
362-67. *a,f,i,j,l*

1830-1835: McCulloch, *Dictionary*
(1837), 678. *a,f,l*

Secondary Works

1697-1850+:   Mitchell and Deane, 279-83. *b,q*

1700-1800: Schumpeter, I-III, 15-16. *b,m,r*

Table 2
(continued)

By official value from Great Britain unless otherwise indicated.
All references to the *Journals of the House of Commons* [*J.H.C.*] are to the
pages in the appendix of the volume.

[a] To each of two dozen countries or places.

[b] Has in addition a separate series for re-exports of "foreign and colonial merchandise."

[c] Exports in this source are only the total of British exports and re-exports of colonial merchandise.

[d] To all parts of the world except Ireland.

[e] Declared as well as official value of exports.

[f] For United Kingdom, not Great Britain.

[g] Differentiating six regions of the world.

[h] For both Great Britain and the United Kingdom.

[i] Differentiating several dozen articles.

[j] By quantities also.

[k] Re-exports only.

[l] Declared value only.

[m] For England and Wales only.

[n] Differentiating England and Scotland.

[o] "By Mr. Chalmers."

[p] Calculated by Beeke by adding 70 per cent to the official values.

[q] 1697-1791, for England and Wales; 1772-1804, Great Britain; 1796-1853, United Kingdom.

[r] Includes a separate series for the exports (including re-exports) of commodities and specie (differentiated).

of *Porter's Tables* and on two other parliamentary returns, set out the paginations in each source for the period 1827-50 for particular industries.
Treatment of various industries later in this work will refer to these tables.

Statistics of shipping have even greater pitfalls than those of commerce.
First, the figure for ship traffic may mean the number of times that ships
entered and cleared the port, or it may mean the number of different vessels
that did so, regardless of how often they entered or cleared. As for the
tonnage data, these are all estimates based on a set average weight for the
type of ship measured. David Macpherson quotes a return of 1760 which noted
that figuring tonnage was " 'seldom done by actual admeasurement' " and adds
that "the real tunnage [*sic*] may in general be reckoned full fifty per cent
above the reputed." G. N. Clark cautions us that, "as to the general value
of such comparisons [of the shipping data], it seems necessary to say, as in
the case of the figures of imports and exports, that they may be drawn much
more confidently over short periods than over long."[94] With these admonitions,
the sources for British shipping (in numbers and tonnage) are set out in TABLE
5. Information also exists for the number of ships built and registered in
Britain or the United Kingdom from 1789 to 1849,[95] and of the number of steamships, British and foreign, entering British ports from 1814 to 1836.[96] For
twelve important tables regarding shipping from 1829 to 1846, see *P.P. 1847*
(588), LX, 140-48.

Related to shipping statistics are figures on the amount of trade in individual English ports. The Customs House Ledgers (1696-1780) furnish annual
data on port statistics. William Vaughan assembled figures comparing the trade
of the port of London with that of the remainder of the English ports, in 1700,

[94]Macpherson, *Annals of Commerce*, III (1805), 340; Clark, 51. See the analysis in "The General Registers of Shipping," in Clark, 45-51.

[95]The longest series, which runs from 1801 to 1849, is in Porter, *Progress*
(1851), 395. For another long series from 1815 to 1849, see *P.P. 1850* (460),
LII, 318. There are various shorter series which may be consulted. For 1789-
1800, see Sir Frederick Morton Eden, *Eight Letters on the Peace* (1802), 61;
for 1801-36, see Porter, *Progress* (3 v., 1836-43), II (1838), 172; for 1814-
24, see Powell, *Statistical Illustrations* (1827), 82; for 1820-31, see *P.T. 1,
P.P. 1833*, XLI, 50-51; for 1825-51, see McCulloch, *Dictionary* (8th ed., 2 v.,
1854), II, 1168.

In addition to the above sources for data on the number of vessels built
and registered in the United Kingdom, there are statistics for the number of
ships in the British Empire. For the period 1803-49, see Porter, *Progress*
(1851), 394; for 1825-51, see McCulloch, *Dictionary* (2 v., 1854), II, 1168.

[96]For British ships from 1814 to 1836, see *P.T. 6, P.P. 1837-38* [137],
XLVII, No. 57, p. 50; for foreign ships for 1820-36, see *P.T. 7, P.P. 1839*
[198], XLV, No. 51, p. 51, which is a corrected return of *P.T. 6, P.P. 1837-
38* [137], XLVII, No. 58, pp. 51-52. Porter, *Progress* (1851), 324, has data
for both British and foreign steamships entering British ports from 1820 to
1849. He also provides figures for the numbers and tonnage of steamships
built and registered in the United Kingdom for 1814-49 (*Progress* [1851], p.
316) and for the numbers belonging to the United Kingdom for 1814-49 (*ibid.*,
p. 317).

Table 3

IMPORTS AND RE-EXPORTS OF FOREIGN AND COLONIAL MERCHANDISE

Years	1827-34	1831-40	1841-50
Source	*Porter's Tables IV, P.P. 1836, XLVI, No. 77, page*	*P.P. 1842 (375), XXXIX, page*	*P.P. 1854-55 (1987), LII, page*
Article			
COPPER, Unwrought	92	12	21-22
COTTON MANUFACTURES OF INDIA	102	20	33-34
COTTON MANUFACTURES (FOREIGN)	102	21-22	35-36
FLAX	106	26	43
IRON, in Bars	119	38	63-64
LEAD, Pig	120	39	65-66
LINENS[a]	124-26	42-46	67-73
SILK, Raw and Waste	144	65	106-07
Thrown	145	66	108-09
Manufactured in Europe	146	67	110-11
Indian	147-50	68-71	112-17
TIN	167	93	145-46
WOOL, Cotton	181	115-16	170-71
Sheep and Lambs	182	117	172-73
YARN, LINEN (Raw)	183	118	174

All figures are for quantities only, imported into and re-exported from the United Kingdom, distinguishing from two to four dozen countries.

[a] This article also includes a series for official values.

Table 4

EXPORTS OF PRODUCE AND MANUFACTURES

Years	1827-34	1831-40	1841-50
Source	*Porter's Tables IV, P.P. 1836,* XLVI, No. 77, page	*P.P. 1842* (375), XXXIX, page	*P.P. 1854-55* (1987), LII, page
Article			
BRASS AND COPPER MANUFACTURES	190	125	186-87
COALS, CULM, AND CINDERS	192	128	190-91
COTTON MANUFACTURES,			
By Yard	194-97	130-31	194-95
Hosiery, Lace[a]	194-97	132	196
Cotton Twist and Yarn	194-97	134-35	198-99
Totals[a]	...	133	197
HARDWARES AND CUTLERY	202	142-43	208-09
IRON AND STEEL,			
Wrought and Unwrought	204	146-47	212-13
LEAD AND SHOT	205	148-49	214-15
LINEN MANUFACTURES,			
By Yard	208-09	152-53	220-21
Thread, Tapes[a]	208-09	154	222
Totals[a]	...	155	223
LINEN YARN	210[b]	156	224-25
MACHINERY AND MILL WORK[a]	210	157	226
SILK MANUFACTURES[a]	214	161	232-33
TIN, Unwrought	218	168	240-41
TIN AND PEWTER WARES[a]	219	169	242-43
WOOL, Sheeps and Lambs	220	170-71	244-45
WOOLEN AND WORSTED YARN	225	170-71	246-47
WOOLEN MANUFACTURES,			
By Piece	221-24	172-73	248-49
By Yard	221-24	174-75	250-51
Hosiery and Small Wares[a]	221-24	176	252
Totals[a]	...	177	253

All figures are for quantity *and* declared value, exported from the United
Kingdom, distinguishing from two to four dozen countries.

[a] By declared value only.   [b] For 1832-34 only.

Table 5

THE SHIPPING OF GREAT BRITAIN

Distinguishing the Number and Tonnage of
Ships, and whether British or Foreign,
clearing inwards and outwards of British Ports

Primary Sources

Government Documents	*Books and Pamphlets*
1789-1800: *J.H.C. 56,* 850-67. *a,b*	1760-1780: Chalmers, *Estimate* (1782), facing 37. *d,f*
1805-1807: *J.H.C. 63,* 705.	1760-1792: Chalmers, *Estimate* (1794), facing 207. *d,f*
1806-1811: *J.H.C. 67,* 767.	1760-1800: Chalmers, *Estimate* (1802), facing 234. *d,f*
1811-1813: *J.H.C. 69,* 720.	1760-1809: Chalmers, *Considerations on Commerce, Bullion and Coin* (1811), App. 1, p. 213 ff. *d,f,g*
1814-1820: *P.P. 1830-31* (47), X, 285-304. *a,c*	
1816-1825: *P.P. 1826* (361), XXII, 322-23. *a,d*	1760-1811: Chalmers, *Historical View of the Domestic Economy* (1812), facing 315. *d,f,g*
1816-1845: *P.P. 1847* (115), LX, 123-26. *c,e*	1760-1811: McCulloch, *Dictionary* (1837), 1021; reprinted in *Dictionary* (2 v., 1854), II, 1167. *d,g*
1820-1831: *P.T. 1, P.P. 1833,* XLI, 50-51. *c*	
1820-1846: *P.P. 1847* (588), LX, 143. *c,d*	1770-1782: Eden, *Eight Letters on the Peace* (1802), 45. *d,f*
1824-1843: "S.C. on British Shipping," *P.P. 1844* (545), VIII, App. 3, pp. 221-30. *a,c*	1770-1824: Powell, *Statistical Illustrations* (1825), 48. *d,g*
1831-1840: *P.P. 1842* [375], XXXIX, 382-92. *a,c*	1789-1800: Eden, *Eight Letters on the Peace* (1802), 46-47, *passim. a,d*
1841-1850: *P.P. 1854-55* [1987], LII, 506-19. *a,c*	

34

Table 5
(continued)

Government Documents	*Books and Pamphlets*
	1790-1802: Courtenay, *Observations upon . . . the Finances* (1803), App. C, p. 95.
	1801-1836: Porter, *Progress* (3 v., 1836-43), II (1838), 174-75. *c*
	1801-1849: Porter, *Progress* (1851), 397-98. *c*
	1814-1824: Powell, *Statistical Illustrations* (1825), 82.
	1814-1831: Marshall, *Digest* (1833), Part 3, p. 207. *h*
	1814-1842: McCulloch, *Dictionary* (2 v., 1854), II, 1167. *c*

Secondary Works

Schumpeter: none.   Mitchell and Deane: none

The statistics refer to Great Britain unless otherwise indicated.

a To and from dozens of countries and places.

b England and Scotland differentiated.

c For the United Kingdom, not Great Britain.

d By tonnage only.

e To and from the twelve principal ports of the United Kingdom.

f For England and Wales only.

g Out of port only.

h Great Britain and Ireland differentiated.

1737, 1756, 1763, 1784, and 1791-92.[97] Chalmers has annual figures for the tonnage clearing five specified British ports for 1750-52 and 1770-72, while a massive parliamentary paper has data for *every* British port for 1790-92 and 1799-1802, annually.[98] *Porter's Tables* gives statistics of the number of vessels (1757-1832) and the tonnage (1800-32) clearing the port of Liverpool.[99] Two parliamentary papers list the number and tonnage of ships clearing the twelve leading ports in the United Kingdom from 1816 to 1850.[100]

The movement of people (cargoes of a different sort) is not strictly pertinent to a study of commerce and shipping, but such information may be found in *Porter's Tables*. One table lists the numbers of emigrants from the United Kingdom from 1825 to 1850, distinguishing the destination (British North America, the United States, Australia or New Zealand, and all others).[101] Another specifies the ports of embarkation in Britain and Ireland for immigrants arriving in Quebec and Montreal between 1831 and 1842;[102] another lists the number of arrivals at New York City from 1829 to 1837.[103] Until 1835 Canada was more popular than the United States, but by 1844 America was receiving twice as many, by 1848, six times as many, emigrants as went to Canada.

(e) *The Uses of Statistics and William Playfair*

Looking over eighteenth-century works on commerce and industry, one is struck by the contrast to nineteenth-century writings. The earlier tracts are discursive, sometimes impressionistic, often unsystematic. A Chalmers or a Macpherson—if we end the century with the Napoleonic Wars—were the exceptions. A more representative figure would be a Malachy Postlethwayt whom we encountered at the outset. His edition of *The Universal Dictionary of Commerce*, though the product of twenty years' labor, includes no statistics, proceeds

[97]"On Wet Docks, Quays, and Warehouses, for the Port of London; with hints respecting trade" (1793), in William Vaughan, *Tracts on Docks and Commerce* (1839), App. A, p. 21. Like Sir Frederick Eden, Vaughan was the head of an insurance company—in this case, the Royal Exchange Assurance Company. For biographical details, see *ibid.*, 1-22.

[98]Chalmers, *Estimate* (1782), table facing 46; the ports are London, Bristol, Liverpool, Newcastle, and Whitehaven. The parliamentary source, extending over several hundred pages, lists the ports alphabetically; see *P.P. 1802-03* (138), VIII.

[99]*P.T. 1, P.P. 1833*, XLI, Part 2, p. 116. Vaughan, "On Wet Docks, Quays, and Warehouses," in Vaughan, *Tracts on Docks and Commerce* (1839), App. F, p. 27, lists the amounts of Liverpool dock duties (1752-93) and the number of ships paying them (1757-93).

[100]*P.P. 1847* (115), LX, 123-25. A series in *P.P. 1851* (656), LII, 213-17, continues the statistics through 1850.

[101]*P.T. 20, P.P. 1852*, LII, No. 230, p. 218. For an earlier series (1825-37), see *P.T. 7, P.P. 1839* [198], XLV, No. 176, p. 195. McCulloch, *Dictionary* (2 v., 1854), II, 962, has differentiated emigration figures for 1815-52.

[102]*P.T. 12, P.P. 1844* [591], XLVI, No. 215, pp. 254-55.

[103]*P.T. 7, P.P. 1839* [198], XLV, No. 183, p. 199.

by no fixed method, and tends to be turgid.[104] Lest we be too harsh, however, we must remember that it was not unusual for writers in Postlethwayt's age to write 1,761,534 as 1761534 or, innocently, to describe a chart or table as, "showing at one view. . . ." It was really not until the 1780's that statistical methods of economic exposition appeared in England. The word 'statistics' was first used in England only in 1787.[105] Count Cavour, looking back from the 1840's, was impressed by "the mathematical ideas which the French Revolution made current." The unidentified author of *Political Geography*, published in London and Dublin in 1789, speaking of tabular presentations, lauded "the advantage of collecting into a small compass and striking point of view the principles of different sciences," with the result, "it has been generally admitted, as tending to impress the mind more forcibly than [if the principles were] in a diffuse state."[106]

The first practitioners of statistical methods worked in political, medical, and demographic subjects. William Petty, who coined the phrase "Political Arithmetick" in 1687, labored in vital statistics and with a miscellany of political and economic figures.[107] John Graunt in 1662 had worked with demo-

[104]Postlethwayt translated and added substantially to Jacques Savary des Bruslons' *Le Dictionnaire Universel du Commerce* (3 v., Paris, 1723-30); see note 1. Savary was inspector of customs at Paris; at his death in 1716, the work was completed by his brother, the Abbé Savary. The first treatise of its kind in modern Europe, the *Dictionnaire* went through numerous editions: Paris, 1748; Geneva, 1750; Copenhagen, 1759 and 1756; and Venice, 1770-71. Malachy Postlethwayt (1707?-67) wrote two books on the African slave trade, *The African Trade the Great Pillar and Support of the British Plantation Trade in America* (1745) and *The Natural and Private Advantages of the African Trade Considered* (1746). In addition, he produced a book on French commerce, *A Short State of the Progress of French Trade and Navigation* (1756), and two books on British Commerce, *Great Britain's True System* (1757) and *Britain's Commercial Interest Explained and Improved* (2 v., 1757).

[105]In Eberhard A. W. von Zimmermann, *Political Survey of the Present State of Europe* (1787). The opinion is that of George Yule, *Journal of the Royal Statistical Society*, LXVIII (1905), 391-96, quoted in H. G. Funkhouser, "The Historical Development of the Graphical Representation of Statistical Data," *Osiris*, III (1937), 280 n. 26. Gottfried Achenwall (1719-72) is credited with coining the word *Statistik*, meaning a comparison of nation-states (*Staatenkunde*) using numbers. See Funkhouser's article [hereafter cited as 'Funkhouser'], pp. 290-91.

[106]Camillo B., conte di Cavour, *Thoughts on Ireland: its present and its future*, tr., W. B. Hodgson (1868), 26. Originally published in Geneva in 1844 because of Piedmontese censorship, the work was first published in Italy in 1855. The anonymous *Political Geography* (1789), 4, has political and military, but no economic statistics.

[107]Petty (1623-87) used the phrase in the title of his work, *Two Essays in Political Arithmetick* (1686). (Arthur Young in his analysis of England in 1774 would later use the phrase as his book title, *Political Arithmetic*.) The son of a clothier, Petty did his first serious work with the English army in Ireland. Though his post was officially that of physician-general, Petty per-

graphic statistics,[108] and Gregory King in 1696 built his famous national table of social rank and income in England.[109] But none of these statisticians did any considerable work with commercial data. Those who did present the data—Davenant, Whitworth, or Chalmers—made little creative use of the statistics.

suaded the Government that his techniques of mapping were the best available. Having conquered Ireland, Cromwell had decided to pay the English officers in forfeited Irish land. To do this properly, the exact location and size of holdings throughout the island had to be determined: the result was Petty's 'Down Survey' (1651), so named because the engineers measured *down* onto maps. Many years later his Irish experiences were abstracted in a brilliant statistical essay; see "The Political Anatomy of Ireland" (written in 1672, but not published until 1691), in *The Economic Writings of Sir William Petty*, ed., Charles H. Hull (2 v., 1899), I, 121-223.

Petty was one of the founders of the Royal Society in 1662, at which time he was knighted. His brilliant *Treatise of Taxes and Contributions* appeared in the same year. Above all, Petty was concerned with general political and social statistics. His two major works are *Two Essays in Political Arithmetick, concerning the People, Housing, Hospitals &c. of London and Paris* (1686) and *Political Arithmetick, or a Discourse concerning the Extent and Value of Lands, People, Buildings; Husbandry, Manufacture, Commerce, Fishery, Artizans, Seamen, Soldiers; Public Revenues, Interest, Taxes. . . .* [written, 1676; posthumously published] (1690). Petty's lifelong interest in statistics, however, was frustrated by the lack of collected data. From the mid-1670's, he advocated the creation of a statistical office in London to collect, count, value, and organize all sorts of data. Unfortunately, it was a century and a half before the government would create such an office, and then only at the Board of Trade (1831). For his life, see *D.N.B.*, XV, 999-1005.

[108]John Graunt (1620-74), of very humble origins in London, was as a child apprenticed to a haberdasher. Later, he became involved in London politics (serving on the City's Common Council), but he is famous for his work in demography. His classic, *Natural and Political Observations mentioned in a following Index, and made upon the Bills of Mortality* (1662; 5th ed., 1676), led to immediate entrance, though he was a shopkeeper, into the Royal Society (February 1662). Charles II is said to have remarked of Graunt's election, that if the Society "found any more such tradesmen, they should be sure to admit them all, without any more adoe." See *D.N.B.*, VIII, 427-28.

[109]In his own lifetime Gregory King (1648-1712), the son of a Staffordshire mathematician, was known as a genealogist and engraver. A quarrel with the Earl Marshal of England over the funeral arrangements for Queen Mary (1694) ended his heraldic concerns. He became secretary to the commissioners of the public accounts until 1712. His new interest led to publication of *Natural and Political Observations and Conclusions upon the State and Condition of England* (1696), a demographic, social, and economic study based on statistics. His income table for 1688 gives a hint of why he has scarcely any commercial or industrial data: the non-agricultural figures are indiscriminately lumped together as "trade, arts, and labours." The work was unknown to the public, for it was not published until George Chalmers appended it to the 1802 edition of his *Estimate of the Comparative Strength of Great-Britain*, pp. 405-

38

At this point it is proper to single out one statistician of commerce who should enjoy a prominence equal to that usually given to Macpherson and Chalmers, McCulloch and Porter. William Playfair (1759-1823)[110] was, on the one hand, a social and antiquarian type and a patriotic Briton,[111] while, on the other, quite a revolutionary. His statistical publications firmly establish him as the inventor of diagrammatic statistics: bar graphs, line graphs, circle charts. By means of "a principle entirely new"—color-tinted, copper-plate graphs—Playfair exulted that the reader could see "with ease and perspicuity" the story contained in tables of figures.

Playfair, like so many other statisticians, was a Scotsman. Born near Dundee in 1759, he was the fourth son of a clergyman. William's brother, James, would become a famous professor of mathematics at Edinburgh; his nephew, William, would be a celebrated architect.[112] William's first job was as an ap-

49. See *D.N.B.*, XI, 131-33.

[110]For his life, see *D.N.B.*, XV, 1300-01. For a list of forty of his works, see *The Gentleman's Magazine*, new ser., XVI (1823), Part 1, pp. 564-66. Under the pseudonym, Jepson Oddy, Playfair may have authored a work called *European Commerce* (1805; 2 v., Philadelphia, 1807); see the Kress Library's *Catalogue 1777-1817* (Boston, 1957), No. B4953, p. 251. The work has trade figures with Russian and East Prussian ports from the 1780's until 1803. William Playfair should not be confused with William Henry Playfair (1789-1857), the architect.

[111]See *A Fair and Candid Address to the British Nobility; accompanied with Illustrations and Proofs of the Advantage of Hereditary Rank and Title in a Free Country* (1809); *A Second Address to the British Nobility* (1810). Both these pamphlets are far less important than his massive *British Family Antiquity* (10 v., 1809-11). The final volume consists of nine beautiful folded copper-plate charts which trace the longevity of each family in each aristocratic rank, from baronetcy to dukedom. It is noteworthy that these works were composed during the Napoleonic Wars, perhaps in response to Napoleon's rewarding his generals with landed titles. The antiquity of the English titles, as anyone studying Playfair's charts could tell, was clearly superior to that of the French ones since the creation of the Empire in 1804. Aside from Arthur Collins' *The Peerage of England* (2 v., 1714; 6th ed., 9 v., 1812), the reference works on the nobility are 19th-century creations. Many short-lived works appeared in the 1790's—perhaps as a reaction to the Revolution in France. The permanent reference works date from the decade in which Playfair's genealogical work appeared; see John Debrett's *The Peerage of England, Scotland, and Ireland* (2 v., 1803; 29th ed., 1847) and *The Baronetage of England* (2 v., 1808; 7th ed., 1835). John Burke's *A General and Heraldic Dictionary of the Peerage and Baronetage of the United Kingdom* was first published in 1826 (7th ed., 1842); his *Genealogical and Heraldic Dictionary of the Landed Gentry* (3 v.) did not appear until 1847-49. Genealogy, like commercial statistics, tended to reassure Englishmen of their place in the world.

[112]The Reverend Charles Rogers, *The Scottish House of Roger* (2nd ed., Edinburgh, 1875), 24.

prentice to Andrew Meikle of Prestonkirk, the inventor of the threshing machine. Then, at age twenty-one, he became a draftsman in the firm of Boulton and Watt in Birmingham. Watt was at this time devising an automatic registering instrument which diagrammed the relationship of steam pressure in the cylinder to the movement of the piston. Another possible influence on Playfair was Joseph Priestley's graphic work with biographical and historical data, e.g., bar graphs representing a man's life span.[113]

With Playfair's publication in 1786 of his classic *Commercial and Political Atlas*, the broken-line and bar graph were introduced to economic historiography. Playfair reasoned that until very recently England was not developed or wealthy enough to require statistical precision. But with Adam Smith's revolution in economics, "like that which was produced by Sir Isaac Newton in mathematics and astronomy," there was now a need

> to render our conceptions as clear, distinct, and easily acquired, as possible. Hitherto few men were much acquainted with the general trade of Britain, or even with any particular branch of it, on account chiefly of the imperfect and difficult way of acquiring the knowledge.[114]

To render a clear account of commercial figures Playfair decided to set out thirty-five plates in the form of broken-line graphs, with time constituting the horizontal axis, and pounds sterling, the vertical. The line of imports Playfair stained yellow; exports, red. A favorable balance of trade he marked by a blue line; an unfavorable one, by a pink line. He employed one bar graph —the first used in economics—to show the trade of Scotland for one year; exports he indicated by a black bar, imports by ribbed lines (hachures).[115] Writing in the preface to the first edition, Playfair was quite explicit as to the purposes of his new methods:

> Information that is imperfectly acquired is generally as imperfectly retained; and a man

[113]Joseph Priestley's *Chart of Biography* (1765) measured two feet by three feet in size, covered 1200 B.C. to 1750 A.D., and contained 2,000 names. Funkhouser, 289 comments that Priestley's writings were "at the height of their popularity at the time Playfair was beginning his work." Playfair never mentions Priestley's example, though he was seldom inclined to credit the work of others.

[114]William Playfair, *The Commercial and Political Atlas* (1786), preface, pp. i-iii.

[115]Playfair was quite aware that this chart "is different from the others in principle, as it does not comprehend any portion of time, and it is much inferior in utility to those that do; for though it gives the extent of the different branches of trade, it does not compare the same branch of commerce with itself at different periods; nor does it imprint upon the mind that distinct idea, in doing which, the chief advantage of Charts consists: for as it wants the dimension that is formed by duration, there is no shape given to the quantities" (*Atlas* [1786], 101).

who has carefully investigated a printed table,
finds, when done, that he has only a very faint
and partial idea of what he has read; and that
like a figure imprinted on sand, is soon totally
erased and defaced. . . . On inspecting any one
of these Charts attentively, a sufficiently
distinct impression will be made, to remain
unimpaired for a considerable time, and the idea
which does remain will be simple and complete,
at once including the duration and the amount . . . .[116]

In the third edition (1801) he was even more specific:

As the eye is the best judge of proportion,
being able to estimate it with more quickness
and accuracy than any other organ, it follows
. . . [that] when a gradual increase or decrease of
any revenue, receipt, or expenditure of money,
or other value, is to be stated, this mode of
representing it is peculiarly applicable; it
gives a simple, accurate, and permanent idea,
by giving form and shape to a number of separate
ideas which are otherwise abstract and unconnected.[117]

Playfair's plates in the 1801 work presented by graphs data on eighteenth-
century English trade (totals to and from eight specific countries), government revenues of England and France (1550-1800), the English national debt
(1688-1800) and its reduction by the Sinking Fund (1786-1801), and Army and
Navy expenditures (1720-1800).[118] One methodological problem with his graph-
ing is that he uses data at ten-year points, rather than annual data or averages of a series of years.

If Playfair hardly achieved overnight fame, as Adam Smith did, a few contemporaries were nevertheless impressed. Gilbert Stuart in his periodical,
The Political Herald, called the new method "the most commodious, as well as
accurate, mode of effecting this object [presenting data] that has hitherto
been thought of."[119] Playfair's *Atlas,* sent by an English nobleman to the
Comte de Vergennes, excited interest in France and a translation by H. Jansen

[116]Playfair, *Atlas* (1786), 3-4.

[117]Playfair, *Atlas* (3rd ed., 1801), preface, p. x.

[118]The first (1786) and second (1787) editions contained the same forty
plates, including "Mr. [James] Corry's Charts of Irish Affairs." The plates
in the second edition were printed only in black (hachures and dots) and white.
The third (1801) edition presents twenty-six colored plates and does not include Corry's Irish graphs.

[119]Gilbert Stuart, *The Political Herald* (3 v., 1785-86), III (1786), 299-
306. This Gilbert Stuart (1742-86), historian and reviewer, should not be
confused with the American Gilbert Stuart (1755-1828), the portrait painter
who worked in England from 1775 to 1792.

appeared in 1789.[120]

Playfair, meanwhile, had become involved in a metalworking business in London which failed and in 1787 he left for France. In Paris he lived by taking out a patent on a rolling mill and acting as agent for a shadowy Ohio land company (Scioto) which would later ruin hundreds of investors. He is reported to have been present at the taking of the Bastille in 1789; he had joined the St. Antoine unit of militia, and nearly all of that unit took part in the assault. But by 1793 the Jacobins were attacking him for mismanagement of Scioto, or, as Playfair claimed, for his own disillusionment with Revolution. He returned to London by way of Frankfort. He soon was in trouble again by falsely claiming to introduce the semaphore telegraph into England. He opened a small loan agency which shortly collapsed. He began writing.

Playfair's political writing combines the qualities of a strong anti-Jacobin and patriotic Briton.[121] Returned from Paris, he remained in London for the rest of his life, with the exception of an unhappy interlude in Paris in 1815-18 as a newspaper editor. It would not be irrelevant to surmise that one reason why Playfair turned to economic statistics was that those statistics demonstrated that England, the bulwark of conservatism in the Napoleonic Wars, was the richest and most powerful nation in the world. "If our *English pseudo patriots*," he wrote in 1796,

> are determined to exhibit to our enemies
> our increasing debts, and to accompany
> their statements with commentaries, fore-
> boding destruction to this nation, I surely
> may be permitted to shew [*sic*] at one single
> view, *that our resources overtop our
> burthens* [*sic*]. . . .[122]

The work contained two colored graphs, one showing the revenue of the English government in the eighteenth century fast closing the gap on its wealthier

[120]As *Tableaux d'Arithmétique linéaire du commerce, des finances, et de la dette nationale de l'Angleterre,* with a preface in French by Playfair. The circumstances are stated in Playfair, *A Real Statement of the Finances and Resources of Great Britain; illustrated by two copper-plate charts* (1796), p. iv, note.

[121]For his views on the French Revolution, see *A General View of the Actual Force and Resources of France* (1793), *Peace with the Jacobins Impossible* (1794), and his vituperative tome of over eight hundred pages, *The History of Jacobinism, its crimes, cruelties, and perfidies: comprising an inquiry into the manner of disseminating, under the appearance of philosophy and virtue, principles which are equally subversive of order, virtue, religion, liberty, and happiness* (1795; 2nd ed., 1798). An edition was published in Philadelphia in 1796 by that English anti-Jacobin William Cobbett, who was then living in America. For Playfair's ideas on political reform in England, see his *Inevitable Consequences of a Reform in Parliament* (1792).

[122]Playfair, *Real Statement of . . . Resources of Great Britain,* introduction, p. vii. He subtitled his work, *For the Use of the Enemies of England.*

neighbor, France, and the other chart presenting the rise in British exports from 1700 to 1795.[123] Playfair hailed the increase in exports as a "glorious" reward for English diligence, while the French were a people who "export nothing of any value." He then acidly observed that

> this chart . . . must, or at least ought, to
> make the greatest impression on our enemies,
> and convince them that if England has
> orators to declaim on her *misery*, she has
> also merchants and manufacturers to support
> her *prosperity*; aye, and to augment it too!![124]

After bring out a translation of Jacob Boetticher's statistical account of Europe as *Statistical Tables* (1800),[125] Playfair issued a third edition (1801) of the *Atlas* and published his *Statistical Breviary*.[126] The latter

[123]Playfair, *Real Statement of . . . Resources of Great Britain* (1796), facing 8.

[124]Playfair, *Real Statement of . . . Resources of Great Britain* (1796), 12-13.

[125]*Statistical Tables: exhibiting a view of all the States of Europe: showing, with the greatest accuracy, their population, military and marine strength, revenue and expenditure, forms of government . . . chief towns, situation, number of houses and inhabitants, historical occurrences, &c., tr. by William Playfair, with a Supplementary Table; containing the Changes since the Publication of the Original Work.* The original work was Jakob Gottlieb Isaak Boetticher's *Statistics Uebersichts-Tabellen aller europeen Staaten* (Leipzig, 1789). This work should not be confused with an anonymous work, *The Political Geography: Introduction to the statistical tables of the principal Empires, Kingdoms, and States in Europe* (1789). Foxwell's note on the inside cover of the *Geography*, that "similar tables were published in 1800," must refer to Playfair's translation in 1800 of Boetticher's work.

[126]The *D.N.B.*, XV, 1301, lists a *Statistical Breviary and Atlas* of 1786. No such work exists. The *D.N.B.* fails to list *The Commercial and Political Atlas* of 1786 and *The Statistical Breviary* of 1801. Funkhouser also makes the mistake. Though he acknowledges the *Atlas* and the *Breviary* in the text (Funkhouser, 281 n. 28; 283 n. 31), he uses the misnomer, *The Statistical Atlas*, in Figures 2 and 4 (Funkhouser, 282, 286). The catalogues of the Kress Library, the Goldsmiths' Library (London), and the British Museum do not list a *Statistical Atlas*. Both the Goldsmiths' Library and the British Museum do have a work called *Lineal Arithmetic* (1798), which is a reprint of the *Commercial Atlas* of 1786 with a title based on the French translation of 1789 (*L' Arithmetique linéaire*). Finally, the problem is slightly confused by Playfair's own reference in *Real Statement of . . . Resources of Great Britain* (1796), p. iv, to his first work as *Lineal Arithmetic, or Charts of Commerce and Revenue*, published in 1785, although no library possesses a work of this title. Perhaps Playfair's memory was clouded by the enthusiastic reception which greeted the translation of the *Atlas* in France in 1789. Louis XVI himself is said to have read and approved the work. On the basis of Playfair's writings, the Academy of Sciences invited him to their meetings in 1787-89.

work introduced to the world the circle graph and the pie diagram. In four color-coded plates Playfair presented the leading countries of the world as circles of sizes proportional to the land areas of the countries; he drew line ordinates rising vertically on the left (population) and right (revenue) of each circle, the lengths of the ordinates being proportional to that country's population and revenue.[127] The *Breviary*, like the *Atlas* earlier, caught on in France, with Donnant issuing a translation in 1802.[128]

The year of the invasion scare in England, 1805, was a prolific one for Playfair. He published his *Inquiry into the Permanent Causes of the Decline and Fall of Powerful and Wealthy Nations* (2nd ed., 1807),[129] issued the eleventh edition of fellow Scot Adam Smith's *Wealth of Nations* (3 v., with supplementary chapters, and a 25-page biography of Smith), and produced *The Statistical Account of the United States of America*,[130] a translation of Donnant's work. By 1805, Playfair had produced his greatest works. His last eighteen years, however, were not totally inactive. In 1813 he sketched the *Outlines of a Plan for a New and Solid Balance of Power in Europe*.[131] In 1821 he published *A Letter on our Agricultural Distresses*, which contained charts of agricultural prices and wages since the sixteenth century;[132] in

[127]Playfair miscalculated when, to suggest the relative harshness of taxation in each country, he drew a line between the tips of the lines of population and revenue, for the diameter of the circle, being the land areas of the country, distorts what he is trying to measure. We may agree with Funkhouser's comment, 285: "That he was able to get all of his data on one graph is proof of his ingenuity. That some of it is a little awkward and misleading is no worse a criticism than can be made of many graphs of today and is certainly not surprising in the first use of a new form."

[128]Denis François Donnant, *Élemens de Statistique, où l'on démontre d'après un principe entièrement neuf, les resources de chaque royaume, état et republique de l'Europe* . . . . *tr. de l'anglais* . . . (Paris, An XI [1802]).

[129]Comment on title page: "Designed to Shew how the Prosperity of the British Empire may be prolonged." The work is illustrated with four engraved charts. The frontispiece consists of a highly imaginative "Chart of Universal Commercial History," or the rise and fall of twenty-one civilizations, from Egypt in 1500 B.C. to the United States of America in 1804. With prescience, Playfair placed England in third place above France, but behind Russia and the United States, to whom he assigned the potential second and first ranks, respectively. Other charts: extent, population, and revenue of twelve leading European nations; exports and imports of England, by official value, 1700-1805; and increase of annual revenues of England and France, 1600-1805.

[130]Denis Francois Donnant, *Statistical Account of the United States of America, tr. from the French By W. Playfair* (1805). The 72-page volume contains a folded color diagram of American economic conditions.

[131]"Dedicated to his Imperial Majesty Alexander I, Emperor of all the Russias." Facing p. 32 is a "Statistical Table, shewing the most important Circumstances that relate to the Power of the different Nations of Europe." Fifteen countries are examined in fourteen categories, from extent in square miles through disposable army to proportional value of money.

[132]*A Letter on Our Agricultural Distresses, their causes and remedies: accompanied with tables and copper-plate charts, shewing and comparing the*

the same year he composed, as a fold-out frontispiece for the *Chronology of Public Events*, a chart which indicated statistical trends and crude correlations for five sets of economic data from 1770 to 1820.[133] For all his labors with statistics, Playfair earned little public recognition or material gain. When he died in 1823, at age sixty-three, he left his wife and four children almost penniless.

(f) The Age of Statistics, 1820-50

At the time of Playfair's death, the educated public was really only beginning to form an interest in statistics. In the 1830's, with the work of Porter and McCulloch, that interest skyrocketed. The more general idea of researching facts and using original sources came of age in the period 1820-40,[134] and statistical investigation was but a part of the awakening. The founders of the Manchester Statistical Society observed, quite simply, in 1833: "A number of gentlemen had been struck with the extreme deficiency of all accurate statistical information regarding this country."[135]

Counting short-lived organizations, the first statistical society was an association in London created as a result of the distresses of 1816-17. The founders, a committee of artisans led by John Powell, sought (in the words of Powell) to investigate the nature and extent of the causes of "the privation

prices of wheat and labour from 1565 to 1821, addressed to the Lords and Commons (1821; 2nd and 3rd eds., 1822). Table 1, facing p. 44, is a black bar graph of wheat prices together with a red line graph of the price of labor, 1565 to 1821 .Table 2, also facing p. 44, is a red line graph of annual average bread prices, 1740 to 1821; Table 3, facing p. 50, is a colored bar graph of the value of a quarter of wheat and of "a mechanic's wages, 1565 to 1821, in bars of widths equalling 25-year periods.

[133]The chart—"Linear Chronology, exhibiting the revenues, expenditure, debt, price of stocks & bread from 1770 to 1820, by William Playfair"—forms the frontispiece of the *Chronology of Public Events and Remarkable Occurrences within the last Fifty Years; or, from 1771 to 1821. With a general chronology from the earliest records to the year 1770* (1821).

[134]Some evidence for this tentative generalization are the figures for the number of visits made for study or research to the Reading Rooms of the British Museum from 1810 to 1845:

1810.......1,950	1830......31,200
1815.......4,300	1835.......63,466
1820.......8,820	1840.......67,542
1825......22,800	1845.......64,427

The number of visits to the general collections, for which we have figures only from 1843, increased from 517,440 in 1843 to 897,985 in 1848. See *P.T. 18, P.P. 1850* [1159], LIV, No. 222, p. 200.

[135]Quoted in the *Journals of the Statistical Society of London,* I (1838), 48. Hereafter cited as *J.S.S.L.*

& misery endured by the productive classes of society."[136] The association published its findings in tabular form in *Statistical Illustrations of . . . the British Empire* (1825). By 1827 the group was calling itself the London Statistical Society. Its namesake successor was rather harsh on this early society. The official *Annals* of the second and lasting London Statistical Society speak of the first society as "hardly of the same standing"—social as well as professional—as the present society. "The tables seem quite honestly handled," the later group admitted, but the association was accused (somewhat contradictorily) of "a tendency to select and accentuate the gloomiest facts and figures of that depressed time." A look through the book will dispel the grounds for that charge. The work is a systematic, fair, and complete representation of figures found in parliamentary papers; it is incorrect to say that "the whole leaves the impression of a controversial and too emotional indictment of things as they were." The harshest indictment by the later London Society seems to have been that the Association was "the private adventure of men of small means," namely, working class radicals, "probably of Owenite leanings."[137] Nothing further is heard from this group after 1827, when it apparently disbanded.

The entirely different Statistical Society of London was founded in March 1834, because the example in Manchester (September 1833) could not pass unanswered and because the British Association for the Advancement of Science, itself created in 1831, wanted a statistical section. The Society became the sixth or F section of the British Association and established a permanent headquarters in London. The group's creator was the Reverend Richard Jones, recently elected to the Chair of Political Economy at King's College in the new London University. Jones was assisted by the well-known Reverend Thomas Malthus, Charles Babbage, the writer on technology and industry, and by Adolphe Quetelet, the astronomer and statistician from Brussels, who was in England for the meetings of the British Association.[138]

The purpose of the Society was to collect, interpret, and publicize statistics of four general kinds: *economic* (manufactures, trade, agriculture, currency), *political* (institutions, law, finance, expenditure), *medical* (birth and death rates, disease), and *moral and intellectual* (literature, education, religion, crime).[139] The first publication of the Society appeared in 1838. It covered all manner of subjects, but over the years medical subjects received the most attention, followed by social and financial affairs. Commerce and industry received surprisingly little attention. Between 1844 and 1863 one hundred and eighty-two papers were published, with the following breakdown by subject:[140]

---

[136]John Powell, *Statistical Illustrations* (1827), p. iii.
[137]*Annals of the Royal Statistical Society, 1834-1934* (1934), 2-3.
[138]*Annals*, 8-9.
[139]*Annals*, 23-24.
[140]*Annals*, 94, furnishes the absolute numbers; percentage calculations are the author's.

Category	Total Number	Percent of Total
Vital	83	45
Moral and Social	32	18
Financial	27	15
Commercial	17	9
Political	15	8
Industrial	8	5

Only 29 per cent of all the papers treated economic affairs, with trade and industry accounting for only 14 per cent of the total and just under half of the papers on economics generally.

The original self-appointed membership of 1834, which totalled three hundred and thirteen, included men from the nobility and landed gentry, politics, the legal and historical professions, the physical sciences, the Church, the Army, philanthropy, finance, and economics and statistics.[141] Among those in the last were Malthus, Babbage, Jones, Senior, Sinclair, McCulloch, Porter, and Tooke. The society, unlike its predecessor, was composed of "noblemen and gentlemen,"[142] and membership, viewed as a high honor, was restricted to the best of a professional elite. Over the next half-century membership was kept at about one thousand. To become a Member one had to be nominated by two or more Fellows of the Society; one was not admitted unless at least sixteen Fellows voted, election being by three-fourths or more of those voting. Not more than fifty Foreign Members could be admitted at a time.[143] To give the Society the proper élan, the Presidency was reserved for the upper ranks of the nobility. The first President was the Marquis of Lansdowne (1834-36), who repeated in 1842-43; Earl Fitzwilliam was President in 1838-40 and 1847-49. The statistician G. R. Porter, a Vice-President at the founding, was Treasurer from 1841 to 1852. A library was also started which by 1885 contained about 20,000 volumes.[144]

Statistical societies in the 1830's were not limited to the metropolis. Manchester organized its statistical society in 1833. Bristol created one in 1836; Liverpool, in 1837.

By the 1850's statistical work was being increasingly consolidated. From 1854, A. W. Fonblanque, Porter's successor as the head of the Statistical Department of the Board of Trade, issued an annual "Statistical Abstract" political, social, and economic activity in Britain for the previous fifteen years.[145] For instance, in the first abstract there is (for our purposes) data for 1839-53 on revenue and expenditure, imports and exports, shipping, excise, the prices

[141]*Annals*, 13. Among the most prominent men were Francis Jeffrey from literature, and Henry Goulburn and Thomas Spring-Rice (later, as Lord Monteagle, President from 1845 to 1847) from politics.

[142]Such were the kinds of persons advertised for at the first meeting in March 1834 (*Annals*, 10-11).

[143]Frederick J. Mouat, *History of the Statistical Society of London* (1885), 5.

[144]Mouat, *History* (1885), frontispiece.

[145]In the index volume for the *Parliamentary Papers* for 1852-99, the listings under "Abstract" cover eight pages (pp. 1310-17) and thirty-eight major subject headings.

and sales of wheat, coinage, savings banks' deposits, the Bank of England, and population.[146]

The 1850's also saw the beginnings of formalized international contacts. The first International Statistical Congress met at Brussels in 1853. From that date until 1876, eight congresses were convened, meeting every two to four years in various European capitals—Paris, Vienna, Budapest, London. From 1885 the meetings were annual, under a new name, the International Institute of Statistics. They took place until the World War.[147]

(g) The Lost Legacy, 1823-1900

From the time of Playfair's death in 1823 until Stanley Jevons' rediscovery of his work in 1879, the technique which Playfair had invented was forgotten.[148] Statisticians continued to confine themselves to tables of figures; lines, circles, bars, and pies were virtually never used to present or explain historical economic data. Although some graphs do appear as early as 1841,[149] there are only fourteen graphic representations in the first fifty volumes (1838-88) of the Statistical society of London--and nine of these deal with vital statistics![150] The first crudely drawn line-graphs of economic data and the first cartogram appear only in 1847.[151]

"Lineal arithmetic," by contrast, flourished on the Continent. The graphic work of Dupin (1819) on illiteracy, of Guerry (1829) on crime, and of Minard

[146]"Statistical Abstract," *P.P. 1854* [1743], XXXIX, 131-58.

[147]Funkhouser, 311.

[148]Funkhouser, 292, says his search turned up no mention of Playfair until Jevons' remarks to the Statistical Society (see *J.S.S.L.*, XLI [1879], 657). In his earlier article in *Economic History*, III (1935), 103-09, Funkhouser was unaware of Jevons' remarks.

[149]These are of vital statistics. See the graph of mortality rates in Limerick, Ireland, compared with England and Wales, in Daniel Griffin, "An Enquiry into the Mortality occurring among the Poor of the City of Limerick," *J.S.S.L.*, III (January 1841), 40-41; see also the two graphs of baptisms and burials in Tavistock, Devon from 1617 to 1836, in Charles Barham, "Remarks on the Abstract of the Parish Registers of Tavistock, Devon," *J.S.S.L.*, IV (April 1841), facing 40-41. The only other graphs before 1847 are six very crude ones correlating mortality with occupations, in William Guy, "Further Contributions to a Knowledge of the Influence of Employments upon Health," *J.S.S.L.*, VI (December 1843), facing 296.

[150]According to Funkhouser, 293-94.

[151]The line graphs are in J. T. Danson, "On the Accounts of the Bank of England under the Operation of the Act 7 & 8 Vict., c. 32," *J.S.S.L.*, X (May 1847), 132-53. The cartogram is in Joseph Fletcher, "Moral and Educational Statistics of England and Wales," *J.S.S.L.*, X (September 1847), facing 193. The map shows educational levels in districts in England, with different washes of color representing different types of counties (agricultural, manufacturing, mixed) and only letters A and B indicating the quality of levels of instruction.

(1845) on railway traffic helped to publicize the usefulness of the techniques devised by Playfair.[152] The French Ministry of Public Works, convinced of the utility of graphics, created in 1878 the *Bureau de la Statistique graphique*. Beginning in the next year, the Bureau published annually until 1897 charts and diagrams of railway statistics in the *Albums de Statistique graphique*. Other countries printed official volumes with bar and line graphs and carto-grams *(cartes figuratives)*. Austria in 1860 issued a population atlas using graphic techniques. Hungary, as early as 1868, printed its social and eco-nomic statistics in graphic form; Prussia, in 1871, issued a similar atlas.[153]

While individuals and governments on the Continent after 1850 increasingly came to use and perfect graphic methods for the representation of data, in England Playfair's methods were almost grudgingly adopted. And the techniques were limited to men working in vital statistics (William Farr), meteorology (Francis Galton), or economic theory (Alfred Marshall, Stanley Jevons). There was, however, *one* field in graphics in which the English economic historians were not retrograde. Indeed, the originator of picture statistics (pictograms) was an Englishman, Michael George Mulhall (1836-1900). His *Dictionary of Statistics* (1883; 4th ed., 1899) rendered all manner of figures into pictograms. Unfortunately, the pictogram is the least reliable graphic representation of data: the reader does not know whether comparison is meant in one, two, or three dimensions, and the eye finds it less easy to compare areas or volumes with each other than to compare lines or bars. (One remedy, found in modern pictograms, is to reduce them to unit size and present them together in the form of a bar graph.) In addition to their inherent problems, the pictograms in Mulhall often simply are not proportional to the data, as, for instance, in the case of the English mercantile fleet, half the size of the world's total, being shown in more space than the world's total. As a French reviewer, Alexandre de Foville, observed in 1887, "The sea has its mirages, and patrio-tism also perhaps."[154] With these warnings in mind, the *Dictionary* is still a fairly useful reference work.

Why did English statisticians of trade and production not adopt serious graphic methods? How could a student of statistics like A. L. Bowley say as late as 1901 that graphics "have their use for popular lectures and hankbooks, but do not add anything to the significance of the figures. . . [while] the use of statistical maps needs only a brief notice"?[155] The answer is not at all clear. But the failure to use graphics to represent commercial and in-dustrial statistics *is* surprising when one considers the favorable light in which it would show Britain's continuing world supremacy and the Englishman's preference for 'hard facts' over theory. By the same token, however, graphic representation may have been viewed as a picturesque, even fictional distor-tion of 'facts' by creating or generalizing from them a 'picture' or impression

---

[152]The discussion of Charles Dupin's map (Funkhouser, 300) cites no book or pamphlet. For Guerry, see Adriano Balbi and Andre Michel Guerry, *Statis-tique comparée de l'instruction et du nombre des crimes* (Paris, 1829); for Charles Joseph Minard, see his retrospective *Des Tableaux graphiques et des cartes figuratives* (Paris, 1861).

[153]Funkhouser, 332-37.

[154]Funkhouser, 347.

[155]Funkhouser, 343.

which did not exist when kept in raw or even tabular form. Morever, especially from the 1880's, graphics must have shown embarrassing trends in the eco-
nomies of Germany and the United States. Besides, the mere fact that graphics
flourished on the Continent may have deterred Englishmen from adopting them,
because other aspects of Continental life —centralization, bureaucracy, and
even 'intellectualism' —were observed and carefully eschewed by Englishmen.
Playfair's work, it may be recalled, went virtually unnoticed in his own land
yet was warmly received in France. His legacy was likewise forgotten until
relatively recently.

II. PRICES

One of the reasons that economic writers from the 1770's onwards concentra-
ted on current prices was that prices were changing so rapidly. Arthur Young
noticed the price increases beginning in the middle of the century, remarking
especially at their rapidity in the period 1760 to 1774.[156] The French Wars
brought further inflation: Joseph Lowe thought that 1814 average prices were
62 per cent above the 1792 level.[157] Prices continued to capture the public's
imagination after 1815, as they fell 43 per cent between 1815 and 1850.[158]
Contemporary writers viewed prices in three ways. First, there was the
practical businessman's handbook of current prices.[159] Secondly, there were
the compilations of epochal price movements from the eleventh century to the
present, mostly for wheat.[160] Bishop William Fleetwood of Ely was the first
eighteenth-century writer to give wheat prices (irregularly) for the period
1125-1598; for 1646-1705, he provides annual average prices.[161] But the first

[156]Arthur Young, *Political Arithmetic* (1774), 37. According to the
Schumpeter-Gilboy index (in Mitchell and Deane, 468), consumer prices (agricultural and non-agricultural) rose in this period by 18 per cent, a revolutionary increase from the stable, moderate prices since 1710.
[157]Joseph Lowe, *The Present State of England* (1822), quoted in Deane and
Cole, 15-16. The Schumpeter-Gilboy index puts the increase at 71 per cent,
while the Gayer-Rostow-Schwartz index registers the increase as 84 per cent
above 1792 price levels (in Mitchell and Deane, 468-70).
[158]Deane and Cole, 16.
[159]For example, *The Builder's Price Book* (1788), by "an Experienced Surveyor", lists prices charged by some thirteen trades. James Dymock, *The Manufacturer's Assistant* (Glasgow, 1798), has tables of current yarn prices. See
also Patrick Kelly, *The Universal Cambist and Commercial Instructor* (1811).
[160]For modern compilations, see Mitchell and Deane, 484-87, for wheat
prices at Exeter (1316-1820), Eton (Windsor Market, 1594-1820), and Winchester
(1594-1817). The outstanding works remain James Edwin Thorold Rogers, *A
History of Agriculture and Prices in England* (7 v., Oxford, 1866-1902) and Sir
William Beveridge, *Prices and Wages in England* (vol. 1, 1939). See also Eric
L. Jones, *Seasons and Prices* (1964).
[161]William Fleetwood, *Chronicon Preciosum: or, an Account of English Gold
and Silver Money; the Price of Corn and other commodities* (1707; reprinted,
1745).

systematic compiler of wheat prices was the great economic theoretician, Adam
Smith, who in *The Wealth of Nations* gives wheat prices at eighty-four points
in time between 1202 and 1601. He sets out prices at Windsor Market from 1595
to 1764.[162] In 1797 Sir Frederick Morton Eden in his *State of the Poor* continues the ancient Windsor Market series through 1796; he also includes prices
for barley and oats for 1732-93.[163] In a work published three years later,
the Earl of Sheffield prints prices which were available in Eden's work but
also adds wheat import and export figures for 1697-1779.[164] David Macpherson
(1805) provides a price series for 1126-1801, incomplete in the early centuries, but with annual figures from 1732, for wheat, rye, barley, oats and
beans.[165] Robert Wilson (1815) furnishes average wheat prices for each quarter of the year from 1780 to 1815,[166] while Tooke in an early work (1824) gives
us a series from 1792 to 1819.[167] Joplin has Eton College wheat prices for
the period 1646-1813, with monthly and yearly averages for 1792-1822;[168] an
anonymous work of 1825 gives Eton College wheat prices for 1697-1792, with
monthly and yearly averages for 1792-1824.[169] Tooke in 1829 provides Winchester

[162]Adam Smith, *An Enquiry into the Wealth of Nations* (2 v., 1776), I, 317-
24.

[163]Sir Frederick Morton Eden, *The State of the Poor* (3 v., 1797), III,
appendix, pp. lxxi-lxxviii, lxxx-lxxxi. The sources which he cites are the
Audit Books of Eton College, Fleetwood's *Chronicon Preciosum* (1745), Smith's
Wealth of Nations, and *Three Tracts on the Corn Trade*. The eldest son of Sir
Robert Eden, Governor of Maryland, Sir Frederick (1766-1809) was a founder,
and later the chairman, of the Globe Insurance Company. He was moved to write
his classic work from concern for effects which high wheat prices in 1794-95
had on the poor. His *State of the Poor* was written from personal visits with,
as well as from research about, the poor of England; clergymen were especially
helpful in compiling the data. The work, completed when Eden was only thirty-
one, is a dictionary of the economic life of the lower classes in England in
the 1790's. Parish baptism, burial, and marriage figures from c. 1760 to 1795
are presented, as well as local food prices and wages in the mid-1790's.
Though there is much valuable information throughout the three volumes, it is
scattered, not systematically arranged. For statistical orderliness, one may
turn to the 400-page appendix in volume three. Karl Marx called Eden "the
only disciple of Adam Smith during the eighteenth century that produced any
work of importance." George Macdonell (in his article on Eden in the *D.N.B.*,
VI, 357) maintains that "to no writer of the time have subsequent investiga-
tors been more indebted."

[164]John Baker Holroyd, 1st Earl of Sheffield, *Remarks on the Deficiency
of Grain, occasioned by the Bad Harvest of 1799* (1800), appendix, facing 120.

[165]David Macpherson, *Annals of Commerce* (4 v., 1805), IV, App. 3.

[166]Robert Wilson, *An Inquiry into the Causes of the High Prices of Corn
and Labour* (Edinburgh, 1815), appendix, Table 1, pp. 77-80.

[167]Thomas Tooke, *Thoughts and Details on the High and Low Prices of the
Thirty Years from 1793 to 1822* (1824), App. 1, No. 5, p. 11.

[168]Thomas Joplin, *Outlines of a System of Political Economy* (1823), App.
2-3, pp. 7-16.

[169]*An Illustration of Mr. Joplin's Views on Currency and Plan for its Improvement* (1825), App. 12, p. 108, and App. 10-11, pp. 104-07.

wheat prices semiannually for 1646-1826 and monthly for 1793-1828.[170] William
Jacob (1831) provides wheat and malt prices at Oxford for 1583-1829,[171] and
Badcock (1832), in addition to furnishing a table of wheat prices for 1100-
1830, provides tables and colored graphs for wheat prices (1600-1825) and prices
of beans, barley, and oats (1790-1830).[172] Bischoff, the great historian of the
woolen industry, gives us wheat prices at Eton College from 1646 to 1840. In
addition, he provides a list of wheat prices at Berlin from 1774 to 1840. Moreover, Bischoff constructs a most useful "comparative table of the annual prices
of wheat in England and Berlin, the weekly rate of wages paid to farming labourers in Sussex and the annual amount of difference between the price of British
wheat and Prussian wheat (if admitted free) from 1791 to 1840."[173] The table
shows that the harshest years for the English wage-earner were 1795-96, 1800-01,
and 1805-15, and not the decades after Waterloo.

Certainly the best writer on prices before 1850 was Thomas Tooke (1774-1858).
The son of William Tooke, an Anglican chaplain who ministered to the spiritual
needs of English businessmen in Germany and later in Russia, Thomas at the age
of fifteen began work in a business firm in St. Petersburg. Later, he returned
to London and eventually became a partner in the firm of Astell, Tooke & Thorn-
ton. Tooke began writing in the 1820's to combat the view that the rapidly-
falling prices resulted from a contraction of the currency due to the return
to cash payments in 1819. All of his writings opposed the 'currency theory'
that prices were directly affected by the state of the circulation of paper
notes and metallic currency. Tooke looked to other causes: more bountiful
harvests, removal of wartime obstructions to trade, and the extension of and
improvements in industry. He began massive researches to determine the nature
of the 'causes' of the price trends. As statistical compilations, two of his
works are of outstanding importance: *Thoughts and Details on the High and Low
Prices of the Thirty Years from 1793 to 1822* (1824) and *A History of Prices*
(1838-57). The latter appeared in six volumes, the last two (1857) being written with the assistance of William Newmarch.[174] For its time, the work was
revolutionary in its subtle integration of text and statistics and in its blend
of (to use Tooke's words) "details in chronological order and in historical connection." Recognition came quickly to Tooke's masterpiece. A typical comment
was that of the Glasgow merchant, James Harley, who said of the *History:* "[It
is] a mass of information of great detail and philosophical research . . . [and]
a work of surpassing merit . . . which, I trust, every liberal merchant, pretend-

[170]Thomas Tooke, *On the Currency in connexion with the Corn Trade; and on
the Corn Laws* (1829), App. 4, pp. 117-19; App. 1, p. 111.
    [171]William Jacob, *An Historical Inquiry into the Production and Consumption
of the Precious Metals* (2 v., 1831), II, App. C-4, pp. 388-91.
    [172]Benjamin Badcock, *Tables Exhibiting the Prices of Wheat, from the year
1100 to 1830; also the Prices of Beans, Barley, and Oats from 1790 to 1830*
(1832), 8 pp.
    [173]James Bischoff, *A Comprehensive History of the Woolen and Worsted Manu-
factures* (2 v., 1842), II, appendix, Tables 8, 10.
    [174]Thomas Tooke, *A History of Prices and of the State of the Circulation
from 1793 to 1837* (2 v., 1838). Additional volumes as follows: III (1840),
IV (1848), V and VI (1857). Volume six has a very full index to the entire
set. 'Prices,' with numerous subheadings, covers pp. 953-58.

ing to any extent of business, will immediately place in his library."[175]

Among Tooke's statistics are price figures for wheat and other grains from 1821 to 1839, with *weekly* price data for the period 1829-47.[176] Especially noteworthy in the monumental 545-page statistical appendix to volume six of the *History*, is a critical and encyclopedic statistical essay which Tooke called "an inquiry concerning the evidence for" the prices of precious metals and wheat in England and France from 1401 until 1855.[177] He examines critically the work of Jacob, Eden, Young, Smith, and the French authorities, the Marquis Garnier, Du Pres de St. Maur, and the French Statistical Commission. Tooke then constructs his own table of English and French wheat prices for the period 1401-1856.[178]

The Government began printing long historical series of wheat prices only in the 1840's. A parliamentary paper of 1843 publishes the Eton College (1646-1770) and Oxford (1697-1770) series and national average prices for 1771-1841.[179] There is also a convenient record of wheat imports and exports for 1697-1840.[180]

The third general category of prices concerns the necessaries of life: bread, meat, cheese and butter, clothing. Several authors furnish series going back to the twelfth century. The first chronicler, Fleetwood, writing in 1707, lists prices for a miscellany of items from 1125 to 1598.[181] Young gives much the same data for the period 1302-1595, while Cunningham sets out prices in greater detail from 1309.[182] Eden presents prices for 1125 – 1619, and,unlike earlier writers, notes the source for most of the prices which he lists.[183] Finally, Cayley in 1830 prints miscellaneous price figures at sixteen dates between 1050 and 1795.[184]

For the prices of bread, there are series for prices of the quartern loaf in the City of London from 1735 to 1848.[185] In addition, the *London Gazette* and *Prince's Prices Current* have complete bread price series. Records also exist for the prices paid for bread by the Commissariat for 1819-31, by the

[175]James Harley, *The Currency* (Glasgow, 1839), 16-17.

[176]Tooke, *History of Prices*, III (1840), 295; IV (1848), 410-13, respectively.

[177]Tooke and Newmarch, *History of Prices*, VI (1857), App. 2, pp. 345-439.

[178]Tooke and Newmarch, *History of Prices*, VI (1857), App. 2, pp. 394-439.

[179]*P.T. 11*, *P.P. 1843*, LVI, Nos. 74-75, p. 69.

[180]For 1697-1814, see *P.T. 3*, *P.P. 1835*, XLIX, No. 231, pp. 213-14; for 1815-40, see *P.T. 10*, *P.P. 1843*, LV, No. 90, p. 73.

[181]William Fleetwood, *Chronicon Preciosum* (1707), 68-124.

[182]Arthur Young, *Political Arithmetic* (1774), 357-59; Timothy Cunningham, *History of our Customs, Aids, . . . and Taxes* (3rd ed., 1778), 422-45.

[183]Eden, *State of the Poor* (3 v., 1797), III, appendix, pp. ix-lxix.

[184]E. S. Cayley, *On Commercial Economy* (1830), facing 91.

[185]For 1735-1808, see the *Assize and Price of Bread* (1808), attributed to John Powell; for 1758-1814, see *P.P. 1814-15* (109), X, 481; for 1781-1815, see *P.P. 1834* (92), XLIX, 321, or *P.T. 3*, *P.P. 1835*, XLIX, No. 317, p. 398; for 1821-48, see *P.T. 18*, *P.P. 1850* [1159], LIV, No. 226, p. 202. Mitchell and Deane, 497-98, print London bread prices from 1545 to 1925. For other London prices at an earlier period, see J. M. Price,"Notes on Some London Price Currents, 1667-1715," *Economic History Review*, 2nd ser., VII (1954), 240-50.

Bethlehem Hospital for 1815-31, and by the Royal Hospital at Greenwich for 1818-42.[186]

There are several series for the prices of meat, a commodity for which Mitchell and Deane give no prices. Young furnishes London beef and pork prices for 1683-1771.[187] Several sources provide the prices of beef and mutton at Smithfield Market from 1796 to 1842.[188] Related to meat prices are figures for the number of cattle and sheep sold at Smithfield from 1730 to 1850.[189] Wholesale *weekly* mutton prices, at Leadenhall Market only, exist for 1803-27.[190] For "butchers' meat," there are price series from 1810 to 1850.[191] Prices for Irish beef and pork exist for 1782-1828.[192]

Further meat prices may be found in the records of various institutions. The Victualling Office of the army has meat prices for 1740 to 1831.[193] Hospital records have prices paid for meat at various times. St. Thomas's Hospital, Southwark, has beef prices since 1688 and mutton prices since 1725.[194]

[186]*P.T. 3, P.P. 1833*, XLI, 163, for the Commissariat and the Bethlehem Hospital. McCulloch, *Dictionary of Commerce* (2 v., 8th ed., 1854), II, 1060-61, has the Greenwich prices, with prices at thirteen dates from 1729 to 1785.

[187]Young, *Political Arithmetic* (1774), 139-42.

[188]For 1796-1824, see Tooke, *History of Prices*, I (1838), App. 6, p. 13; for 1813-31, see *P.T. 1, P.P. 1833*, XLI, 166; for 1819-32, see "Select Committee on the Bank of England Charter," *P.P. 1831-32* (722), VI, App. 92, pp. 92-93. For mutton prices only, for 1803-41, see Bischoff, *Comprehensive History* (2 v., 1842), II, appendix, Table 9.

[189]For 1730-70, see Anderson, *Origin of Commerce* (4 v., 1787-89), IV (1789), 156. Tooke, *History of Prices*, III (1840), App. 16, p. 38, has a long series from 1732 to 1823. John Powell, *Statistical Illustrations* (3rd ed., 1827), 61; for 1820-31, see *P.T. 1, P.P. 1833*, XLI, 166; for 1833-39, see *P.T. 9, P.P. 1841* [303], XXIV, No. 438, p. 383. For 1840-54, see Mitchell and Deane, 354, whose list runs from 1732 to 1854.

[190]The evidence of R. Hulme, salesman, in "Select Committee on the Wool Trade," *P.P. 1828* (515), VIII, 637-38.

[191]For 1810-32, see Edward Baines, *History of the Cotton Manufactures in Great Britain* (1835), 433, 439; for 1834-56, see Tooke and Newmarch, *History of Prices*, VI (1857), 455-56; for 1840-50, monthly averages, see *P.P. 1850* (460), LII, 311-13; for 1842-48, see *P.T. 18, P.P. 1850* [1159], LIV, No. 224, p. 200; for 1843-50, see *P.T. 20, P.P. 1852*, LII, No. 226, p. 215.

[192]For 1782-1822, see Tooke, *Thoughts and Details* (1824), App. 4, No. 1, pp. 30-33; for 1783-1828, see the evidence of Edward Hohler in the "Select Committee on the Wool Trade," *P.P. 1828* (515), VIII, 727. Henry James, *State of the Nation* (1835), table facing 1, has figures for 1790-1828.

[193]For 1740-95, see Frederick Eden, *State of the Poor* (3 v., 1797), III, appendix, pp. lxxxvi-vii. Eden comments that the Office paid 3½ *d.* for every 7 *d.* that the consumer, buying retail, usually paid. For 1790-1823, see *J.H.C. 78*, 625-27; for 1819-31, see *P.T. 1, P.P. 1833*, XLI, 163.

[194]For prices through 1831, see *P.T. 1, P.P. 1833*, XLI, 164. G. R. Porter, *Progress of the Nation* (3 v., 1836-43), III (1843), 112-13, has prices for 1801-42, while *P.P. 1850* (460), LII, 314, and Porter, *Progress* (1851), 589, have prices for 1800-49.

Chelsea Hospital has prices for 1730-32 and 1791-93,[195] while in *Porter's Tables* there are prices for Bethlehem and Greenwich Hospitals for 1815-31. McCulloch has prices for Greenwich Hospital continuous from 1805 to 1842, with earlier prices irregularly from 1729 to 1800.[196]

Arthur Young tried to establish an index of the cost of meat over the eighteenth century. Dividing the period into five sections (1701-66, 1767-89, 1767-1800, 1790-1803, and 1804-10) and measuring beef, mutton, veal, pork, and bacon prices, he calculated that meat prices rose almost 200 per cent from 1701/66 to 1804/10.[197]

Prices of butter and cheese at Smithfield Market exist for 1819-32, as do prices in "London markets" for 1813-31.[198] The Victualling Office has a series for 1749-95.[199] Chelsea Hospital has prices for 1730-32 and 1791-93; Greenwich Hospital, for 1729-1842; Bethlehem Hospital, for 1815-31.[200] Prices for Irish butter exist from 1782 to 1832.[201]

For clothing, there are series of prices paid by institutions: Greenwich (1800-38), Bethlehem (1814-35), and Chelsea (1815-35) Hospitals.[202]

Outside London perhaps the most accessible printed series of retail prices for flour, butter, potatoes, and meat are those for Manchester and environs, from 1810 to 1832.[203]

The outstanding compilations of prices for a wide variety of articles are

[195]Jacob, *Historical Inquiry into . . . the Precious Metals* (2 v., 1831), II, App. C-6, p. 393.

[196]*P.T. 1, P.P. 1833*, XLI, 162-63; McCulloch, *Dictionary* (2 v., 1854 ed.), II, 1060.

[197]Arthur Young, *An Enquiry into the Progressive Value of Money in England, as marked by the price of agricultural products* (1812), 137. The Schumpeter-Gilboy indexes (1661-1823) would suggest that the estimate is too high, almost by half; see Mitchell and Deane, 468-69.

[198]See "The Select Committee on the Bank of England Charter," *P.P. 1831-32* (722), VI, App. 92, pp. 92-93; *P.T. 1, P.P. 1833*, XLI, 166, respectively.

[199]Eden, *State of the Poor* (3 v., 1797), III, appendix, pp. lxxxvi-vii.

[200]For Chelsea, see Jacob, *Historical Inquiry into . . . the Precious Metals* (2 v., 1831), II, App. C-6, p. 393. For Greenwich, for 1729-1800 (irregularly) and 1805-42 (annually), see McCulloch, *Dictionary* (2 v., 1854 ed.), II, 1060; for 1800-35, see Bischoff, *Comprehensive History* (2 v., 1842), II, 419; for 1818-31, see "Select Committee on the Bank of England Charter," *P.P. 1831-32* (722), VI, App. 91, pp. 90-91. For Bethlehem, see *P.T. 1, P.P. 1833*, XLI, 163.

[201]For 1782-1822, see Tooke, *Thoughts and Details* (1824), App. 4, No. 1, pp. 30-33; for 1783-1828, see "Select Committee on the Wool Trade," *P.P. 1828* (515), 727; for 1790-1828, see James, *State of the Nation* (1835), table facing 1; for 1810-32, see Baines, *Cotton Manufactures* (1835), 433, 439.

[202]For Greenwich, for 1815-31, see *P.T. 1, P.P. 1833*, XLI, 162-63; for 1800-38, see Porter, *Progress*, (3 v., 1836-43), III (1843), 114. For Bethlehem, see *P.T. 1, P.P. 1833*, XLI, 161; and for Bethlehem and Chelsea, see Porter *Progress*, III (1843), 115, or *Progress* (1851), 590-92.

[203]For 1810-19, see Tooke, *Thoughts and Details* (1824), Table 9, facing p. 21. For 1810-25, see *P.T. 1, P.P. 1833*, XLI, 165; for 1826-32, see *P.T. 3, P.P. 1835*, XLIX, No. 326, p. 403, or J. R. McCulloch, *Statistical Account of the British Empire* (2 v., 1837), II, 82.

the work of Thomas Tooke: *Thoughts and Details on the High and Low Prices of the Thirty Years from 1793 to 1822* (1824) and the six-volume *History of Prices* (1838-57). He has price data for dozens of articles, from "Ashes" to "Wool," for 1782-1822 and 1838-47.[204] Many modern writers have relied on Tooke to construct price indexes.[205]

Obviously prices change greatly over the centuries and with them the value of money. Contemporaries, confronted with wheat prices stretching back seven centuries, went about setting up price indexes to obtain some understanding of the secular inflation of prices. Eden (1797) has a conversion table of ten columns for the average value of money every fifty years, from 1066 to 1796.[206] Sir George Shuckburgh Evelyn in 1798 presented a table of monetary depreciation at various dates from 1050 to 1800.[207] Wheatley (1803) gives proportions of monetary value at twenty-five points in time, from 26 in 1050 to 562 in 1800, but he gives no prices themselves.[208] Arthur Young (1812) sets out "proportions in twenty" for various articles of consumption at several periods, from the thirteenth through the eighteenth century.[209] Cayley (1830), citing ten sources for his table, presents prices and proportions for fourteen items from 1050 to 1795. He calculated that since 1550 the price of consumer articles had increased by 652 per cent, while the price of labor had increased only 331 per cent.[210] Finally, a parliamentary committee in 1848 presents a large table of

[204]See Tooke, *Thoughts and Details* (1824), App. 4, No. 1, pp. 1-72; Tooke, *History of Prices*, III (1840), 297, and IV (1848), 426-34. The items include brandy, rum, East Indian tea, sugar, tobacco, Dutch butter, coffee. For the prices of twenty-four articles used in Greenwich Hospital from 1729 to 1842 (annual prices from 1805), see McCulloch, *Dictionary* (2 v., 1854 ed.), II, 1060-61.

[205]See Norman J. Silberling, "British Prices and Business Cycles, 1779-1850," *Review of Economic Statistics*, V (1923), Supplement 2, pp. 219-62; Elizabeth B. Schumpeter, "English Prices and Public Finance, 1660-1822," *Review of Economic Statistics*, XX (1938), 21-37; and A. P. Gayer, W. W. Rostow, and A. J. Schwartz, *The Growth and Fluctuation of the British Economy, 1790-1850* (2 v., Oxford, 1953). Gayer *et. al.*, *Growth and Fluctuation*, I, 475-78, list the price series available to the historian.

[206]Eden, *State of the Poor* (3 v., 1797), III, appendix, facing p. viii.

[207]Sir George Shuckburgh Evelyn, "An account of some Endeavours to ascertain a Standard Weight and Measure," *Philosophical Transactions of the Royal Society of London*, LXXXVIII (1798), facing 176. Reprinted in Sir John Sinclair, *History of the Public Revenue of the British Empire* (3 v., 1803-04), II (1803), App. 3, pp. 49-50.

[208]John Wheatley, *Remarks on Currency and Commerce* (1803), 261-62. Reprinted in Sinclair, *History of the Public Revenue*, II (1803), App. 3, p. 50. Wheatley, in another work, *Essay on the Theory of Money and the Principles of Commerce* (1807), facing 248, prints a chart of agricultural prices at sixteen dates from 1050 to 1795.

[209]Young, *Enquiry into the Progressive Value of Money* (1812), 82, **137**.

[210]E. S. Cayley, *On Commercial Economy* (1830), facing 91. See also his 'British Depreciation Table,' facing 135, for price index trends from 1803 to 1822 for butter, wheat, meat, and gold. Compare Tooke, *History of Prices*, VI (1857), App. 2, No. 19, p. 389.

the prices of ninety leading articles of commerce, "expressed in Centesimal Proportions," at eight seven-year periods of time from 1784 to 1837.[211]

Wages, unlike prices, are not directly related to the subjects of this bibliography, but a few of the many contemporary sources for wage data may be mentioned. Fleetwood has some figures for 1351-60, 1389, 1446, and 1514.[212] Eden (again citing his authorities) gives wage data for 1126 to 1610 (irregularly), 1661, 1682, and 1725.[213] Young has averages for eleven periods from 1200 to 1810.[214] Almost all of these are wages for forms of agricultural labor. Young also provides some dubious average wages for 'artisans' (carpenter and mason) for five centuries, from the fourteenth through the eighteenth, and averages for five more recent periods from 1730 to 1810.[215] Rooke has some data on wages in northern England from 1730 to 1823.[216] Eden has wage data scattered throughout his *State of the Poor*; Arthur Young records the wages encountered on any one of his *Tours*[217] or in the *Annals of Agriculture* (46 volumes), the monthly periodical which he edited from 1784 to 1815; William Cobbett's *Rural Rides* (1830) has scattered wage data. G. R. Porter has wages for many kinds of urban workers in various cities from 1805 to 1836, as do many Government publications.[218] Sir William Beveridge's *Prices and Wages in England* (vol. 1, 1939) remains the best comprehensive study of wages in our period. A. L. Bowley's *Wages in the United Kingdom in the Nineteenth Century* (1900) and Mitchell and Deane's *Abstract of British Historical Statistics* (1962) should also be consulted.

III.   THE TEXTILE INDUSTRIES

(a) Wool and Woolens

Because of the primacy of the woolen industry, British wool was for over a

[211]In the evidence of J. Taylor before the "Select Committee on Commerical Distress,"*P.P. 1847-48* (395), VIII, Part 1, 466-68.

[212]Fleetwood, *Chronicon Preciosum* (1707), 158-63.

[213]Eden, *State of the Poor*, III (1797), appendix, pp. ix-lxix, cii-cx.

[214]Young, *Enquiry into the Progressive Value of Money* (1812), 88. For a discussion of these figures, see Tooke and Newmarch, *History of Prices*, VI (1857), App. 2, No. 19, pp. 388-92.

[215]Young, *Enquiry into the Progressive Value of Money* (1812), 93-94.

[216]John Rooke, *An Inquiry into the Principles of National Wealth* (Edinburgh, 1824), 432-33, 444-45.

[217]*A Six Weeks' Tour through the Southern Counties of England and Wales* (1768); *A Six Months' Tour through the North of England* (4 v., 1770); *The Farmers' Tour through the East of England* (4 v., 1771). See also Young's *A Tour in Ireland* (2 v., 1780).

[218]Porter, *Progress*, (3 v., 1836-43), II (1838), 251-54, or *Progress* (1851), 443-46. For parliamentary compilations, see the indexes to the *Parliamentary Papers*, and Mitchell and Deane, 359-60. McCulloch, *Dictionary* (2 v., 1854 ed.), II, 1061, has the daily wages of carpenters, bricklayers, masons, and plumbers hired by Greenwich Hospital from 1729 to 1842 (annual average daily wages from 1805).

century and a half—from 1660 to 1825—prohibited from export.[219] The import of foreign wool was free of duty until 1802; in that year, however, to aid domestic sheep-growers, Government imposed a small duty, which was increased in 1813 and again in 1819, so that by the latter year foreign wool was quite expensive. This was unfortunate for, owing to the deterioration and amount of wastage in British wool production, the use of foreign wool was becoming almost indispensable in British woolen manufactures. The high rate of duty (6 d./lb.) in 1819 was reduced by five-sixths (to 1 d./lb.) in 1824, with colonial wool entering free of duty after 1825. Rates on foreign wool were finally abolished in 1844. Imports of wool, which had declined at a great rate in the early eighteenth century, began to increase in the 1760's, so that by 1805 30 per cent of all the wool used by the woolen industry was imported; by 1850, fully 50 per cent was imported.[220] Until 1814, most foreign wool came from Spain. After that date, Germany and Russia were the chief suppliers until the 1840's when Australia became Britain's chief source of wool imports.[221]

Sources for the prices of raw wool are numerous. First, there are the sources with generalized prices. John Smith, the leading writer on wool before Bischoff, provides us with prices at twenty-nine dates from 1198 to 1753.[222]

[219]An act of 1788 prohibited the shearing of sheep within five miles of the coast "except in the presence of a revenue officer." It also specified the manner by which wool could be shipped from one British port to another. But Ashton (in Schumpeter, 6) concludes that wool smuggling was of minimal importance. See Ephraim Lipson, *The Economic History of England* (3 v., 1937-43), III (1943), 22-30.

[220]Deane and Cole, Table 47, p. 196.

[221]The standard work is Herbert Heaton, *The Yorkshire Woollen and Worsted Industries* (Oxford, 1920). J. Burnley's *History of Wool and Woolcombing* (1889) is a substantial technical and scientific history of the industry but has no trade or industrial statistics. Neither of Ephraim Lipson's works—*A Short History of Wool and its Manufacture* (Cambridge, Mass., 1953) and *The History of the Woollen and Worsted Industries* (1921)—has any statistical tables. J. H. Clapham's *The Woollen and Worsted Industries* (1907) is, in the author's own words, "a sketch, not a fully finished picture" (p. v). The work, lacking a bibliography and footnotes, concentrates on late-nineteenth century developments and has no statistical tables. For good modern studies on wool, see G. P. Fussell and C. Goodman, "Eighteenth-century Estimates of British Sheep and Wool Production," *Agricultural History,* IV (1930), 131-51; on woolens, see Phyllis Deane, "The Output of the British Woollen Industry in the Eighteenth Century," *Journal of Economic History,* XVII (1957), 207-23.

[222]John Smith, *Memoirs of Wool* (2 v., 1757), II, 241-43. John Smith, born c. 1700 and educated at Trinity Hall, Cambridge, wrote his *Chronicon Rusticum-Commerciale, or Memoirs of Wool* (2 v., 1747; 2nd ed., 2 v., 1757) to oppose the restrictions on the exportation of wool, for he believed that wool merchants could obtain a higher price for their wool on the Continent than in England. His book is a compendium of the literature on wool since the early seventeenth century. Arthur Young believed it was invaluable, while McCulloch judged it "one of the most carefully compiled and valuable works that has been published on the history of any branch of trade" *(Literature of Political Economy* [1845], 237-38). On Smith, see *D.N.B.*, XVIII, 486-87.

In the modern period he gives us prices from many places "for near 40 Years successively," starting in 1706.[223] Arthur Young offers six prices between 1198 and 1533 and prices at seventeen dates between 1581 and 1743, six of them falling in the eighteenth century.[224] Then Sir Joseph Banks[225] gives us "successive prices of wool in England" in 1697-98, 1706-07, 1712, and 1714.[226] Finally, Eden offers a list of wool prices from 1229 to 1760,[227] and Bischoff, the premier historian of wool, has a series from 1741 to 1790.[228]

There are several regional price series. Temple lists Herefordshire wool prices for 1724, 1727-44, and 1748.[229] James has prices for Nottinghamshire and Leicestershire wool from 1780 to 1799.[230] Smith gives us a series for Lincolnshire wool for 1718-44,[231] Banks has a series for 1717-81,[232] Eden has a series for 1724-44,[233] and James provides prices for 1789 to 1828.[234] Eden

[223]Smith, *Memoirs of Wool*, (2 v., 1757), II, 205-12.

[224]Arthur Young, *Political Arithmetic* (1774), 151-52.

[225]*The Propriety of Allowing a Qualified Exportation of Wool* (1782) is attributed to Banks by Samuel Halkett and John Laing, *Dictionary of Anonymous and Pseudonymous English Literature* (new ed. by J. Kennedy, W. A. Smith, and A. F. Johnson, 9 v., Edinburgh and London, 1926-62), IV (1928), 447, and by the British Museum Catalogue, the Kress Library Catalogue, and Mitchell and Deane, 212. But the authorship is by no means undisputed. Many writers believe George Chalmers was the author. See Palgrave, *Dictionary of Political Economy* (2 v., 1919), I, 254-55; Grace Cockroft, *The Public Life of George Chalmers* (New York, 1939), 66 n. 53; and *D.N.B.*, III, 1355. Cockroft's claim is solidly researched and should be seriously considered.

[226]Sir Joseph Banks, *The Propriety of Allowing a Qualified Exportation of Wool* (1782), 83-85. This series is printed in Mitchell and Deane, 494.

[227]Sir Frederick Morton Eden, *State of the Poor* (3 v., 1797), III, appendix, pp. lxxxii-iii.

[228]James Bischoff, *A Comprehensive History of the Woollen and Worsted Manufactures* (2 v., 1842), II, appendix, Table 6. James Bischoff (1776-1845) grew up in a German family which had settled at Leeds in 1718. Beginning in 1816 he wrote letters and pamphlets against the tax on foreign wool imports, and in the last year of his life saw the introduction of free imports of wool. His early mercantile concerns were wool and woolens, but in later life he was a merchant and insurance broker in London (see *D.N.B.*, II, 550-51).

[229]William Temple, "gentleman" clothier of Trowbridge, *A Refutation of One of the Principal Arguments in the Reverend Mr. Smith's Memoirs of Wool* (1750), 10-11.

[230]John James, *History of the Worsted Manufacture in England* (1857), 317.

[231]Smith, *Memoirs of Wool* (2 v., 1757), II, 210.

[232]Banks, *Propriety of Allowing a Qualified Exportation of Wool* (1782), 83-85.

[233]Eden, *State of the Poor* (3 v., 1797), III, appendix, pp. lxxxiv-v. For a later period, 1804-27, see "Select Committee on the Wool Trade," *P.P. 1828* (515), VIII, 470.

[234]James, *History of the Worsted Manufacture in England* (1857), 317, 382, 422.

also gives the prices for Lewes fine wool for 1770-92 and 1794.[235] For Scottish wool, Bischoff provides prices for Cheviot and for White and Laid Highland wool for the period 1797-1827; for Highland wool alone, he has figures for 1801-40.[236] Tooke presents prices for Spanish and German wool from 1782 to 1822.[237] TABLE 6 sets out wool prices in various areas of England.

The figures for the imports of wool before 1771 remained buried in the Custom House records until publication of Schumpeter's book. Mitchell and Deane rely entirely on her researches for their wool import figures before 1796,[238] but for the period 1771-1841 Bischoff's excellent work of 1842 may be consulted.[239] Bischoff also provides a table indicating forty countries of origin for the import of raw wool at every fifth year from 1800 to 1840.[240] For 1833-41, he gives a full series of the amounts imported from Germany, Spain, Austria, the Cape of Good Hope, and "other countries."[241] Schumpeter provides quantity figures for Irish and Spanish wool imports in 1700-71, 1775, and 1780.[242] Several parliamentary papers indicate some two dozen places of origin for wool imports from 1802 to 1831.[243] There is a record of the amounts imported from British colonies as opposed to foreign countries, from 1818 to 1845;[244] we also

[235]Eden, *State of the Poor* (3 v., 1797), III, appendix, pp. lxxxiv-v.

[236]Bischoff, *Comprehensive History*, II, 131, and appendix, Table 6, respectively. These figures are probably based on J. Sutcliffe's evidence in the "Select Committee on the Wool Trade," *P.P. 1828* (515), VIII, 628. Bischoff's figures, like Sutcliffe's (1797-1827), give one price for White and Laid Highland wool together. In later evidence before the same committee, though, Thomas Cook, using data from Messrs. Maxwell in Liverpool, provides separate prices for White Highland and Laid Highland wool for 1807-28 (*ibid.*, p. 664).

[237]Thomas Tooke, *Thoughts and Details* (1824), App. 4, No. 1, pp. 62-65. The Spanish series is continued through 1838 in Tooke, *History of Prices*, II (1838), 420. There is a series for 1811-24 for Merino wool, in *P.P. 1828* (515), VIII, 517-18. E. C. Hohler (in *ibid.*, p. 729) gives figures for "foreign" wool for 1783-1828, but the type of wool is not stated, so the series is not very useful.

[238]Mitchell and Deane, 191.

[239]Bischoff, *Comprehensive History*, II, appendix, Tables 2 and 6.

[240]Bischoff, *Comprehensive History*, II, appendix, Table 3. A later historian, John James, *History of the Worsted Manufacture in England* (1857), appendix, 37, has only quinquennial figures for 1800-55, differentiating two dozen countries of origin.

[241]Bischoff, *Comprehensive History*, II, appendix, Table 2. For a long run (1815-49), distinguishing these same areas, see *P.P. 1850* (460), LII, 316. John Powell, *Statistical Illustrations* (1827), 59, has a series for 1816-22, differentiating fifteen places of origin. McCulloch, *Dictionary* (1837), 1263, has figures from twenty-two places, but only for 1810, 1820, 1825, 1830, 1832, and 1833.

[242]Schumpeter, XVI, 52-55.

[243]See for 1802-11, *J.H.C. 67*, 759; for 1811-14, *J.H.C. 70*, 854; for 1816-22, *J.H.C. 78*, 879; and for 1820-31, *P.T. 1*, *P.P. 1833*, XLI, 70a-70d. See also for 1809-12, *P.P. 1813-14* (310), XII, 207; for 1812-15, *P.P. 1814-15* (465), X, 457; for 1816-19, *P.P. 1819* (278), XVI, 151; for 1820-27, see "Select Committee on the Wool Trade," *P.P. 1828* (515), VIII, App. 1, pp. 782-87.

[244]*P.P. 1846* (109), XLIV, 15.

know, for 1821-27, the amounts entering some thirty ports in England, four in Scotland, and four in Ireland.[245] The gross totals of wool imports annually from 1771 to 1849 are indicated in TABLE 7. There are no printed or parliamentary records of the official value of wool imports. But Schumpeter has figures for the period 1700-1808.[246] Mitchell and Deane reprint her statistics and, for the period 1808-56, set out figures from the Trade and Navigation Accounts.[247]

For the rates of duty on the importation of wool between 1815 and 1849, see *P.P. 1850* (460), LII, 316.

Far fewer sources exist for the exports of English wool, since it was prohibited until 1825. There are quantity figures for the period 1825-50 which distinguish some two dozen countries of destination.[248] There is also a series of declared value for 1825-50.[249]

A few parliamentary papers provide statistics of imports, re-exports, and the amounts retained for domestic consumption from 1820 to 1843.[250]

Textile industries of course did not begin in England in the eighteenth century. The woolen industry had existed for five centuries when the revolution in cotton production began in the late eighteenth century. From the year 1275 we have statistics for exports of wool; for exports of woolen cloth, the series, beginning in 1347, is virtually complete.[251]

Already by the late fifteenth century woolen cloth formed almost 90 per cent of the total exports of England. By 1700, other articles of export had gained importance, but woolens still accounted for 57 per cent of total national exports. In the eighteenth and nineteenth centuries, however, the record is one of a long decline in the share of woolens, as TABLE 8 indicates.

---

[245]*P.P. 1826-27* (230), XVIII, 386.

[246]Schumpeter, XV, 48-51; XVII, 56-59.

[247]Mitchell and Deane, 285-91.

[248]For 1825-27, see *P.P. 1826-27* (230), XVIII, 387; for 1826-43, see *P.P. 1844* (306), XLV, 247-48; for 1827-50, see the sources in Table 4 in this essay. James, *History of the Worsted Manufacture in England* (1857), 36, has statistics for 1825-56. Mitchell and Deane, 192-93, have figures for 1825-50+.

[249]For 1825-27, see "Select Committee on the Wool Trade," *P.P. 1828* (515), VIII, App. 3, pp. 804-05. For 1827-50, see the sources in Table 4 in this essay. Mitchell and Deane present no data on this subject.

[250]For 1820-31, see *P.T. 1, P.P. 1833*, XLI, 131; for 1826-43, see *P.P. 1844* (306), XLV, 245-46. Mitchell and Deane have import figures from 1816, re-export data from 1820, and export figures from 1826, but do not give domestic consumption figures.

[251]See Eleanora M. Carus-Wilson and Olive Coleman, *England's Export Trade, 1275-1547* (Oxford, 1963). The book differentiates "denizen" and "alien" wool and "denizen" and "alien" woolens exported from each of fourteen and fifteen ports, respectively, Michaelmas every year. Clear and fully annotated, the work benefits from numerous graphs.

Table 6

PRICES OF SHEEPS AND LAMBS WOOL
(price per lb.)

Government Documents	*Books and Pamphlets*

Kent Long

1759-1827: "S.C. on Wool Trade," P.P. *1828* (515), VIII, 507.

Kent Long

1759-1799: James, *Worsted Manufacture* (1857), 316-17.

1801-1815: "S.C. on Seeds and Wool," P.P. *1816* (272), VI, 150.

1759-1827: Marshall, *Digest* (1833), Part 3, p. 119; see also Bischoff, *Comprehensive History* (2 v., 1842), II, 125-26.

1818-1845: P.P. *1846* (109), XLIV, 15.

1791-1840: Bischoff, *Comprehensive History* (2 v., 1842), appendix, Table 6.

1817-1828: James, *Worsted Manufacture* (1857), 422.

1818-1845: McCulloch, *Dictionary* (2 v., 1854), II, 1425.

Norfolk

1770-1815: "S.C. on Seeds and Wool," P.P. *1816* (272), VI, 152-53.

1808-1828: "S.C. on Wool Trade," P.P. *1828* (515), VIII, 659.

Norfolk/Suffolk

1815-1835: "S.C. on Agricultural Distress," P.P. *1836* (465), VIII Part 2, App. 20, p. 543

South Down

1759-1827: "S.C. on Wool Trade," P.P. *1828* (515), VIII, 457, 486, 507.

South Down

1759-1827: Marshall, *Digest* (1833), Part 3, p. 119; see also Bischoff, *Comprehensive History* (2 v., 1842), II, 125-26, 129.

1818-1845: P.P. *1846* (109), XLIV, 15.

1784-1833: McCulloch, *Dictionary* (1837), 1263.

Table 6
(continued)

Government Documents	*Books and Pamphlets*

Books and Pamphlets

South Down
1791-1840: Bischoff, *Comprehensive History* (2 v., 1842), II, appendix, Table 6.

1818-1845: McCulloch, *Dictionary* (2 v., 1854), II, 1425.

Suffolk
1770-1815: "S.C. on Seeds and Wool," *P.P. 1816* (272), VI, 152-53.

1799-1827: "S.C. on Wool Trade," *P.P. 1828* (515), VIII, 571.

Suffolk
1747-1788: Eden, *State of the Poor* (3 v., 1797), III, appendix, pp. lxxxiv-lxxxv.

1774-1789: Marshall, *Digest* (1833), Part 3, p.119.

1809-1824: Bischoff, *Comprehensive History* (2 v., 1842), II, 128.

Sussex
1793-1827: "S.C. on Wool Trade," *P.P. 1828* (515), VIII, 664.

1801-1815: "S.C. on Seeds and Wool," *P.P. 1816* (272), VI, 150.

Sussex
1793-1827: Bischoff, *Comprehensive History* (2 v., 1842), II, 130.

Wiltshire
1803-1812: "S.C. on Wool Trade," *P.P. 1828* (515), VIII, App. 14, p. 821.

Wiltshire
1768-1791: Marshall, *Digest* (1833), Part 3, p. 119.

Yorkshire, Northumberland, Scotland
1780-1815: "S.C. on Seeds and Wool," *P.P. 1816* (272), VI, 148.

Yorkshire, Northumberland, Scotland
1780-1815: James, *Worsted Manufacture* (1857), 317, 382.

Secondary Works

Kent Long
1759-1845: Mitchell and Deane, 495.

South Down
1759-1845: Mitchell and Deane, 495.

Deane and Cole present no wool prices.

Table 7

IMPORTS OF SHEEPS WOOL
(in lbs.)

Primary Sources

Government Documents

1781-1806: *J.H.C. 62*, 904; also in
P.P. 1807 (45), IV, 79. *a*

1790-1798: *A.& P. 1799-1800* (1018 a,
1019), LI. *b*

1796-1805: *P.P. 1806* (29), XII, 199.
b,c

1800-1820: *J.H.C. 76*, 1066; also in
P.P. 1821 (467), XVII, 223. *d*

1802-1811: *P.P. 1812* (243), X, 55. *c*

1809-1812: *P.P. 1813-14* (310), XII,
207. *c*

1811-1814: *P.P. 1814-15* (465), X, 457.
c

1815-1818: *P.P. 1819* (278), XVI, 151.
c

1815-1849: *P.P. 1850* (460), LII, 316.
e,f

1818-1845: *P.P. 1846* (109), XLIV, 15.
e

1820-1826: *P.P. 1826-27* (230), XVIII,
385-87. *c,e,g,h*

1820-1831: *P.T. 1, P.P. 1833*, XLI,
70a-70d, 131. *c,e,g*

Books and Pamphlets

1771-1841: Bischoff, *Comprehensive
History* (2 v., 1842), II, appendix,
Tables 2, 6.

1771-1856: James, *Worsted Manufacture*
(1857), appendix, p. 36. *g*

1796-1831: Marshall, *Digest* (1833),
Part 3, p. 115. *c*

1801-1835: Porter, *Progress* (3 v.,
1836-43), I (1836), 198.

1801-1849: Porter, *Progress* (1851),
173.

1814-1831: Marshall, *Digest* (1833),
Part 3, pp. 58-61. *c*

1816-1822: Powell, *Statistical
Illustrations* (1825), 59. *c*

1818-1845: McCulloch, *Dictionary*
(2 v., 1854), II, 1425. *e,i*

Table 7
(continued)

Government Documents   *Books and Pamphlets*

1827-1850:   See Table 3. *c,e,g*

Secondary Works

1700-1808:   Schumpeter, XVI, 52-55; XVII, 56-59. *a*

1700-1850+:   Mitchell and Deane, 190-92. *b,d,g,j*

Imported into Great Britain unless otherwise noted.

a England and Wales only.

b Imports from Spain are distinguished from the total.

c From two dozen countries.

d Imports distinguished as "foreign" or from Ireland.

e United Kingdom.

f From nine parts of the world.

g Includes a series for re-exports; no re-export data before 1820.

h Distinguishes three dozen ports of entry.

i Distinguishes colonial from foreign wool.

j 1700-1792, England and Wales; 1792-1824, Great Britain; 1816-1850+, United Kingdom.

Table 8
EXPORTS OF ENGLISH TEXTILES
AS A PERCENTAGE OF TOTAL EXPORTS

	1772	*1790*	*1800*	*1830*	*1850*	*1870*
Woolens	42.2	34.8	28.5	12.7	14.1	13.4
Linens	7.3	4.2	3.3	5.4	6.8	4.8
Cottons	2.3	10.0	21.9	50.8	39.6	35.8

The figures are for yarn and manufactures combined. For 1772-
1800, they are for England; for 1830-70, for the United Kingdom.
Sources. For 1772, 1790, and 1800, see Ashton, in Schumpeter, 12.
For 1830, 1850, and 1870, see Deane and Cole, Table 9, p. 31.

Eighteenth-century export figures for woolens began to be published around
mid-century. Joseph Massie, the prolific writer on trade and finance,[252] printed a short series in 1757, and John Smith set out a slightly longer one in the
second (1757) edition of his *Memoirs of Wool*. Then in 1782 Sir Joseph Banks
printed a ninety-year annual seris. Macpherson in 1805 set out a series for
the 1790's. Bischoff in 1842 printed a series that was complete from 1741.
The official valuations of woolens were the only ones to change after 1705, but
they, too, remained constant after 1715.[253] See TABLES 9 and 10.

[252]Joseph Massie (d. 1784) penned over a dozen significant works. One of
the most useful is a bibliography of economic literature from 1557 to 1763
(Landsdowne MS 1049, British Museum; published as *Bibliography of the Collection
of Books and Tracts on Commerce, Currency, and Poor Law, 1557 to 1763*, by Joseph
Massie, with transcription and an introduction by William Shaw, 1937). Massie's
mind ranged over finance, taxation, commerce and custom duties, various industries, humanitarian concerns for seamen and prostitutes, and the poor laws. In
his *A Representation Concerning the Knowledge of Commerce as a National Concern
pointing out the proper Means of Promoting such Knowledge in this Kingdom* (1760),
Massie proposed that a research team begin a systematic collection of facts relating to industries under sixteen headings. Like Petty before and Playfair
after him, though, Massie became dejected by the lack of interest shown by both
the public and the Government in his proposal. His last publication was in 1764,
twenty years before his death. For a list of his works, see *D.N.B.*, XIII, 8-9.
For an examination of Massie's studies of the social classes in England, see
Peter Mathias, "The Social Structure in the Eighteenth Century: a Calculation
by Joseph Massie," *Economic History Review*, 2nd ser., X (1957), 30-45.

[253]Ashton, in Schumpeter, 3. See Schumpeter, XLVI, 70, for the values assigned to fifty-one types of woolens in 1660, 1697-1702 (annually), and 1703-08.

Exports of yarn are included in the figures for manufactures until 1814 when a separate series becomes available. See TABLE 11.

Some miscellaneous export series may be of interest. A parliamentary paper, perhaps prepared to show the economic results of the Union, furnishes figures for the exports of woolens from Ireland for the period 1800-20 (all kinds differentiated, by quantity, official value).[254] Another fairly recondite series is that for 1830-42 for re-exports (declared value) of foreign woolens from warehouses in the United Kingdom, distinguishing 'made up' from 'not made up.'[255]

Since England was a seller, not a buyer, of manufactured products, there were few imports of woolen yarn or manufactures. But these are important for they give us a sense of the magnitude of the proportion of England as the workshop of the world. Schumpeter has yarn figures for the eighteenth century, while for woolen manufactures there are statistics for 1812-26 in a parliamentary report of 1828.[256]

On one particular aspect of the process of working up wool into cloth in Yorkshire there is a long statistical series. Figures exist from 1738 for both broad cloth and narrow cloth in pieces, and from 1769, also in yards. The width of the cloth varied even within its category (until its abolition in 1765, the legal minimum for broad was 49½ inches), but an average was usually 27 inches for narrow and 54 inches for broad cloth. As to problems in the statistics, Joseph Massie pointed out in 1757 that the pieces were 33 or 34 yards long until 1733 or 1734, "but since then the said *Lengths* have been gradually increased, and each *Piece* now manufactured is near *Seventy Yards long*: So that the *Increase in these Manufacturies* is about double in Quantity to what it appears to be, by the Increase in the Number of *Pieces* of *Cloth*." Apart from this defect, concluded Massie, "I have good Reasons for believing that it is a just Account."[257] Massie was the first to provide statistics of this production; Eden was the first to print the figures in yards. Other writers continued to record the production, as TABLE 12 indicates.

There are scattered statistics for the value of wool and the woolen manufactures. For wool, one may turn to Laybourne's estimate of 1744, Luccock's of 1805, and Hubbard's of 1828.[258] For woolens, there is John London's es-

---

[254]*J.H.C. 76*, 1060-64. For 1801-21, see *P.P. 1821* (647), XX, 97-100. For Irish exports to Britain from 1764 to 1778, see John Hely-Hutchinson, *The Commercial Restraints of Ireland Considered* (Dublin, 1779), App. 1, facing p. 240. Mitchell and Deane have no separate series for Ireland.

[255]*P.P. 1843* (312), LII, 359.

[256]"Select Committee on the Wool Trade," *P.P. 1828* (515), VIII, App. 6, pp. 808-09 (official value only, distinguishing fourteen places of origin). On yarn for 1700-71, see Schumpeter, XV, 48-51, for official values; XVI, 52-55, for quantities. For values and quantities from 1772 to 1808, see *ibid.*, XVII, 56-59.

[257]Joseph Massie, *Ways and Means for Raising the Extraordinary Supplies to Carry on the War, &c.* (1757), 60-61. Mitchell and Deane, 189, make no mention of this problem in their series.

[258]Henry Laybourne, *Tracts upon our Wool, and Woollen Trade* (1744), 16, 40; John Luccock, "woolstapler," *The Nature and Properties of Wool* (Leeds, 1805 ["printed by Edward Baines"]), table facing 338. Hubbard's estimate is in "Select Committee on the Wool Trade," *P.P. 1828* (515), VIII, 684-85. Both es-

Table 9

OFFICIAL VALUE OF EXPORTS OF WOOLENS

Primary Sources

Government Documents	*Books and Pamphlets*
1790-1799: *A.& P. 1799-1800* (1018), LI. *a*	1697-1780: Banks, *Propriety of* . . . *Exportation of Wool* (1782), 83-85. *c*
1800-1820: *P.P. 1821* (621), XVII, 227.	
1816-1826: *P.P. 1826-27* (532), XVIII, 404-05. *a*	1718-1724, 1738-1743: Massie, *Ways and Means* (1757), 59-60. *c*
1818-1827: "S.C. on Wool Trade," *P.P. 1828* (515), VIII, App. 4, p. 806. *b*	1718-1724, 1738-1753: Smith, *Memoirs of Wool* (2 v., 1757), II, 210, 280. *c*
	1772-1776: Bischoff, *Comprehensive History* (2 v., 1842), I, 176. *a,c*
	1790-1799: Eden, *Eight Letters on the Peace* (1802), 98; reprinted in Macpherson, *Annals of Commerce* (4 v., 1805), IV, 489, and in Bischoff, *Comprehensive History* (2 v., 1842), I, 328. *a*
	1791-1840: Bischoff, *Comprehensive History* (2 v., 1842), II, appendix, Table 6.
	1805-1831: Marshall, *Digest* (1833), Part 3, pp. 64-65, 81.
	1816-1832: McCulloch, *Dictionary* (1837), 445.

Secondary Works

1697-1807: Schumpeter, XII, 35-38; XIII, 39-43. *d*

1697-1829: Mitchell and Deane, 293-95. *d*

Table 9
(Continued)

Exports are from Great Britain unless otherwise noted.

a To two dozen countries.   *c* From England and Wales.

b From the United Kingdom.   *d* 1697-1791, England and Wales;
                                          1792 and after, Great Britain.

---

timate of 1740,[259] an anonymous estimate of 1741 criticizing London's figures,[260]
Anderson's estimate of 1783,[261] Colquhoun's of 1812,[262] Youatt's of 1834,[263] and
McCulloch's of 1837.[264] The problem with all of these estimates is that they
are really guesses, since they base the value of the final product on a multiplier of the value of the wool inputs. Deane and Cole discuss these problems.[265]
    Finally, there are some miscellaneous statistics of interest. One is a list
of the proprietors, the number of looms, and the value of the woolen and worsted manufactures in Ireland in 1783.[266] For employment and wage statistics,
there is a detailed wages chart which Bischoff compiled for twenty-two jobs in
the manufacture of woolen cloth in the county of Gloucester for 1808-38, "show-

timates are presented in McCulloch, *Dictionary* (1837), 1262, and in Bischoff,
Comprehensive History (1842), II, appendix, Table 1. Bischoff called Luccock's
work "deservedly the standard book upon wool" (*Comprehensive History*, I, 371).
James, *History of the Worsted Manufacture in England* (1857), 321, 423-24, prints
the estimates of Luccock and Hubbard and describes the latter as "a high authority on the subject."
    [259]John London, *Some Considerations on the Importance of the Woollen Manufac-
tures* (1740), 26.
    [260]"A Lover of His Country," *A Short Essay upon Trade in General* (1741), 9
pp.
    [261]Adam Anderson, *Origin of Commerce* (2nd ed., 4 v., 1787-89), IV (1789), 522.
    [262]Patrick Colquhoun, *A Treatise on the Wealth, Power, and Resources of the
British Empire* (1814), 91. His estimates are suspiciously rounded, his sources
are unlisted, and his reasoning is often inferred rather than explained.
    [263]In William Waterston, *Cyclopaedia of Commerce* (1843), 671.
    [264]J. R. McCulloch, *Statistical Account of the British Empire* (1837), II,
48. See also the subsequent 2nd ed., 1839, I, 626; 3rd ed., 1847, I, 650. In
the first two editions, McCulloch chose the multiplier of 3; in the 1847 edition
he rejected this method and arrived at a final value roughly twice the value of
the wool. In his *Dictionary of Commerce* (1837), 1265-66, he set out Campbell's
estimate of 1774 and Edward Law's of 1800.
    [265]*British Economic Growth, 1688-1959* (2nd ed., Cambridge, 1967), 192-201,
and Tables 47 and 52. Mitchell and Deane provide no statistics for the value
of the woolen industry.
    [266]Ireland, Trustees of the Linen and Hempen Manufactures, *To the Right Hon-
ourable, the Trustees of the Linen Board, the Report of John Arbuthnot, Esq.,
Inspector-General for the Provinces of Leinster, Munster, and Connaught* (Dublin,
1783), 81-83.

Table 10

EXPORTS OF WOOLENS
BY QUANTITY AND DECLARED VALUE

Primary Sources

Government Documents	*Books and Pamphlets*

By Quantity

1698-1702: *J.H.C. 17*, 366-67. *a,b,c*

1815-1820: *P.P. 1821* (621), XVII, 228-29. *c,d*

1815-1827: "S.C. on Wool Trade," *P.P. 1828* (515), VIII, App. 3, pp. 790-806. *b,c*

1820-1831: *P.T. 1, P.P. 1833*, XLI, 71-82. *b,c,e*

1826-1843: *P.P. 1844* (306), XLV, 250-51. *e,f*

1827-1850: See Table 4. *b,e*

By Quantity

1815-1834: Porter, *Progress* (3 v., 1836-43), I (1836), 192. *c*

1815-1840: Bischoff, *Comprehensive History* (2 v., 1842), II, appendix, Table 7. *c*

1815-1849: Porter, *Progress* (1851), 170. *c*

1820-1851: James, *Worsted Manufacture* (1857), 410, 431, 449, 493, 502, 517. *b*

By Declared Value

1814-1820: *J.H.C. 76*, 1066; also in *P.P. 1821* (621), XVII, 227.

1818-1845: *P.P. 1846* (109), XLIV, 15. *e*

1820-1831: *P.T. 1, P.P. 1833*, XLI, 71-82. *b,e*

1826-1843: *P.P. 1844* (306), XLV, 250-51. *e,f*

1827-1850: See Table 4. *b,e*

By Declared Value

1741-1790: Bischoff, *Comprehensive History* (2 v., 1842), II, appendix, Tables 6, 7. *h*

1814-1831: Marshall, *Digest* (1833), Part 3, pp. 64-65, 81.

1815-1849: Porter, *Progress* (1851), 170.

Table 10
(continued)

Secondary Works

By Quantity
1697-1807: Schumpeter, XIII, 39-43; XIV, 44-47. *c*

1815-1850+:   Mitchell and Deane, 195-96.

By Declared Value
1814-1850+ : Mitchell and Deane, 302-03. *i*

Exports are from Great Britain unless otherwise noted.

a From England and Wales.

b To two dozen countries.

c Distinguishes a dozen types of woolens.

d To four parts of the world.

e From United Kingdom.

f Distinguishes whether to British possessions or to foreign countries.

g 1697-1791, England and Wales; 1792-1807, Great Britain.

h A series at this early date is either a misprint or a calculation computed by Bischoff.

i 1814-29, Great Britain; 1826-1850+, United Kingdom.

Table 11

EXPORTS OF WOOLEN AND BAY YARN

Primary Sources

| *Government Documents* | *Books and Pamphlets* |

By Quantity
1815-1818: *P.P. 1819* (277), XVI, 148. *a*

1815-1827: "S.C. on Wool Trade," *P.P. 1828* (515), VIII, App. 3, pp. 790-805. *a*

1820-1831: *P.T. 1, P.P. 1833,* XLI, 70a-70d. *a,b*

1826-1843: *P.P. 1844* (306), XLV, 248-49. *a,b*

1827-1850: See Table 4. *a,b*

By Quantity
1815-1840: Bischoff, *Comprehensive History* (2 v., 1842), II, appendix, Tables 6,7.

1820-1827: James, *Worsted Manufacture* (1857), 419.

By Declared Value
1815-1827: "S.C. on Wool Trade," *P.P. 1828* (515), VIII, App. 3, pp. 790-805. *a*

1827-1850: See Table 4. *a,b*

1831-1845: *P.P. 1846* (109), XLIV, 15. *b*

By Declared Value
1820-1827: James, *Worsted Manufacture* (1857), 419.

Secondary Works

By Quantity
Schumpeter: none
1819-1850+ : Mitchell and Deane, 195-96. *b*

By Declared Value
Schumpeter: none.
Mitchell and Deane: none.

Exports are from Great Britain unless otherwise noted.

a To two dozen countries.   *b* From the United Kingdom.

Table 12

AMOUNTS OF CLOTH MADE AT THE FULLING
MILLS IN THE WEST RIDING OF YORKSHIRE

Primary Sources

Government Documents

1726-1799	B ^{p}	
1738-1799	N ^{p}	A. & P. *1799-1800*
1769-1799	B ^{y}	(1020), LI, p. 11.
1769-1799	N ^{y}	
1726-1805	B ^{p}	"S.C. on Woollen
1738-1805	N ^{p}	Manufacture," *P.P.*
1769-1805	B ^{y}	*1806* (268), I, 25.
1769-1805	N ^{y}	
1790-1819	B ^{p,y}	*J.H.C. 75*, 768; also
1790-1819	N ^{p,y}	in *P.P. 1820* (88),
		XII, 89.

Books and Pamphlets

1726-1750	B ^{p}	Massie, *Ways and*
1739-1750	N ^{p}	*Means* (1757), 61-62.
1726-1770	B ^{p}	Anderson, *Origin of*
1738-1770	N ^{p}	*Commerce* (4 v., 1787-
		89), IV (1789), 146-
		47.
1726-1795	B ^{p}	Eden, *State of the*
1738-1795	N ^{p}	*Poor* (3 v., 1797),
1769-1795	B ^{y}	III, appendix, p.
1769-1795	N ^{y}	ccclxiii.
1726-1813	B ^{p}	McCulloch, *Statisti-*
1738-1813	N ^{p}	*cal Account of*
1769-1813	B ^{y}	*British Empire* (2 v.,
1769-1813	N ^{y}	1837), II, 52.
1726-1820	B ^{p}	Bischoff, *Compre-*
1738-1820	N ^{p}	*hensive History*
1769-1820	B ^{y}	(2 v., 1842), II,
1769-1820	N ^{y}	appendix, Table 4.
1769-1819	B ^{p,y}	Marshall, *Digest*
1769-1819	N ^{p,y}	(1833), Part 3, p.
		120.
1784-1800	B ^{p,y}	Macpherson, *Annals*
1784-1800	N ^{p,y}	*of Commerce* (4 v.,
		1805), IV, 525.

Secondary Works

1726-1820	B ^{p}	
1739-1820	N ^{p}	Mitchell and Deane, 189.
1769-1820	B ^{y}	
1769-1820	N ^{y}	

^{B} Broad Cloth. ^{N} Narrow Cloth. ^{p} In pieces. ^{y} In yards.

ing the Decrease per Cent. in the Wages of each Class."[267] A parliamentary paper furnishes wages for all the hands in a worsted factory in Bradford from 1824 to 1831.[268] Porter gives us the number of woolen factories and the numbers employed in each county in the United Kingdom in 1835.[269]

(b) Linens

Before the revolution in cotton at the end of the eighteenth century, the linen industry was important for it provided the middle classes and the well-to-do with the kind of light, moderately expensive, washable clothing which woolens, by their nature, could never be. But the linen industry never achieved its full promise. The appearance of several inventions—Hargreaves' spinning jenny (c. 1765), Arkwright's water frame (1769), Crompton's mule (1779)—revolutionized the production of its chief rival, the cotton textile industry. The spinning jenny, for instance, offered a mechanical advantage of up to twenty-four to one over the traditional hand spinning wheel, while the water frame gave an advantage of several hundred to one![270] Linens, caught in the middle between cottons and woolens, never grew substantially in output, even after woolens began their precipitous decline in the 1770's (see above, Table 8).

The industry in England since the Glorious Revolution was a minor one. In the early eighteenth century, to encourage the English woolen industry, English linens had been exposed to competition from Ireland, on the theory that this would induce many to put their investments into English woolens. William III had told Parliament in 1698, "I shall do all that in me lies to discourage the woollen manufactures in Ireland, and encourage the linen manufactures [there], and to promote the trade of England!"[271] In the same spirit, Acts of 1701 and 1721 barred the selling or wearing of Indian piece-goods and calicoes in England. In 1742 an additional duty was placed on the import of foreign linens and the proceeds of this were used to pay a bounty on the export of Irish (as well as British) linens. The trade statistics show the result. The share of Irish linens in the total imports of linens into England changed from 1 per cent in 1700 to 18 per cent in 1750, 46 per cent in 1772, and 70 per cent in 1800.[272]

When, therefore, English cottons cornered the linen market at the end of the eighteenth century, it was an old story, for decades earlier English linens had been sacrificed to Irish in order to discourage the Irish and encourage the English woolen industry. English linens suffered again, but, more importantly, for

[267]Bischoff, *Comprehensive History* (1842), II, 416.
[268]*P.T. 3, P.P. 1835*, XLIX, Nos. 361-65, pp. 418-19.
[269]G. R. Porter, *Progress of the Nation* (3 v., 1836-43), I (1836), 196-97. These figures are from the first report of the government factory inspectors, *P.P. 1835* (342), XL, 689. Further reports (on the cotton, flax, and silk industries as well) were made annually from 1836; these are listed in the *General Index to Accounts and Papers &c. . . . . of the House of Commons, 1801-52* (1938), 364.
[270]David Landes, *The Unbound Prometheus* (Cambridge, 1969), 83-85.
[271]Quoted in J. R. McCulloch, *Dictionary* (1837), 761.
[272]T. S. Ashton, in Schumpeter, 12.

the history of Ireland so did that island's only textile industry. Little solace was it to Irishmen—this poetic justice of the English woolen industry, supported by the destruction of Irish competition, now in its turn heavily damaged by the competition with English cottons!

Price series for flax and linen are random and miscellaneous. A series exists of average annual flax prices (at Marienberg) from 1783 to 1816.[273] For Russian flax (at Riga and St. Petersburg), there are monthly averages twice a year, in January and July, from 1810 to 1822, while Tooke has the quarterly average price for flax and hemp at St. Petersburg for 1782-1825 and 1838-47.[274] For linen yarn there is a curious series of prices of "an average bundle" (place not specified) for 1813-33.[275]

The great growth of the Irish linen industry came in the early eighteenth century. In printing the figure of over seven million yards of linen cloth exported from Ireland to all countries in 1756, Joseph Massie (1757) observed that this was *Three Hundred Times* the Quantity yearly exported Eighty-eight Years ago." Since the bulk of the exports went to England, Massie rejoiced in the *"one common Interest* in three Kingdoms," for England, in no longer buying linens from Continental nations, was investing in the economic well-being of her sister lands. Each would buy from the other, linens for woolens: "these *Linen Manufactures* do not interfere with any, but help some of the *English Manufactures.*"[276] The bargain worked, at least until the cotton revolution. TABLE 13 sets out the sources for imports of linens (by quantity) into Great Britain from Ireland. Gill, a modern authority, has graphed the quinquennial figures of exports of linens and linen yarn from Ireland from 1712 to 1821. He also shows, for selected years, the amounts of linens leaving the ports of Belfast, Londonderry, Newry, and Dublin.[277]

Though by far the bulk of the Irish linens went to England, some cloth was exported from Ireland to the rest of the world (see TABLE 14).

Certain sources may be mentioned for Irish linen yarn (as distinct from linen cloth) exported to Great Britain in the eighteenth century,[278] and for Irish yarn exported to the rest of the world.[279]

---

[273]Price per ton, separate figures for hemp, in the evidence of E. C. Hohler, extracted from *Prince's Prices Current*, in "Select Committee on the Wool Trade," *P.P. 1828* (515), VIII, 726.

[274]Respectively: *J.H.C. 77*, 1015; Tooke, *Thoughts and Details* (1824), App. 4, pp. 1-72, and Tooke, *History of Prices*, III (1840), 297, and IV (1848), 426-34. Conrad Gill, *The Rise of the Irish Linen Industry* (Oxford, 1925), 223, has graphed the prices of Russian flax from 1782 to 1825.

[275]*P.T. 3, P.P. 1835*, XLIX, No. 314, p. 395. A series for 1813-32 is reprinted in Porter, *Progress*, I (1836), 268. There are no flax or linen prices in Mitchell and Deane.

[276]Massie, *Ways and Means* (1757), 84-85. The third kingdom would be Scotland.

[277]Conrad Gill, *Rise of the Irish Linen Industry* (Oxford, 1925), 339, 184, respectively. The selected years: 1773, 1782, 1792, 1801, 1807, 1810.

[278]For 1701-71 (official value), see "Report relative to the Linen Trade of Great Britain and Ireland (1773)," *Commons' Committees*, III, 116; for 1731-50 (quantity), see the "Report relative to Chequed and Striped Linens (1751)," *Commons' Committees*, II, 310.

[279]For 1701-71 (official value), see "Report relative to the Linen Trade of Great Britain and Ireland (1773)," *Commons' Committees*, III, 116; for 1710-50, decennially, and 1760-71 (official value), see Macpherson, *Annals of Commerce*

Table 13

IMPORTS OF LINENS INTO GREAT BRITAIN FROM IRELAND
(by quantity in yards)

Primary Sources

Government Documents

1725-1740: "Report relating to Linens, Threads, and Tapes (1744)," *Commons' Committees*, II, 69. *a*

1727-1748: "Report relating to Chequed and Striped Linens (1751)," *Commons' Committees*, II, 301. *a,b*

1789-1798: Great Britain, Parliament, House of Lords, *Accounts respecting . . . Britain and Ireland* (1799), No. 8, p. 19.

1801-1812: *J.H.C. 68*, 858; also in *P.P. 1812-13* (272), XII, 449. *c*

1810-1819: *J.H.C. 75*, 753.

1820-1825: *P.T. 1, P.P. 1833*, XLI, 83. *d,e*

Books and Pamphlets

1705-1742: Hely-Hutchinson, *Commercial Restraints of Ireland* (1779), App. 3, facing p. 240. *a*

1731-1750: Savary des Bruslons, *Universal Dictionary* (2 v., 1751-55), II (1755), 83. *a,f*

1757-1773: Glover, *Substance of the Evidence* (1774), 60. *a*

1800-1825: Porter, *Progress* (3 v., 1836-43), I (1836), 265; also in *Progress* (1851), 225.

1800-1825: McCulloch, *Statistical Account of British Empire* (2 v., 1837), II, 93.

Secondary Works

Mitchell and Deane: none.

Horner, *Linen Trade of Europe* (1920); Gill, *Rise of Irish Linen Industry* (1925): none.

After 1825 no figures are available, as the Irish linen trade was recorded with the coasting trade of Britain.

a England and Wales only.

b Not annual figures but averages for three periods: 1727-33, 1734-40, 1742-48.

c Series of re-exports also.

d United Kingdom.

e Series also for amount retained for domestic consumption.

f Linen yarn only.

Table 14

EXPORTS OF LINENS FROM IRELAND TO ALL PARTS OF THE WORLD

Primary Sources

Government Documents	Books and Pamphlets

Government Documents

1701-1771: "Report relating to the Linen Trade of Great Britain and Ireland (1773)," *Commons' Committees,* III, 116. *a*

1800-1803: *J.H.C. 59,* 679. *a,b,c*

1803-1814: *J.H.C. 71,* 903-04. *a,d,e*

1808-1822: *J.H.C. 78,* 883-91. *a,e,f*

1810-1819: *J.H.C. 75,* 752. *a,d,f*

Books and Pamphlets

1705-1742: Hely-Hutchinson, *Commercial Restraints of Ireland* (1779), App. 3, facing p. 240. *b,g*

1752-1773: Glover, *Substance of the Evidence* (1774), 58. *b*

1760-1771: Macpherson, *Annals of Commerce* (4 v., 1805), III, 515. *a,b*

1800-1825: Porter, *Progress* (3 v., 1836-43), I (1836), 265; also in *Progress* (1851), 225. *b,g*

1800-1825: McCulloch, *Dictionary* (1837), 762; also in his *Statistical Account of British Empire* (2 v., 1837), II, 93. *b,g*

1814-1823: Powell, *Statistical Illustrations* (1825), 52-53. *a,f*

Secondary Works

1712-1821: Horner, *Linen Trade of Europe* (1920), 201-04; also in Gill, *Rise of Irish Linen Industry* (1925), App. 2, pp. 341-43. *h*

Mitchell and Deane: none.

a By official value.
b By quantity in yards.
c Distinguishes to Britain, British colonies, the United States, and other.
d Differentiating colored and plain linen.

e Distinguishes two dozen countries.
f By declared value.
g Distinguishes Great Britain and foreign parts.
h A series for yarn (in cwts.) as well as for linen (in yds.); also for the period 1787-1821 a series for flax (in cwts.).

Statistics exist for the output of the Irish linen industry. For 1770 a parliamentary account provides the value of linen cloth sent to market, by each county.[280] For 1783 there are figures for the number of pieces and value of linens in Leinster, Munster, and Connaught, distinguishing counties, names of proprietors, and types of articles; also, for the amount of linen yarn spun in Leinster and Connaught.[281] For a later period, 1821-24, there are annual figures for the value of brown (unbleached) linens sold at specified market towns in each county of Ireland.[282]

The English linen industry, though less important than the Irish, has left us many statistics simply because it existed in England. TABLE 15 shows the record of imports of flax into England from 1700 until 1850. Most series are for totals only, but some (as indicated) specify countries of origin. There is also a series of flax imports into Ireland for 1745-51 and 1814-23.[283]

TABLE 16 sets out the sources for the imports of linen yarn into England. There is also a series (1810-19) which sets out the imports of linen yarn into Ireland and which, for yarn imported into Britain in the same years, distinguishes British from foreign ships as carriers.[284]

TABLE 17 indicates the sources for the imports (and, in some cases, re-exports) of foreign linens. One series also gives the rates of duty and revenue thus raised for 1820-31.[285]

Export figures of linen yarn are scarce, but there is a series for 1833-37.[286]

(1805), III, 515; for 1701-71, decennially (by quantity, in pieces), see Anderson, *Origin of Commerce* (4 v., 1787-89), IV (1789), 147; for 1741-47 (by quantity), see *State of Facts relating to the Linen-Manufacture of Great Britain and Ireland* (1750?), n.p.; and for 1814-23 (declared value), see John Powell, *Statistical Illustrations* (1825); Gill, *Rise of the Irish Linen Industry* (Oxford, 1925), 91, 222, has quinquennial averages for 1731-60 and 1791-1820, respectively.

[280]"Report relative to the Linen Trade of Great Britain and Ireland (1773)," in *Commons' Committees*, III, 117 (evidence of Robert Stephenson). Printed also in *Reports 1773* (30), III, App. 10, p. 39.

[281][Ireland,] Trustees of the Linen and Hempen Manufactures, *To the Right Honourable and Honourable, the Trustees of the Linen Board. The Report of John Arbuthnot, Esq., Inspector-General for the Provinces of Leinster, Munster, and Connaught* (n.p., 1783), 71-77, 80-81. Gill, *Rise of the Irish Linen Industry* (Oxford, 1925), 160-62, gives reasons why he feels Stephenson's estimates of 1770 and 1784 are too high.

[282]"Select Committee on the Linen Trade of Ireland," *P.P. 1825* (463), V, App. 1, pp. 851-55. Porter, *Progress*, I (1836), 266, reprints these figures for 1821-24 by province and comments, "There is not any document in existence which brings this information down to a later date." Gill, *Rise of the Irish Linen Industry* (Oxford, 1925), App. 1, pp. 335-38, lists the weekly sales at markets in each county in 1784, 1816, 1820, and 1821. He also provides figures for the number of linen and cotton looms in Belfast at eight dates from 1760 to 1810 (*ibid.*, 239).

[283]For 1745-51, by quantity, see Robert Stephenson, *An Inquiry into the State and Progress of the Linen Manufacture of Ireland* (Dublin, 1757), 92; for 1814-23, by official value, see Powell, *Statistical Illustrations* (1825), 50. Gill, *Rise of the Irish Linen Industry* (Oxford, 1925), App. 2, pp. 341-43, has figures (in cwts.) for flax exports from Ireland from 1787 to 1821.

[284]By quantity (cwts.), in *J.H.C. 75*, 752.

[285]*P.T. 1, P.P. 1833*, XLI, 86.

[286]*P.P. 1837-38* (343), XLV, 232-33.

Table 15

IMPORTS OF FLAX
(by quantity, in cwts.)

Primary Sources

Government Documents

1709-1711: *J.H.C. 17*, 351. *a,b*

1792-1801: *J.H.C. 58*, 778-79. *c,d*

1806-1808: *J.H.C. 64*, 640. *e,f*

1810-1819: *J.H.C. 75*, 755. *g,h*

1819-1822: *J.H.C. 78*, 881-82. *i,j*

1827-1850: See Table 3. *i,k,l*

Books and Pamphlets

1814-1831: Marshall, *Digest* (1833)
Part 3, pp. 56-61. *l,m*

1820-1835: Porter, *Progress* (3 v.,
1836-43), I (1836), 270. *k*

1820-1849: Porter, *Progress* (1851),
229. *k*

Secondary Works

1700-1808: Schumpeter, XV-XVII, 48-59. *n,o*

1700-1856: Mitchell and Deane, 287-91. *m,p*

Imports are into Great Britain unless otherwise noted.

a England and Wales only.

b Distinguishes flax from hemp.

c Distinguishes flax from flaxen yarn.

d Differentiates from nine countries.

e Flax seed only (in bushels).

f From Europe, the United States, and
other.

g Distinguishes dressed from undressed
flax.

h Differentiates foreign flax and Irish
flax.

i Distinguishes two dozen countries.

j Distinguishes the imports of undressed flax into three dozen ports.

k United Kingdom.

l Series of re-exports also.

m By official value only.

n By official value as well as by
quantity.

o 1700-1791, England and Wales;
1792-1808, Great Britain.

p 1700-1791, England and Wales;
1792-1829, Great Britain;
1826-1856, United Kingdom.

Table 16

IMPORTS OF LINEN YARN
(by quantity, in cwts.)

Primary Sources

Government Documents

1752-1771: "Report relating to the Linen Trade of Great Britain and Ireland (1773)," *Commons Committees*, III, 131; also in *Reports 1773* (30), III, App. 14, p. 43. *a,b*

1792-1801: *J.H.C. 57*, 938-39. *c,d,e*

1810-1819: *J.H.C. 75*, 755. *c*

1819-1822: *J.H.C. 78*, 882. *c*

1827-1850: See Table 3. *f,g,h*

Books and Pamphlets

1814-1823: Powell, *Statistical Illustrations* (1825), 55.

1814-1831: Marshall, *Digest* (1833), Part 3, pp. 58-59. *i*

Secondary Works

1700-1808: Schumpeter, XV-XVII, 48-59. *e,j*

1700-1856: Mitchell and Deane, 287-91. *i,k*

Imports (by quantity, in cwts.) are into Great Britain unless otherwise noted.

a England and Wales only.

b Quantity is in lbs.

c Distinguishes from ten countries.

d Series includes hempen as well as linen yarn.

e By official value as well as by quantity.

f United Kingdom.

g Distinguishes from two to four dozen countries.

h Series of re-exports also.

i By official value only.

j 1700-1791, England and Wales; 1792-1808, Great Britain.

k 1700-1791, England and Wales; 1792-1829, Great Britain; 1826-1856, United Kingdom.

Table 17

IMPORTS OF FOREIGN LINENS

Primary Sources

Government Documents	Books and Pamphlets

Government Documents

1752-1771: "Report relating to the Linen Trade of Great Britain and Ireland (1773)," *Commons' Committees*, III, 119-30; also in *Reports 1773* (30), III, App. 12-13, pp. 47-48. *a,b,c*

1789-1797: Great Britain, Parliament, House of Lords, *Accounts respecting . . . Britain and Ireland* (1799), Nos. 10-11, pp. 22-24. *b,c,d,e,*

1801-1812: *P.P. 1812-13* (271), XII, 446-47. *b,d,f,g*

1810-1819: *J.H.C. 75*, 753-54. *b,d,e,f*

1820-1831: *P.T. 1*, *P.P. 1833*, XLI, 84-85. *b,d,f,h*

1827-1850: See Table 3. *b,d,e,f,h,i*

Books and Pamphlets

1752-1771: Young, *Political Arithmetic* (1774), 316. *a,b*

1752-1773: Glover, *Substance of the Evidence* (1774), 56-57. *a,b*

1762-1771: Anderson, *Origin of Commerce* (4 v., 1787-89), IV (1789), 149; also in Macpherson, *Annals of Commerce* (4 v., 1805), III, 516. *a*

1814-1831: Marshall, *Digest* (1833), Part 3, pp. 58-59. *j*

Secondary Works

Schumpeter: none.   Mitchell and Deane: none.

Imports (by quantity, in yards) are into Great Britain unless otherwise noted.

a England and Wales only.

b Series of re-exports also.

c Distinguishes two dozen kinds of linens.

d Quantity in ells, pieces, and yards.

e By official value as well as by quantity.

f Distinguishes one dozen kinds of linens.

g Distinguishes from three countries.

h United Kingdom.

i From two to four dozen countries.

j By official value only.

Table 18

EXPORTS OF LINENS

Primary Sources

Government Documents

1743-1771: "Report relating to the Linen Trade of Great Britain and Ireland (1773)," *Commons' Committees*, III, 133; also in *Reports 1773* (30), III, App. 17, p. 46. *a,b,c*

1746-1750: "Report relating to Chequed and Striped Linens (1751)," *Commons' Committees*, II, 290. *d,e*

1789-1798: Great Britain, Parliament, House of Lords, *Accounts respecting . . . Britain and Ireland* (1799), No. 9, p. 20. *b,f*

1797-1815: *J.H.C. 71*, 902; also in *P.P. 1816* (309), XIV, 413. *c,d,g*

1799-1819: "S.C. on Foreign Trade," *P.P. 1820* (300), II, App. 8, p. 500. *b,c*

1801-1812: *P.P. 1812-13* (273), XII, 451. *f*

1808-1822: *J.H.C. 78*, 883-91. *c,h,i,j*

1820-1831: *P.T. 1*, *P.P. 1833*, XLI, 83. *b,c,k*

1827-1850: See Table 4. *b,i,k,l*

Books and Pamphlets

1743-1771: Young, *Political Arithmetic* (1774), 314-15; also in Anderson, *Origin of Commerce* (4 v., 1787-89), IV (1789), 148, and in Macpherson, *Annals of Commerce* (4 v., 1805), III, 515-16. *a,b,c*

1757-1773: Glover, *Substance of the Evidence* (1774), 61. *b,c*

1805-1827: Marshall, *Digest* (1833), Part 3, p. 81. *d*

1816-1832: McCulloch, *Dictionary* (1837), 445. *h*

1820-1833: Porter, *Progress* (3 v., 1836-43), I (1836), 265. *b,c,k*

Table 18
(continued)

Secondary Works

1697-1807: Schumpeter, X, 29-30; XI, 31-34; XIV, 44-47. *b,c,m*

1697-1850+: Mitchell and Deane, 201-02. *b,n*

1697-1829: Mitchell and Deane, 293-95. *d,o,p*

1814-1850+: Mitchell and Deane, 302-03. *l,p,q*

Exports are from Great Britain unless otherwise noted.

a England and Wales only.

b By quantity in yards.

c Includes a series for exports of Irish as well as British linens from Great Britain.

d By official value only.

e English exports of chequed and striped linens made only from Irish yarn in Lancashire, England.

f Exports from Great Britain of Irish linens only.

g Includes a series for the re-exports of foreign linens.

h By declared value as well as by official value.

i Distinguishes exports to two dozen countries.

j Distinguishes exports from England and Wales, Scotland, and Ireland.

k United Kingdom.

l By declared value.

m 1697-1791, England and Wales; 1792-1807, Great Britain.

n 1697-1791, England and Wales; 1792-1825, Great Britain; 1826-1850+, United Kingdom.

o 1697-1791, England and Wales; 1792-1829, Great Britain.

p These figures include linen yarn as well as manufactures.

q 1814-1829, Great Britain; 1826-1850+, United Kingdom.

Sources for the exports of linens from England appear in TABLE 18. Many different types of linens were designated starting in 1751, so that we have a century-long series of finely differentiated figures through (and beyond) 1850.[287] Schumpeter provides twenty quinquennial figures in the eighteenth century of exports to eight geographical areas of the world from 1700 to 1800.[288]

(c) Cottons

The use of the word 'cotton' by Lewes Roberts in 1641 appears to have been the first mention of that staple in England.[289] From then until the 1770's, cotton remained a minor industry, its development held back by the delicate nature of the fibre, the undesirability of the coarse product when interwoven with linen, and the relative unproductivity of the hand spinning wheel. But beginning in the 1780's, the growth of the industry was rapid, as a direct result of "the influence of the stupendous discoveries and inventions of Hargreaves, Arkwright, Crompton, Cartwright and others."[290] McCulloch, who wrote those words, believed the "rapid growth and prodigious magnitude" of the cotton manufacture to be "beyond all question, the most extraordinary phenomena in the history of industry." Cotton, he noted, also contributed "in no common degree to raise the British nation to the high and conspicuous place she now occupies."[291]

In the 1830's the cotton industry found its first historians. Edward Baines (1774-1848), author of the *History of the Cotton Manufacture in Great Britain* (1835), was the son of a Preston tradesman. Most famous perhaps as the proprietor of the *Leeds Mercury*, a paper which he crafted into a liberal Whig journal, Baines was liked by workers and employers alike. He believed that the revolution in the cotton industry helped all classes of Englishmen. A Member of Parliament from 1834 to 1841, Baines contended for various liberal causes as well as for factory reform and free trade.

Andrew Ure (1778-1857), Scottish author of *The Cotton Manufacture of Great Britain* (1836), was a chemist and scientific writer. Ure's economic writings were really a sideline to his work in physics and chemistry. If his *Philosophy of Manufactures* (1835) is best remembered for its passages on the 'euphoric' lives of the cotton workers, his work on *The Cotton Manufacture* does contain many useful statistical series. Baines and Ure furnish much data, but the most comprehensive statistical writer before Ellison[292] must be Richard Burn,

[287]T. S. Ashton, in Schumpeter, 4.

[288]Schumpeter, XXXIV, 66.

[289]In his *Treasure of Trafficke* (1641), 32. The reference is to the purchase in London markets of cotton wool from Smyrna and Cyprus. The opinion is that of J. R. McCulloch, *Dictionary of Commerce* (2 v., 1854 edn.), I, 452.

[290]For a list of the fifty patents taken out for improvements in cotton spinning between 1800 and 1836, see Andrew Ure, *The Cotton Manufacture of Great Britain* (2 v., 1836), I, 315-18. Thomas Ellison, *The Cotton Trade of Great Britain* (1886), 29, presents the dates of inventions next to the amounts of cotton imported from 1738 to 1800.

[291]McCulloch, *Dictionary* (2 v., 1854), I, 451.

[292]Thomas Ellison's two great works on cotton were *A Handbook of the Cotton Trade* (1858) and *The Cotton Trade of Great Britain* (1886).

the editor of *The Commercial Glance*, a businessman's newspaper in Manchester. Burn's *Statistics of the Cotton Trade* (1847) consists of thirty-four tables in twenty-seven concise pages. "I have adopted the tabular form," he explained in the preface, "in order that the reader may at one view, see the progress of each separate article, and the great value of statistical works being in their conciseness, I have confined myself to that point as much as possible." He compiles the works of others, acknowledging McCulloch, Porter, Baines, Ure, "and many others," and furnishes many new figures.

There are many series of cotton wool prices. These comprise cotton prices from fourteen regions of the world and of prices in the Liverpool and Manchester markets. Tooke, in 1824, was the first writer to present a long series of cotton wool prices.[293] Select Committees in 1828 and 1832 printed series, as did Baines and Ure in the 1830's and Burn in 1847. These and other series for various types of cotton wool are set out in TABLE 19. A colored graph by J. F. Royle dramatically presents the annual price movements of Indian and American Upland cotton from 1806 to 1846.[294] In their modern work, Wadsworth and Mann present cotton prices at various dates between 1607 and 1780.[295]

For other cotton prices, there is the work of Baines who provides prices of warp, weft, and cotton wool for 1815-33.[296] Ure, using figures from Samuel Greg & Company, gives prices of cotton wool compared to prices of twist, from 1805 to 1832; Porter has a similar series for 1802-32.[297] Fielden compares the prices of Upland cotton, 20 hanks water twist, three-quarters velveteens, and 9/8 shirtings for each month in every year in the period 1827-33.[298]

For cotton yarn, Ure has prices of the yarn sold by the East India Company from 1706 to 1759; Burn has a similar but less complete series.[299] Burn provides a table comparing cotton yarn with cotton wool prices from 1809 to 1847.[300] For the most common type of yarn, one hundred hanks to the pound, Baines gives prices from an early date, 1786, to 1832; Burn, who gives prices for 1786-1807, carries the figures from 1832 to 1846.[301]

[293]Thomas Tooke, *Thoughts and Details* (1824), App. 4, No. 1, pp. 10-15.

[294]"Select Committee Report on the Growth of Cotton in India," *P.P. 1847-48* (511), IX, facing 544. The work also graphs data on the quantity of imports of Indian as opposed to American cotton.

[295]A. P. Wadsworth and Julia DeLacy Mann, *The Cotton Trade and Industrial Lancashire, 1600-1780* (Manchester, 1931), App. H, pp. 522-23.

[296]Edward Baines, *A History of the Cotton Manufacture in Great Britain* (1835), 355; Thomas Hopkins, *Great Britain for the Last Forty Years* (1834), 276, has a similar series for 1814-33.

[297]Andrew Ure, *The Cotton Manufacture of Great Britain* (2 v., 1836), II, 431; Porter, *Progress* (3 v., 1836-43), I (1836), 213.

[298]John Fielden's letter and statistics are in W. Fitton, *National Regeneration* (1834), App. 7, pp. 24-25. Fielden was the famous Radical cotton manufacturer at Todmorden.

[299]Ure, *Cotton Manufacture* (2 v., 1836), I, 322; Richard Burn, *Statistics of the Cotton Trade arranged in a Tabular Form* (1847), table, p. 11.

[300]Burn, *Statistics* (1847), table, p. 13.

[301]Baines, *Cotton Manufacture* (1835), 357; Burn, *Statistics* (1847), table, p. 10. Porter, *Progress* (3 v., 1836-43), I (1836), 212, has prices only for 1786-1807, 1829 and 1832. Michael Edwards, *The Growth of the British Cotton Trade, 1780-1815* (Manchester, 1967), App. C, p. 253, gives prices for 1786-1815;

Table 19

PRICES OF COTTON WOOL

Primary Sources

Government Documents	*Books and Pamphlets*	
1783-1828: "S.C. on Wool Trade," *P.P. 1828* (515), VIII, 726. *a*	1782-1822 (*a,g,h*) 1788-1822 (*i*) 1790-1822 (*j*) 1793-1822 (*c*)	Tooke, *Thoughts and Details* (1824), App. 4, No. 1, pp. 10-17.
1810-1822: *J.H.C. 77,* 1015. *b,c,d*		
1819-1832: "S.C. on Bank of England Charter," *P.P. 1831-32* (722), VI, App. 92, p. 94. *b,c,d*	1782-1825 (*a,g,h*) 1788-1825 (*i*) 1790-1825 (*j*) 1793-1846 (*e*)	Burn, *Statistics* (1847), 14, 20.
1836-1846: *P.T. 16, P.P. 1847-48* (982), LXII, No. 201, p. 236. *e,f*	1800-1857 (*e,i,k,l, m*):	Ellison, *Handbook* (1858), Table B, section 1, facing p. 191.
	1806-1833 (*e,i,k,l n,o,p,q, r*):	Baines, *Cotton Manufacture* (1835), 314; identical series for the period 1806-35 is re-printed in Ure, *Cotton Manufacture* (2 v., 1836), I, 157, and for 1806-36, in Burn, *Statistics* (1847), 21.
	1814-1828 (*c,l*):	Marshall, *Digest* (1833), Part 3, p. 49.
	1824-1835 (*c,i,k,m, n,p,s,t, u*):	Ure, *Cotton Manufacture* (2 v., 1836), I, 156.

Table 19
(continued)

Government Documents   *Books and Pamphlets*

1827-1833 *(e,f)*:   Fielden, in Fitton,
                      National Regenera-
                      tion (1834), App.
                      7, pp. 24-25.

Secondary Works

1782-1820   *(a,g,h)*
1788-1820   *(i)*   Mitchell and Deane, 490-91.
1798-1850+ *(c,e)*

1791-1815 *(e,l,n)*: Edwards, *Growth of British Cotton Trade* (1967), App. C, p.
    253.

---

a West Indian.

b Average price in months of January
   and July.

c Bowed Georgia.

d Bengal.

e Upland Bowed.

f Average monthly prices.

g Surinam.

h Berbice.

i Pernambuco.

j Bengal and Surat.

k Surat only.

l Highest and lowest annual price.

m Annual average price.

n New Orleans.

o Sea Island.

p Maranham.

q Demerara.

r Prices specifically in the
   Liverpool market.

s Egyptian.

t Bengal only.

u Prices on December 1 of each year.

There are many price series for calicoes. Baines gives the cost and selling price of one piece of calico for 1814-33, as does Fielden (1815-32), specifying third 74 s. calico.[302] Porter furnishes the selling prices of 72 7/8 calicoes from 1814 to 1831.[303] Fielden has many other calico prices. He gives the cost of 72 s. calicoes, half-ell velveteens, and 30 hanks water twist made by power loom in 1815, 1824, 1831, and 1832;[304] he provides the prices obtained for second-quality 74 s. calico from 1820 to 1833[305] and the prices of 30 hanks water twist, 1818-33.[306] All of these figures apply for northeast Lancashire and the West Riding of Yorkshire.

Finally, the prices of manufactured cotton goods may be mentioned. Porter provides general prices paid for cotton goods from 1814 to 1831, and Burn gives us the average annual price of seventeen types of cotton manufactures exported from England from 1831 to 1846.[307] A modern writer has discussed in a critical appendix the prices of cotton cloth.[308]

There are numerous sources for the figures of cotton wool imports. As Mc-Culloch observed, the statistics until 1770 "have been but imperfectly preserved" due to the unimportance of the industry before that date; but some figures do exist.[309] Some of the sources also break down the statistics into five world regions--America, Egypt, Brazil, the West Indies, and the East Indies. There are figures at a variety of dates in addition to the series set out in TABLE 20. Burn has data for 1697, 1701, 1702-05 (average), 1710-20 (average), 1730, 1741, 1743-49 (annually), 1751, 1764, 1771-75 (totals), and 1776-80 (totals).[310] Ure has five-yearly averages for 1701-1800.[311] The figures are usually broken down geographically into five or six world regions, but McCulloch differentiates twenty-seven places of origin for 1829-34.[312] Ure may be consulted for figures of annual imports *from India only* from 1700 to 1760.[313] Modern authorities pre-

he cites as his sources Baines' book and the McConnell and Kennedy papers at the University of Manchester Library.

[302]Baines, *Cotton Manufacture* (1835), 356; Fielden, in Fitton, *National Regeneration* (1834), Table 1, p. 7.

[303]Porter, *Progress* (3 v., 1836-43), I (1836), 215.

[304]Fielden, in Fitton, *National Regeneration* (1834), Table 2, p. 8.

[305]Fielden, in Fitton, *National Regeneration* (1834), App. 1 and 2, p. 22; probably based on the evidence of George Smith, in "Select Committee on Manufactures, Commerce, and Shipping," P.P. *1833* (690), III, 568.

[306]Fielden, in Fitton, *National Regeneration* (1834), App. 3, p. 22; probably based on figures in P.P. *1833* (690), III, 569-70.

[307]Porter, *Progress* (3 v., 1836-43), I (1836), 215; Burn, *Statistics* (1847), table, p. 7.

[308]Michael Edwards, *The Growth of the British Cotton Trade, 1780-1815* (Manchester, 1967), App. A, pp. 239-42.

[309]J. R. McCulloch, *Dictionary* (2 v., 1854), I, 452. For the rates of duty for 1798-1833, see Baines, *Cotton Manufacture* (1835), 326-27, or Ure, *Cotton Manufacture* (2 v., 1836), II, 438-39. Burn, *Statistics* (1847), table, p. 24, carries the figures to 1845, after which importation was free.

[310]Burn, *Statistics* (1847), table, p. 14.

[311]Ure, *Cotton Manufacture* (2 v., 1836), I, 161.

[312]McCulloch, *Dictionary* (1836), 440.

[313]Ure, *Cotton Manufacture* (2 v., 1836), I, 321.

sent data by line graphs for imports from the West Indies and the Levant (differentiated) from 1698 to 1780.[314] There is also a colored graphic representation of the imports from Calcutta, Madras, and Bombay from 1796 to 1846 (see above, note 294). For import data from the United States probably the most convenient source, covering 1785-1847, is a parliamentary inquiry into economic distress in 1847-48.[315] Baines also has figures from 1791 to 1820, while Ure has statistics for 1794-1835.[316] The American figures are particularly important, for by the 1830's two-thirds of America's raw cotton exports went to England: in 1832, some 210 million of £ 313 million total. Baines gives figures (in bales) for the size of American crops from 1819 to 1832, while Ellison has crop figures for 1824-57.[317]

The direction of flow of imports into Great Britain can be measured, for in some cases we are told the ports of entry. Thus, for 1812-17, the total imports are broken down among nine English ports.[318] For a period a few years later (1823-32), Ure provides figures (in bales) of imports into London, Liverpool, and Glasgow.[319] He gives data in a longer series (1791-1835), but for cotton imports into Liverpool only.[320]

Before the revolution in the cotton industry brought the avalanche of cotton wool imports there was a large importation of cotton yarn. Burn gives us figures for the cotton yarn imports *from India* in 1703-07 and 1713-60.[321] Parliamentary records contain data for imports of cotton yarn and twist (from each of twelve countries) and for re-exports (to nine countries) from 1750 to 1780.[322] By 1847, in an entirely new cotton climate, Burn furnishes statistics of the quantity of cotton yarn spun annually from 1830 to 1846 in Britain, distinguishing England from Scotland.[323] These two sets of figures reflect the momentous changes in technology from 1760 to 1830.

[314]Wadsworth and Mann, *Cotton Trade and Industrial Lancashire, 1600-1780* (Manchester, 1931), 184. Unfortunately, the value of the vertical axis (imports) is not specified.

[315]"Select Committee (Secret) on Commercial Distress," *P.P. 1847-48* (395), VIII Part 2, App. 44, p. 371. There is also a shorter series for East Indian cotton imports, 1834-47 (*ibid.*, App. 45, p. 372). Ellison, *Handbook of the Cotton Trade* (1858), Table A, facing p. 191, also has American cotton export data to England for 1827-57. For 1788-1815, see Edwards, *Growth of the British Cotton Trade* (Manchester, 1967), App. C, p. 251.

[316]Baines, *Cotton Manufacture* (1835), 302; Ure, *Cotton Manufacture* (2 v., 1836), I, 147.

[317]Baines, *Cotton Manufacture* (1835), 303; Thomas Ellison, *Handbook of the Cotton Trade* (1858), Table A, facing p. 191 (state-by-state figures); Edwards, *Growth of the British Cotton Trade, 1780-1815* (Manchester, 1967), 96, provides state-by-state figures for 1791, 1801, 1811, and 1821. Ellison, *Cotton Trade of Great Britain* (1886), Table 3, facing p. 355, gives data for American crops and exports from 1826 to 1884. (One bale equals 300 lbs. avoirdupois.)

[318]*P.P. 1819* (276), XVI, 83-91.

[319]Ure, *Cotton Manufacture* (2 v., 1836), I, 152.

[320]Ure, *Cotton Manufacture* (2 v., 1836), I, 160.

[321]Burn, *Statistics* (1847), table, p. 11.

[322]*J.H.C. 58*, 893. For the eighteenth-century figures of cotton yarn imports (by quantity and value), from 1700 to 1808, see Schumpeter, XV-XVII, 48-59.

[323]Burn, *Statistics* (1847), table, p. 18.

Table 20

IMPORTS OF COTTON WOOL

Primary Sources

Government Documents	Books and Pamphlets

<table>
<tr><td>

Government Documents

1743-1749: "Report relating to Chequed and Striped Linens, (1751)," *Commons' Committees*, II, 311. *a*

1771-1790: "S.C. on the Export Trade from Great Britain to the East Indies," *A.& P. 1792-93* (774c), XXXVIII, p. 2.

1791-1802: *J.H.C. 58*, 892.

1792-1811: *J.H.C. 67*, 760; also in *P.P. 1812* (278), X, 57.

1806-1808: *J.H.C. 64*, 640. *b*

1807-1817: *P.P. 1818* (102), XIV, 177.

1809-1814: *J.H.C. 70*, 850. *b*

1810-1815: *P.P. 1817* (210), X, 448-49. *b*

1812-1817: *P.P. 1819* (276), XVI, 83-91; also in *J.H.C. 74*, 931-33. *c,d*

</td><td>

Books and Pamphlets

1743-1749: Savary des Bruslons, *Universal Dictionary* (2 v., 1751-55), II, (1755), 84. *a*

1768-1779: Macpherson, *Annals of Commerce* (4 v., 1805), III, 650. *g,h*

1771-1787: *Considerations relative to . . . the Cotton Manufactury* (1788), App. 2, p. 45. *h*

1781-1800: MacGregor, *Commercial Statistics* (4 v., 1847-48), IV (1848), 754.

1781-1832: McCulloch, *Dictionary* (1837), 439.

1781-1833: Baines, *Cotton Manufacture* (1835), 347.

1781-1834: McCulloch, *Statistical Account of British Empire* (2 v., 1837), II, 68-69.

</td></tr>
</table>

Table 20
(continued)

Government Documents	*Books and Pamphlets*
1815-1847: *P.P. 1847-48* (383), LVIII, 326-27. *b,e*	1781-1846: Burn, *Statistics* (1847), 14. *i*
1820-1831: *P.T. 1, P.P. 1833*, XLI, 101. *e,f*	1798-1830: Marshall, *Digest* (1833), Part 3, p. 112.
1827-1850: See Table 3. *c,e*	1800-1857: Ellison, *Handbook* (1858), Table B, section 1, facing p. 191. *b,e,i*
	1801-1835: Porter, *Progress* (3 v., 1836-43), I (1836), 205. *j*
	1801-1846: MacGregor, *Commercial Statistics* (4 v., 1847-48), IV (1848), 754. *j*
	1801-1849: Porter, *Progress* (1851), 178.
	1802-1823: Powell, *Statistical Illustrations* (1825), 58. *b,i,j*
	1806-1835: Ure, *Cotton Manufacture* (2 v., 1836), I, 161. *b*
	1814-1830: Marshall, *Digest* (1833), Part 3, p. 113. *b*

Table 20
(continued)

Government Documents   *Books and Pamphlets*

1820-1833: Baines, *Cotton Manufacture* (1835), 309, 347. *b*

1820-1846: Burn, *Statistics* (1847), 17. *b*

1827-1834: Ure, *Cotton Manufacture* (2 v., 1836), I, 155. *b*

Secondary Works

1697-1780: Wadsworth and Mann, *Cotton Trade* (1931), App. G, pp. 520-21. *k*

1697-1850+: Mitchell and Deane, 177-78, 180-81. *l,m*

1772-1808: Schumpeter, XVII, 56-59. *n*

1772-1856: Mitchell and Deane, 286, 289, 291. *j,o*

1780-1815: Edwards, *Growth of British Cotton Trade* (1967), App. C, pp. 250-51. *p*

1811-1884: Ellison, *Cotton Trade of Great Britain* (1886), Table 1, facing p. 355. *b,e*

Table 20
(continued)

Imports (by quantity, in lbs.) are into Great Britain unless otherwise noted.

^a Stated to be for Great Britain, but the figures must be for England and Wales, as British series do not exist for the mid-century.

^b Differentiates imports from six parts of the world (the United States, Brazil, Egypt, West Indies, East Indies, other).

^c Distinguishes from two dozen countries.

^d Distinguishes imports into one dozen British ports.

^e United Kingdom.

^f Differentiates from four foreign countries and three British colonies.

^g Distinguishes foreign from British colonial cotton wool.

^h Distinguishes imports into Scotland from imports into England and Wales.

ⁱ Quantity in bales as well as in pounds.

^j By official value only.

^k Distinguishes cotton wool from the Levant, the West Indies, Europe, and Africa; and prize wool.

^l 1697-1819, Great Britain; 1815-1850+, United Kingdom.

^m For 1815-50+, the imports from the United States are distinguished from the total.

ⁿ By official value as well as by quantity (lbs.).

^o 1792-1829, Great Britain; 1826-1856, United Kingdom.

^p Differentiates from British West Indies, the East Indies, and the United States.

Table 21

EXPORTS OF COTTON MANUFACTURES
BY QUANTITY

Primary Sources

Government Documents

1762-1771: "Report relating to the Linen Trade of Great Britain and Ireland (1773)," *Commons' Committees*, III, 131. *a,b*

1791-1802: *J.H.C. 58*, 894.

1812-1817: *J.H.C. 74*, 934-46; also in *P.P. 1819* (300), XVI, 95-119. *c,d*

1814-1845: *P.P. 1846* (291), XLIV, 147. *e*

1815-1847: *P.P. 1847-48* (383), LVIII, 328. *e*

1818-1826: *P.P. 1828* (553), XIX, 285-99. *c,d*

1820-1831: *P.T. 1, P.P. 1833*, XLI, 65-70. *c,d,e*

1827-1850: See Table 4. *c,d,e*

Books and Pamphlets

1814-1828: Marshall, *Digest* (1833), Part 3, pp. 50-51. *c,d*

1814-1850: McCulloch, *Dictionary* (2 v., 1854), I, 460. *e*

1814-1857: Ellison, *Handbook* (1858), Table B, section 2, facing p. 191. *e*

1820-1834: Porter, *Progress* (3 v., 1836-43), I (1836), 208. *c,e*

1820-1849: Porter, *Progress* (1851), 180. *c,e*

1827-1834: Ure, *Cotton Manufacture* (2 v., 1836), I, 326-33. *c,d,e*

1831-1846: Burn, *Statistics* (1847), 3-6. *c,d,e*

Secondary Works

1697-1807: Schumpeter, XI, 31-34; XIV, 44-47. *c,f*

1800-1850+: Robson, *Cotton Industry in Britain* (1957), 331-33. *e*

1815-1850+: Mitchell and Deane, 182-83. *e*

Table 21
(continued)

Exports (by quantity, in yards) are from Great Britain unless otherwise noted.

a
England and Wales only.

b
A combination of printed cottons
and linens.

c
Distinguishes several different types
of cottons.

d
Distinguishes to two dozen countries.

e
United Kingdom.

f
1697-1791, England and Wales;
1792-1807, Great Britain.

Exports of cotton manufactures, inconsiderable in 1780, by 1800 equalled the amount of woolens exported, and by 1850 cotton exports were three times greater than woolens and constituted half the total exports of the nation. Sources for the exports of cotton manufactures, by quantity, are set out in TABLE 21.

Sources for the valuations of cotton manufacture exports appear in TABLE 22. For the first three-quarters of the eighteenth century, the basic differentiations in the figures are checked cotton, checked cotton and linen, printed cotton and linen, dimity, and fustian. Beginning in 1772, more types of cottons appear in the records, including "Manchester cottons and velverets."[324] Schumpeter lists all the different types.[325] In addition to the figures available in Baines' book, which are listed in Table 22, are scattered data for 1697, 1701, 1710-40 (decennially only), 1751, 1764-66 (annually), and 1780. Statistics of declared value were not kept until 1798; a fire destroyed the records of 1798-1813, however, so the series actually begins in 1814. A modern writer has calculated the percentage which cottons annually comprised of all exports from 1814 to 1955.[326] One source, as a long footnote to its record of total exports for 1815-47, gives detailed treatment to the American market over this period.[327] There is also some data on Irish cottons exported from Ireland from 1810 to

[324]T. S. Ashton, in Schumpeter, 4.

[325]For the export of fustians to eight geographical areas quinquennially from 1700 to 1800, see Schumpeter, XXXII, 66; for printed cotton and linen, from 1765 to 1800, quinquennially, see Schumpeter, XXXVII, 67. Edwards, *Growth of the British Cotton Trade, 1780-1815* (Manchester, 1967), App. B, p. 247, sets out by bar graph the increasing diversification of the cotton manufactures exported from 1780 to 1807.

[326]Robert Robson, *The Cotton Industry in Britain* (1957), 334-35.

[327]*P.P. 1847-48* (383), LVIII, 329, has quantity and declared value figures for the exports of cottons, cotton thread, and cotton twist and yarn to this country.

Table 22

EXPORTS OF COTTON MANUFACTURES
BY VALUE

Primary Sources

Government Documents

1789-1798: Great Britain, Parliament, House of Lords, *Accounts respecting . . . Britain and Ireland* (1799), No. 3, p. 8. *a*

1791-1802: *J.H.C. 58*, 892. *a,b*

1798-1829: *P.P. 1830-31* (145), X, 398. *a*

1810-1814: *J.H.C. 70*, 851. *a,b,c*

1811-1815: *P.P. 1817* (266), X, 453. *a,b*

1812-1817: *J.H.C. 74*, 935-47; also in *P.P. 1819* (300), XVI, 95-119. *a,b,d,e*

1814-1829: *P.P. 1830-31* (145), X, 398. *e*

1814-1845: *P.P. 1844* (291), XLVI, 147. *e,f*

1815-1847: *P.P. 1847-48* (383), LVIII, 328. *e,f*

1818-1826: *P.P. 1828* (553), XIX, 258-99. *a,b,d,e*

1820-1831: *P.T. 1*, *P.P. 1833*, XLI, 65-70. *b,d,e,f*

1827-1850: See Table 4. *b,d,e,f*

Books and Pamphlets

1785-1800: MacGregor, *Commercial Statistics* (4 v., 1847-48), IV (1848), 768. *a*

1785-1830: Burn, *Statistics* (1847), 8. *a*

1785-1833: Baines, *Cotton Manufacture* (1835), 349-50. *a*

1800-1857: Ellison, *Handbook* (1858), Table B, section 2, facing p. 191. *a,f*

1801-1849: Porter, *Progress* (1851), 178. *a,f*

1814-1823: Powell, *Statistical Illustrations* (1825), 58. *a,e*

1814-1830: Burn, *Statistics* (1847), 8. *e*

1814-1833: Baines, *Cotton Manufacture* (1835), 350. *e*

1814-1849: Porter, *Progress* (1851), 178. *e,f*

1814-1850: McCulloch, *Dictionary* (2 v., 1854), I, 460. *e,f*

1814-1857: Ellison, *Handbook* (1858), Table B, section 2, facing p. 191. *e*

Table 22
(Continued)

Government Documents   *Books and Pamphlets*

1816-1832: McCulloch, *Dictionary* (1837), 445. *a,e*

1820-1834: Porter, *Progress* (3 v., 1836-43), I (1836), 208. *d,e,f*

1820-1849: Porter, *Progress* (1851), 180. *d,e,f*

1827-1834: Ure, *Cotton Manufacture* (2 v., 1836), I, 326-33. *b,e,f*

1831-1846: Burn, *Statistics* (1847), 9. *d,e,f*

Secondary Works

1697-1807: Schumpeter, X-XI, 29-34. *a,d,g*

1697-1829: Mitchell and Deane, 293-95. *a,d,g*

1731-1780: Wadsworth and Mann, *Cotton Trade* (1931), 153, 167. *a*

1780-1807: Edwards, *Growth of British Cotton Trade* (1967), App. B, pp. 243-46. *d,h*

1814-1850+: Mitchell and Deane, 302-03; also in Robson, *Cotton Industry in Britain* (1957), 334-35. *e,i*

Exports (by official, declared value) are from Great Britain unless otherwise noted.

a By official value.

b Distinguishes to two dozen countries.

c Includes cotton yarn as well as manufactures.

d Distinguishes several different types of cottons.

e By declared value.

f United Kingdom.

g 1697-1791, England and Wales; 1792 and after, Great Britain.

h Figures for alternate years only; distinguishes exports to five regions of the world.

i 1814-1829, Great Britain; 1826-1850+, United Kingdom.

Table 23

EXPORTS OF COTTON TWIST AND YARN

Primary Sources

Government Documents

1790-1802: *J.H.C.* 58, 890. *a,b*

1798-1829: *P.P. 1830-31* (145), X, 399. *c*

1812-1817: *J.H.C. 74*, 948-53. *b,c,d, e,f*

1814-1829: *P.P. 1830-31* (145), X, 399. *f*

1814-1845: *P.P. 1846* (291), XLIV, 149. *d,f,g*

1815-1847: *P.P. 1847-48* (383), LVIII, 328. *d,f,g*

1818-1826: *P.P. 1828* (553), XIX, 314-32. *b,d,f*

1820-1831: *P.T. 1*, *P.P. 1833*, XLI, 65-70. *b,d,f,g*

1827-1850: See Table 4. *b,d,f,g*

Books and Pamphlets

1798-1830: Burn, *Statistics* (1847), 8. *c*

1798-1833: Baines, *Cotton Manufacture* (1835), 350. *c*

1798-1834: McCulloch, *Statistical Account of British Empire* (2 v., 1837), II, 73. *c*

1814-1823: Powell, *Statistical Illustrations* (1825), 58. *c,f*

1814-1828: Marshall, *Digest* (1833), Part 3, p. 49. *b,c,d,f*

1814-1830: Burn, *Statistics* (1847), 8. *f*

1814-1833: Baines, *Cotton Manufacture* (1835), 350. *f*

1814-1834: McCulloch, *Statistical Account of British Empire* (2 v., 1837), II, 73. *f*

1814-1850: McCulloch, *Dictionary* (2 v., 1854), I, 460. *d,f,g*

1815-1857: Ellison, *Handbook* (1858), Table B, section 2, facing p. 191. *b,d,f,g*

1816-1832: McCulloch, *Dictionary* (1837), 445. *c,f*

Table 23
(continued)

Government Documents   *Books and Pamphlets*

1820-1849: Porter, *Progress* (1851), 180. *d,f,g*

1827-1834: Ure, *Cotton Manufacture* (2 v., 1836), I, 326-33. *b,d,f,g*

1831-1846: Burn, *Statistics* (1847), 1. *b,d,g*

Secondary Works

Schumpeter: none.

Mitchell and Deane: none.

1800-1850+: Robson, *Cotton Industry in Britain* (1957), 331-33. *d,g*

1821-1884: Ellison, *Cotton Trade of Great Britain* (1886), Table 2, facing p. 355. *d,f,g*

Exports are from Great Britain unless otherwise noted.

[a] By quantity in cwts.

[b] Distinguishes to two dozen countries.

[c] By official value.

[d] By quantity in lbs.

[e] Distinguishes exports from five British ports.

[f] By declared value.

[g] United Kingdom.

99

Table 24

RE-EXPORTS OF COTTON WOOL

Primary Sources

Government Documents	*Books and Pamphlets*
1743-1749: "Report relating to Chequed and Striped Linens (1751)," *Commons' Committees*, II, 311. *a*	1743-1749; Savary des Bruslons, *Universal Dictionary* (2 v., 1751-55), II (1755), 84.
1790-1802: *J.H.C. 58*, 889. *b*	1771-1787: *Considerations relative to . . . the Cotton Manufactury* (1788), App. 2, p. 45. *g*
1807-1817: *P.P. 1818* (102), XIV, 177.	
1809-1814: *J.H.C. 70*, 850. *c*	1781-1800: MacGregor, *Commercial Statistics* (4 v., 1847-48), IV (1848), 754.
1812-1817: *J.H.C. 74*, 930-31; also in *P.P. 1819* (275), XVI, 79-81. *b,d*	
1820-1831: *P.T. 1*, *P.P. 1833*, XLI, 101. *e,f*	1781-1832: McCulloch, *Dictionary* (1837), 439.
1827-1850: See Table 3. *b,e,f*	1781-1833: Baines, *Cotton Manufacture* (1835), 347.
	1781-1834: McCulloch, *Statistical Account of British Empire* (2 v., 1837), II, 68-69.
	1781-1846: Burn, *Statistics* (1847), 14.
	1798-1830: Marshall, *Digest* (1833), Part 3, p. 113.
	1800-1857: Ellison, *Handbook* (1858), Table B, section 1, facing p. 191. *e,f*
	1801-1835: Porter, *Progress* (3 v., 1836-43), I (1836), 205. *e*
	1801-1849: Porter, *Progress* (1851), 178. *e*

Table 24
(Continued)

Government Documents   *Books and Pamphlets*

1820-1833: Baines, *Cotton Manufacture* (1835), 347. *e*

1820-1834: McCulloch, *Statistical Account of British Empire* (2 v., 1837), II, 69. *e*

1837-1846: Burn, *Statistics* (1847), 15-16. *b*

Secondary Works

1697-1780: Wadsworth and Mann, *Cotton Trade* (1931), App. G, pp. 520-21.

1697-1850+: Mitchell and Deane, 177-78, 180-81. *h*

1700-1808: Schumpeter, XVIII, 61-62. *e,i*

1800-1850+: Mitchell and Deane, 179. *f,j*

1811-1884: Ellison, *Cotton Trade of Great Britain* (1886), Table 1, facing p. 355. *e*

Re-exports (by quantity, in lbs.) are from Great Britain unless otherwise noted.

a Stated to be for Great Britain, but the figures must be for England and Wales, as British series do not exist for the mid-century.

b Distinguishes to two dozen countries.

c Distinguishes to Ireland and the rest of the world.

d Distinguishes from six British ports.

e Includes a separate series of the amounts taken for domestic consumption.

f United Kingdom.

g Distinguishes Scotland from England and Wales.

h 1697-1819, Great Britain; 1815-1850+, United Kingdom.

i 1700-1791, England and Wales; 1792-1808, Great Britain.

j This series is for domestic consumption only.

1821.[328]

Not all of the cotton wool which was made into yarn was used at home. The statistics which exist for the exports of cotton yarn appear in TABLE 23. One source gives the amounts leaving each British port from 1814 to 1817.[329] Another source provides the *price* of cotton yarn exported from 1814 to 1828.[330]

Roughly 5 per cent of all cotton wool imports were re-exported. TABLE 24 presents the sources for these re-export data. It is, again, for Regency-period statistics that we have printed records of the distribution of the re-exports from British ports: in this case, from the port of London, nine other English ports, and all Scottish ports to nineteen foreign countries from 1812 to 1817.[331]

It is possible to calculate the amount of cotton wool used in British textile industries by deducting the figures set out in the sources in Table 24 (re-exports) from those in Table 20 (imports). Baines does this in a chart listing cotton wool imports, re-exports, consumption, and prices from 1816 to 1833. Burn calculates the amount retained for domestic consumption for 1832-47, while Ellison has figures for 1815-57.[332] McCulloch lists the amounts left in stock in British ports at the end of each year, 1814-32; Ellison, differentiating American and East Indian cotton, has figures for 1815-57; Burn, in figures for 1829-47, differentiates the stock left in ports in London, Liverpool, Glasgow, and all of Britain.[333] Finally, Burn has an interesting table of the transactions in the Liverpool cotton market for every three months from 1838 to 1847, specifying the number of bales sold to spinners and dealers, the reported sales to exporters and speculators, and the average price of Upland cotton.[334] Ellison has figures for the total number of bales sold annually to speculators in Liverpool from 1816 to 1857.[335]

Another measurement of the scale of the cotton industry is the number and distribution of factories. A pamphlet of 1788 estimates the number of cotton factories and hand engines in each county in England.[336] Baines prints figures

[328]For 1810-14, see *J.H.C. 70*, 852; for 1816-21, see *J.H.C. 76*, 1118-25 (quantities only).
[329]*P.P. 1819* (301), XVI, 121-30.
[330]Marshall, *Digest* (1833), Part 3, p. 49.
[331]*P.P. 1819* (275), XVI, 79-81.
[332]Baines, *Cotton Manufacture* (1835), 315; Burn, *Statistics* (1847), table, p. 12; Ellison, *Handbook of the Cotton Trade* (1858), Table B, section 1, facing p. 191. A modern writer, Neil Smelser, *Social Change in the Industrial Revolution* (Chicago and London, 1959), 120, gives figures for consumption for 1801-15, while Robert Robson, *The Cotton Industry in Britain* (1957), 331-33, sets out data for 1800-1955.
[333]McCulloch, *Dictionary* (1837), 439; Ellison, *Handbook of the Cotton Trade* (1858), Table B, section 1, facing p. 191; Burn, *Statistics* (1847), table, p. 18. Ellison, *Cotton Trade of Great Britain* (1886), Table 1, facing p. 355, has figures for the stock (in bales) in British ports on December 31, for every year from 1811 to 1884, distinguishing American, East Indian, and all other types of cotton.
[334]Burn, *Statistics* (1847), table, p. 23.
[335]Ellison, *Handbook of the Cotton Trade* (1858), Table B, section 1, facing p. 191.
[336]*Considerations relative to a Plan of Relief for the Cotton Manufactury* (1788), App. 1, pp. 43-44. This pamphlet is sometimes attributed to Patrick

for the distribution of factories in Manchester, Salford, and nearby townships in 1820, 1823, 1826, 1829, and 1832.[337] He also gives us Stanway's estimate of the number of water-powered and steam-driven cotton mills in Lancashire towns in 1833.[338] Using returns provided by the factory inspectors appointed by the Factory Act of 1833, Ure furnishes figures for the number of textile mills (differentiated by industry and the numbers employed) in each county in the United Kingdom in 1835.[339] Burn provides similar figures, for cotton mills only, in 1838.[340]

The number of power looms is another index of the growth of the cotton industry. Baines has statistics for England and Scotland in 1820, 1829, and 1833. Porter, using the factory inspectors' returns, provides figures for the number in each textile industry in each county in the United Kingdom in 1835.[341]

The cotton industry, though strong and healthy, was not a success story for everyone, whether worker or employer. Many employers went bankrupt, as may be seen in a sixty-year series which Burn provides of bankruptcies (by number of firms and of partners) in the cotton trade from 1786 to 1846.[342]

A few sources of wages in cotton weaving and spinning may be mentioned here. Young and Eden give wages in the pre-factory weaving of cotton.[343] Baines has figures for the weaving of cambrics (60-reed) in Bolton from 1795 to 1834, while Marshall has a series (place unspecified) for 1798-1831.[344] Fielden

Colquhoun. These figures also appear in another pamphlet, *An Important Crisis, in the Callico and Muslin Manufactory in Great Britain, explained* (1788), 5. Deane and Cole, 184-85, cite this work but do not reproduce the table. The pamphlet, *An Important Crisis*, is not at Harvard, but the table in the pamphlet is reprinted in Sydney J. Chapman, *The Lancashire Cotton Industry* (Manchester, 1904), 149 n. 1, and in Paul Mantoux, *The Industrial Revolution in the Eighteenth Century* (1962 ed.), 248 n. 2.

[337]Baines, *Cotton Manufacture* (1835), 395; Burn, *Statistics* (1847), table, p. 26. *P.T. 3, P.P. 1835*, XLIX, No. 328, p. 404, gives the number of textile mills (differentiated) at work in Manchester and a half-dozen nearby towns from 1820 to 1832.

[338]Baines, *Cotton Manufacture* (1835), 386.

[339]Ure, *Cotton Manufacture* (2 v., 1836), I, 353-54; Burn, *Statistics* (1847), table, p. 26.

[340]Burn, *Statistics* (1847), table, p. 26. Chapman, *Lancashire Cotton Industry* (Manchester, 1904), 149, reprints these figures.

[341]Baines, *Cotton Manufacture* (1835), 235, 237; Porter, *Progress* (3 v., 1836-43), I (1836), 240. On the transition to power-looms, see A. J. Taylor, "Concentration and Specialization in the Lancashire Cotton Industry, 1825-1850," *Economic History Review*, 2nd ser., I (1949), 114-22. Smelser, *Social Change in the Industrial Revolution* (Chicago and London, 1959), 148, has data at nine dates from 1813 to 1850.

[342]Burn, *Statistics* (1847), table, p. 25.

[343]See any one of Arthur Young's tours (1768-80): note 217; see also Eden, *State of the Poor* (3 v., 1797), *passim*.

[344]Baines, *Cotton Manufacture* (1835), 489; Marshall, *Digest* (1833), Part 3, p. 48. These figures are probably based on data for 1795-1833 in the "Select Committee on Manufactures, Commerce, and Shipping," *P.P. 1833* (690), III, 699-700. The wage for 60-reed cambrics, according to Richard Needham of Great Bolton, "regulates all the plain cambrics in the cotton trade; it is a sort of standard or average rate" (*ibid.*, 699).

lists the wages paid by a Lancashire manufacturer named William Cannon for 48-, 56-, and 70-reed cambrics from 1811 to 1833.[345] Porter furnishes figures for wages to weavers for 1814-31, types of work and places unspecified; he also lists the wages for weaving 24 yards of cambric at Stockport, 1802-12.[346] For the weaving of calicoes, Yates gives the wages for weaving 74 printing calicoes at Burnley from 1792 to 1814.[347] Baines provides wages for the weaving of second-quality 74 calicoes near Burnley and Skipton annually from 1802 to 1833,[348] and Fielden has wages at Burnley for third-quality 74 calicoes from 1814 to 1820 and a series with place unspecified for 1821 to 1833. Fielden also estimates individual average weekly earnings, the average weekly income of a family of six (if five were weaving), and the weekly money needs of that family for rent and looms, food and clothing.[349] Local diet costs, item by item, for 1814-33, are also furnished.[350]

Wages for the spinning, weaving, printing, and bleaching of cottons in and around Manchester from 1810 to 1819 are provided by Tooke;[351] the series, compiled by the city's Chamber of Commerce, is continued by Baines through 1825.[352] Baines also gives wages for the cotton spinners of Mr. Thomas Houldsworth (Manchester) in 1804, 1814, and 1833, and of spinners, dressers, and weavers in Cheshire (firms and places unspecified) in 1816, 1821, 1826, and 1831-32.[353] He lists, too, cotton weavers' wages in Glasgow for 1810-19 and 1831-32.[354] Ure has wage figures gathered by Mr. Stanway for all persons connected with cotton in 1833, correlating average wages in each of 151 mills in Lancashire with type of work (e.g., carding, mule-spinning, throstle-spinning, weaving), seats of the manufacture, total numbers employed, and total hours.[355] Porter prints data from the factory inspectors' reports, enumerating the employees in all cotton mills in the United Kingdom in 1835.[356] *Porter's Tables* has the "nett earnings" of several types of factory workers at Manchester, from carders' assistants to spinners, from 1844 to 1849.[357] Probably the best modern

[345]Fielden, in Fitton, *National Regeneration* (1834), App. 13, p. 30. These are based on the statistics in *P.P. 1833* (690), III, 701.

[346]Porter, *Progress* (3 v., 1836-43), I (1836), 215. See also *P.T. 3, P.P. 1835,* XLIX, No. 331, p. 406.

[347]John Ashton Yates, *A Letter on the Distresses of the Country* (1817), App. F, p. 15. The figures are for April in each year.

[348]Baines, *Cotton Manufacture* (1835), 490. Compare the figures in *P.P. 1833* (690), III, 564.

[349]Fielden, in Fitton, *National Regeneration* (1834), App. 8, p. 26.

[350]Fielden, in Fitton, *National Regeneration* (1834), App. 9, p. 27.

[351]Tooke, *Thoughts and Details* (1824), appendix, Table 9, facing p. 21.

[352]Baines, *Cotton Manufacture* (1835), 433. Baines' complex table (1810-25) lists figures for six types of spinning and ten types of weaving. Wages for other kinds of workers: fustian cutters, warpers, dressers, dyers; calico printers, bleachers, and finishers; tailors; porters; packers; shoemakers; ironfounders; whitesmiths; sawyers; carpenters; stonemasons, bricklayers, painters, slaters, plasterers, and bricklayers' labourers.

[353]Baines, *Cotton Manufacture* (1835), 443, 445, respectively. Mr. Houldsworth's figures are reprinted in Ure, *Cotton Manufacture* (2 v., 1836), II, 447.

[354]Baines, *Cotton Manufacture* (1835), 441, 488.

[355]Ure, *Cotton Manufacture* (2 v., 1836), I, 334-42.

[356]Porter, *Progress* (3 v., 1836-43), I (1836), 224-28.

[357]*P.T. 18, P.P. 1850* [1159], LIV, No. 207, p. 195.

compendium of wages in the industry remains Wood's work which contains forty-nine tables, while Collier's book for the crucial half-century, 1784 to 1833, is also valuable.[358]

For the darkest side of the picture—the handloom weavers—Fielden has compiled a chart (in eleven columns) of their wages and costs in the village of Crompton, Yorkshire, from 1814 to 1833.[359] For international comparisons, Ure has set up a comparative table of wages for carders, drawers, spinners, piecers, and weavers in 1833 in England, America, France, Prussia, Switzerland, and six other countries.[360]

(d) Silk

The English silk industry, though its origins dated to the fifteenth century, had always competed unfavorably with the French industry, due to the lower labor costs, cheaper raw materials, and superior workmanship in France. Raw and thrown silk could legally be imported into England, but foreign silk manufactures were barred by acts of 1697 and 1701. Despite this protective legislation, the English industry did not prosper, owing to the demand for smuggled French silks[361] and, from the 1780's, English cottons. Finally, in 1826, the prohibition was repealed, but the new *ad valorem* import duty of 30 per cent was still high enough to make smuggling profitable; in 1845 the duty was reduced to 15 per cent.[362] Though the silk industry trebled in value from 1820 to 1860, it remained of minor importance because, as a luxury item, demand was inelastic, consumers preferred the French product, and the raw material did not lend itself to mechanization.[363]

A parliamentary paper gives silk prices from 1783 to 1828,[364] and another specifies London prices (including consignees' charges and duty) for Milan thrown and raw silk for 1819-31.[365]

[358]George Henry Wood, *The History of Wages in the Cotton Trade during the Past Hundred Years* (1910); Frances Collier, *The Family Economy of the Working Classes in the Cotton Industry, 1784-1833* (Manchester, 1964).

[359]Fielden, in Fitton, *National Regeneration* (1834), App. 12, p. 29. These statistics are extracted from *P.P. 1833* (690), III, 661. Smelser, *Social Change in the Industrial Revolution* (Chicago and London, 1959), 137, 140, has data on the numbers (1806-20) and wages (1797-1838) of handloom weavers. See especially Duncan Bythell's *The Handloom Weavers* (Cambridge, 1969).

[360]Ure, *Cotton Manufacture* (2 v., 1836), I, p. xliii.

[361]In the period 1688-1741 silk valued at £ 500,000 was smuggled into England *every* year! As little as 5 per cent of the annual total would be seized by Customs Officers (McCulloch, *Dictionary* [2 v., 1854], II, 1183, 1186).

[362]Smuggling costs were usually about 15 per cent of the value of the silk, so the 1845 act effectively ended the large-scale smuggling industry (*ibid.*, II, 1185).

[363]Deane and Cole, 207-11. The only adequate book on the industry is Sir Frank Warren's *The Silk Industry of the United Kingdom* (1921), a long (664 pages) work without tables of statistics.

[364]"Select Committee on the Wool Trade," *P.P. 1828* (515), VIII, 727. Hohler's evidence is based on *Prince's Prices Current*. Hohler does not specify the type of silk; the place may be London.

[365]"Select Committee on the Silk Trade," *P.P. 1831-32* (678), XIX, 181. See

Table 25

IMPORTS OF SILK

Primary Sources

Government Documents	*Books and Pamphlets*

Government Documents

1715-1719: *J.H.C. 19*, 190. *a,b*

1760-1772: *J.H.C. 34*, 242. *a,c*

1786-1805: *J.H.C. 61*, 854-55. *b,d,e*

1806-1816: *J.H.C. 72*, 738-39. *b,d,e*

1814-1831: "S.C. on Silk Trade," *P.P. 1831-32* (678), XIX, p. 10, and App. A, pp. 918-19. *b,f,g,h*

1814-1841: *P.P. 1842* (296), XXXIX, 539-40. *b,f,g,h*

1814-1844: *P.P. 1846* (109), XLIV, 12. *g,h,i*

1817-1818: *J.H.C. 74*, 963. *d,e*

1820-1831: "S.C. on Silk Trade," *P.P. 1831-32* (678), XIX, App. C, pp. 922-25. *h,i*

1820-1831: *P.T. 1, P.P. 1833*, XLI, 87-89. *h,k*

1827-1850: See Table 3. *b,h,i,l*

Books and Pamphlets

1814-1831: Marshall, *Digest* (1833), Part 3, pp. 56-57. *m*

1814-1833: McCulloch, *Dictionary* (1837), 1035. *i*

1814-1835: Porter, *Progress* (3 v., 836-43), I (1836), 254. *i*

1814-1849: Porter, *Progress* (1851), 215. *i*

Secondary Works

1700-1808: Schumpeter, XVI-XVII, 52-59. *n,o*

1700-1850+: Mitchell and Deane, 205-07. *b,p,q*

1700-1856: Mitchell and Deane, 285-92. *m,r*

Table 25
(continued)

Imports (by quantity, in lbs.) are into Great Britain unless otherwise noted.

[a] England and Wales.

[b] Series of re-exports also.

[c] Distinguishes raw silk from thrown silk.

[d] By official value as well as by quantity.

[e] Raw silk imports are distinguished as from Bengal, China, and Italy/Turkey; totals only for thrown organzine.

[f] Raw, waste, and thrown silk are each differentiated as from East Indies/China/St. Helena/Cape of Good Hope, Turkey, and other.

[g] Series also for the amounts of domestic consumption.

[h] United Kingdom.

[i] Distinguishes raw, waste, and thrown silk.

[j] Raw, waste, organzine, tram, and singles silk are each differentiated as from India, Cape of Good Hope, China, Turkey, Italy, France, and other.

[k] Differentiating for raw silk. India, Cape of Good Hope, China, Turkey, Italy, France, and other; for waste and knubbs: India, China, Italy, France, and other; for thrown silk: Italy, France, and other.

[l] Distinguishes several countries.

[m] By official value only.

[n] 1700-1791, England and Wales; 1792-1808, Great Britain.

[o] Distinguishes as follows: for raw silk, Bengal/Chinese and Turkish/Italian/miscellaneous; thrown silk; wrought East Indian silk; wrought Italian/Dutch/miscellaneous silk.

[p] Distinguishes raw from thrown silk.

[q] 1700-1791, England and Wales; 1792-1825, Great Britain; 1814-1850+, United Kingdom.

[r] 1700-1791, England and Wales; 1792-1829, Great Britain; 1826-1856, United Kingdom.

There are many sources for the importation of raw, waste, and thrown silk. A select committee has figures on the rates of duty on imports of thrown and raw silk from 1660 to 1825.[366] Schumpeter prints official values as well as the quantities of raw and thrown silk imports from 1700 to 1808.[367] TABLE 25 sets out the sources for quantities of silk imports. The detailed notes are necessary because of the changing geographical categories in the sources. There are also some averages of silk imports. A select committee prints the averages for raw and thrown silk (differentiated) for 1765-67, 1785-87, 1801-12, 1815-17, 1821-23, 1829-31, and 1830-31, and for waste silk for 1815-17, 1821-23, 1829-31, and 1830-31; all but the last two averages appear in Porter.[368]

Official figures for the import of foreign silk manufactures date from 1826. *Porter's Tables* lists fifteen kinds of silks imported from Europe and five kinds from India from 1826 to 1831;[369] McCulloch prints the annual gross totals for 1826-32.[370] There is data also on silk imports from China for 1830-42.[371] For 1833-37, there are statistics of various silks from France, Holland and Belgium, and "the Hanseatic towns."[372] Finally, a parliamentary paper of 1846 provides a long series of imports of foreign silks and the amounts retained for home consumption from 1826 to 1845.[373] See also the sources in Table 3 for imports from 1827 to 1850.

Because of the 30 per cent duty placed on silk imports from 1826, smuggling remained extensive, so that there is data on the amount of foreign silks seized by the Government between 1826 and 1841.[374]

There is no accessible published original source for the exports of British silk manufactures in the eighteenth century, so the reader must consult Schumpeter for data for 1700 to 1807.[375] The Government began to publish figures

Marshall, *Digest* (1833), Part 3, p. 180, for the prices of Bengal and Chinese raw silk sold by the East India Company (1799-1831).

[366]*P.P. 1831-32* (678), XIX, 265-66.

[367]For 1700-72, by official value: Schumpeter, XV, 48-51; for 1700-72, by quantity: Schumpeter, XVI, 52-55; for 1772-1808, by value and quantity: Schumpeter, XVII, 56-59.

[368]*P.P. 1831-32* (678), XIX, 10; Porter, *Progress* (3 v., 1836-43), I (1836), 254.

[369]*P.T. 1, P.P. 1833*, XLI, 88-89 (for re-exports, see p. 87).

[370]McCulloch, *Dictionary* (1837), 1036.

[371]*P.P. 1843* (257), LII, 26.

[372]*P.P. 1837-38* (458), XLV, 439-44.

[373]*P.P. 1846* (109), XLIV, 13.

[374]For 1826-31, see *P.P. 1831-32* (389), XXXIV, 500; for 1832-41, see *P.P. 1842* (306), XXXIX, 547.

[375]For quantity statistics, from 1697 to 1771, see Schumpeter, XIV, 44-47 (differentiating thrown and wrought silk exports). For figures by official value, from 1697 to 1772, she discriminates thrown, wrought, and miscellaneous (X, 29-30). For figures by quantity and value, 1772-1807, for thrown, wrought, and miscellaneous silk, see Schumpeter, XI, 31-34. Finally, she has figures for wrought silk exports quinquennially from 1700 to 1800 to eight regions of the world (XXXV, 67). Mitchell and Deane have valuation figures for 1697-1829 (pp. 293-95) and quantity figures for 1697-1823 and 1840-50 (pp. 209-10).

in 1815, with a series from that date through 1831 being published in 1832.[376]
Porter's Tables has declared value figures for 1820-31, and a select committee
report provides official values for 1821-31.[377] There are declared value figures for 1824-26, and a longer series for 1826-44, for exports to six parts of
the world.[378] Table 4 sets out the sources for data from 1827 to 1850. Various
contemporary authors furnish export figures. Porter provides declared values
for 1820-49; McCulloch has official and declared values for 1816-32, and declared values for exports to thirty-seven places from 1827 to 1834.[379]
    The number of silk factories, and the age and number of employees in every
county in England in 1835, is recorded by Porter.[380]
    Finally, there is a detailed, multi-column tabular comparison between "the
Progress of the Silk and Cotton Manufactures, 1815-31."[381]

IV. THE MINING INDUSTRIES

(a) Copper

    Though in existence for many centuries, the copper mines in England "were
not wrought with much spirit" before the eighteenth century. Until the end
of that century, England was a net importer of copper. From the 1770's, production in Cornwall quickened, so that by 1800 the annual output of copper was
seven times the amount produced in 1730; by 1850 the annual output was twice
as great as in 1800. Cornwall was always the leading county of production,
with Devonshire next at about one-sixth the level of the Cornish output; Scotland and Ireland produced only negligible amounts.[382]
    William Pryce — antiquary, surgeon, apothecary, and owner of part of a
copper mine[383] — was the first writer to publish (1778) the prices of copper

[376]*P.P. 1831-32* (391), XXXIV, 496. Official and declared values but no
quantity data, for pure and mixed silks.
[377]*P.T. 1, P.P. 1833*, XLI, 87; *P.P.* 1831-32 (678), XIX, 14.
[378]For 1824-26, see *P.P. 1826-27* (295), XVIII, 320-26; for 1826-44, see
P.P. 1846 (109), XLIV, 13.
[379]Porter, *Progress* (3 v., 1836-43), I (1836), 260, and *Progress* (1851),
219; for 1816-32, see McCulloch, *Dictionary* (1837), 445; for 1827-34, see
McCulloch, *Statistical Account of the British Empire* (2 v., 1837), II, 104.
[380]Porter, *Progress* (3 v., 1836-43), I (1836), 260. Subsequent annual reports by the factory inspectors are cited in the index to the *Parliamentary
Papers*.
[381]*P.P. 1831-32* (678), XIX, App. F, pp. 934-37. As a minor footnote to the
silk industry, see the figures for Irish silk exports from 1816 to 1820 (by
quantity), in *J.H.C. 76*, 1118-25.
[382]McCulloch, *Dictionary* (2 v., 1854), I, 407. The output in Cornwall accounted for about 80 per cent of the total output in the British Isles. The
leading modern works on copper are Henry Hamilton, *The English Brass and Copper
Industries to 1800* (1926), and John Rowe, *Cornwall in the Age of the Industrial
Revolution* (Liverpool, 1953).
[383]Pryce (1725?-1790), a resident of Redruth, owned part of a mine at Dol-

ore in Cornwall. He sets out five decennial averages between 1726 and 1775.[384] A parliamentary committee report provides annual prices for 1784-99,[385] and another has prices for 1783-1828.[386] Tooke provides prices for 1800-22; McCulloch lists prices for 1800-52; and Salt has prices for 1828-37.[387] Marshall provides, not average prices, but the highest and lowest annual prices for 1786-1828.[388] Finally, two writers in 1838 set out long price series: Sir Charles Lemon[389] has prices for 1771-1837 and J. S. Courtenay provides prices for 1726-70 and 1823-38.[390] A modern writer provides annual copper ore prices for 1779-89, 1794-98, and 1801-29.[391]

TABLE 26 sets out the sources containing figures for the imports of copper ore and unwrought and wrought copper. In addition, there are earlier decennial statistics for copper and brass manufactured imports (1740-70), unwrought copper

coath in Cornwall. This co-ownership undoubtedly stimulated his interest in Cornish copper. William Courtney has judged Pryce's *Mineralogia Cornubiensis* as "still of value, both for historical purposes and for practical mining" (*D.N.B.*, XVI, 429). Pryce had interests other than business and economic history: his *Archaeologia Cornu-Britannica* (1790) studied the vocabulary and grammar of the dying Cornish language.

[384]Pryce, *Mineralogia Cornubiensis; a treatise on minerals, mines, and mining* (1778), table facing p. xiv. The prices are per ton for ore sold at "publick ticketings."

[385]"Select Committee on Copper Mines and the Copper Trade, 1800," *Commons' Committees*, X, No. 9, p. 702. For 1784-97, see the committee report of 1799 on the copper trade, in *Accounts & Papers 1799*, App. 9, p. 139; this table is reprinted in Henry Hamilton, *The English Brass and Copper Industries to 1800* (1926), App. 11, p. 366.

[386]"Select Committee on the Wool Trade," *P.P. 1828* (515), VIII, 725. This source also gives the price of foreign copper per ton (with duty paid) for 1807-28.

[387]Tooke, *Thoughts and Details* (1824), App. 4, No. 5, p. 77; McCulloch, *Dictionary* (1837), 399, for 1800-31, and *Dictionary* (2 v., 1854), I, 408, for 1800-52; Samuel Salt, *Statistics and Calculations* (1845), 66, with prices also at every even year between 1800 and 1826.

[388]Marshall, *Digest* (1833), Part 3, p. 33.

[389]Sir Charles Lemon (1784-1868), third son of William Lemon (1748-1824), was educated at Harrow and Cambridge. He had a long career (1807-12, 1830-57) as Member of Parliament from three different seats in Cornwall. One of the founders of the Statistical Society of London in 1834, Lemon was also President of the Royal Cornwall Polytechnic Society from 1833 to his death in 1868. On his life, see Frederic Boase, *Modern English Biography* (6 v., Truro, 1892-1921), II (1897), 386.

[390]Sir Charles Lemon, "Statistics of the Copper Mines of Cornwall," *J.S.S.L.*, I (1838), 70; J. S. Courtenay, "A Treatise on the Statistics of Cornwall," in *The Sixth Annual Report of the Royal Cornwall Polytechnic Society* (Falmouth, 1838), 136-38, bound in *Royal Cornwall Polytechnic Society, Reports, 1833-1838*. Courtenay's prices for 1726-70 are decennial averages; for 1823-38 they are annual.

[391]John Rowe, *Cornwall in the Age of the Industrial Revolution* (Liverpool, 1953), 76 n. 2, and App. 3, p. 331.

imports (1710-90), and copper ore imports (1730-90).[392]

Sources for export figures of British wrought and unwrought copper and of brass and copper manufactures are set out in TABLE 27. Schumpeter provides quinquennial quantity figures for wrought copper exports in the eighteenth century to eight geographical regions of the world.[393]

National output figures do not exist before 1815, but statistics of copper ore production in Cornwall date from 1726; see TABLE 28. William Pryce provides us with *annual* tonnage figures from 1726 to 1775 and *decennial* averages of the value of the ore sold in Cornwall at five periods from 1726 to 1775.[394] The Royal Geological Society of Cornwall, founded in 1814, began printing in 1818 the annual county production (in tons) from 1815 to 1832.[395] In 1846 the Society printed statistics of the amount of copper ore (in tons) sold at "publick ticketings" in Cornwall and at Swansea (where the ore was sent for smelting) from 1832 to 1846. All of the above figures are for public sales of copper ore, but there is a series for 1841-46 which indicates the amount of "private sales." In this period they amount to one-tenth of the ore sold at public sales, or one-eleventh of total (public and private) sales.[396]

For comprehensive surveys, company by company, of the state of the Cornish copper mines in the 1790's, two detailed parliamentary studies should be consulted.[397] The Royal Geological Society of Cornwall also published figures for the tons of copper ore and copper produced *by each mine* in Cornwall annually

[392]*Commons' Committees*, X, No. 37, p. 727. Reprinted in Hamilton, *English Brass and Copper Industries* (1926), App. 9, p. 364.

[393]Schumpeter, XXI, 63.

[394]Pryce, *Mineralogia Cornubiensis* (1778), table facing p. xiv. Rowe, *Cornwall* (1953), 76 n. 2, has figures for the tons of copper ore and copper sold in Cornwall for 1779-89 and 1794-98.

[395]June was the end of the business year, so for June 1815 to June 1817, see *Transactions of the Royal Geological Society of Cornwall* [hereafter, *T.R.G.S.C.*], I (1818), 262-63; for 1817-22, *T.R.G.S.C.*, II (1822), 440-44; for 1822-27, *T.R.G.S.C.*, III (1828), 354-58; and for 1827-32, *T.R.G.S.C.*, IV (1832), 497. Also listed for the period 1817-32 are the amounts of ore which were purchased by individually identified companies for smelting into metallic copper.

[396]*T.R.G.S.C.*, VI (1846), 357. Robert Hunt, *British Mining* (1884), App. 15, p. 893, prints the amount of copper ore sold at Swansea ticketings annually from 1804 to 1863. Hunt's book was the definitive study of mining in Britain up to that time. Formerly Secretary of the Royal Cornwall Polytechnic Society, Hunt was Professor of Experimental Science in the Royal School of Mines, "the Keeper of Mining Records," and the originator of the official annual recording of *Mineral Statistics of the United Kingdom* (1854). Mitchell and Deane, 150, comment that "until well into the nineteenth century. . . . by far the greatest proportion of British copper was sold at public ticketings," and add that "for a long period this proportion was fairly constant." Changes occurred rapidly in the later 1840's, however, for by 1854-56 almost one-third of the copper ore was sold by private contract.

[397]See the "Report from the Committee on Copper Mines and the Copper Trade, 1799," *Accounts & Papers 1799*, App. 17, p. 18; and the "Report from the Select Committee on Copper Mines and the Copper Trade, 1800," *Commons' Committees*, X, 682-83, 709-15.

from 1814 to 1832.[398] There are also interesting miscellaneous series. For instance, data exists for the number of steam engines used in every year in the Cornish mines from 1813 to 1837.[399] W. J. Henwood, in a short article of 1843, lists the numbers of persons employed, the engines working, and the quantities of copper ore produced *in each mine* in Cornwall and Devon in 1837-38.[400] Finally, there is an interesting table first published by Sir Charles Lemon in 1838 which sets out the business records of the "Consolidated Mines" in Cornwall from 1819 to 1836. The table states for each year the amount of capital and compound interest invested, the "cost," the "lords' dues," the value of the copper ores, the tons of ore, and the wages paid over this period.[401]

G. R. Porter claimed in 1836 that no national output figures existed before 1820. This unfortunate fact did not deter him from extrapolating backwards: judging non-Cornish production as 20 per cent of the national total, he offered national annual output figures from 1801 to 1819.[402] Porter's belief was, however, mistaken. In 1818, the Royal Geological Society of Cornwall began publishing production figures dating from 1815, not only for copper ore production (in tons) for Cornwall, but also for Devonshire, the rest of England, Anglesea, the rest of Wales, Ireland, and the Isle of Man; by 1832 the series stretched from 1815 to 1832.[403] Porter in his *Tables* (1833) gives tonnage and value figures for copper ore production in Swansea, Devon, and Anglesea from 1820 to 1831;[404] in two volumes of *Progress of the Nation* (1836, 1843), he provides regional and national output figures for 1820-34 and 1820-40.[405] McCulloch has regional figures for 1820-34; Salt has regional data for a shorter period, 1828-

---

[398]For June 1814 to June 1817, see *T.R.G.S.C.*, I (1818), 252-61; for 1817-22, *T.R.G.S.C.*, II (1822), 428-37; for 1822-27, *T.R.G.S.C.*, III (1828), 342-53; and for 1827-32, *T.R.G.S.C.*, IV (1832), 492-96.

[399]Lemon, "Statistics of the Copper Mines of Cornwall," *J.S.S.L.*, I (1838), 67; Great Britain, *Geological Survey Memoirs: Report on the Geology of Cornwall, Devon, and West Somerset* (1839), 554. The author of the 1839 *Report* was Sir Henry Thomas de la Bêche (1796-1855). Son of an army colonel resident in Jamaica, de la Bêche studied geology in southwest England, Pembrokeshire, Switzerland, and France. In 1832, he helped in the government survey of Cornwall and Devon, and in 1840 became Director-General of the Ordnance Survey, a post he held until his death in 1855. He was President of the Geological Society in 1847 and 1848, and founded the Geological Museum in Jermyn Street, London in 1851. Besides numerous articles in scientific journals and his *Report* of 1839, de la Bêche authored *Researches in Theoretical Geology* (1834) and *How to Observe Geology* (1835). On his life, see Frederic Boase, *Modern English Biography* (6 v., Truro, 1892-1921), I (1892), 849.

[400]W. J. Henwood, "Statistical Notices of the Mines in Cornwall and Devon," *T.R.G.S.C.*, V (1843), 461-82.

[401]Lemon, "Statistics of the Copper Mines of Cornwall," *J.S.S.L.*, I (1838), 77. Also in *Geological Survey Memoirs: Report on the Geology of Cornwall, Devon, and West Somerset* (1839), 603; and Hunt, *British Mining* (1884), App. 17, p. 894. Hunt incorrectly cites the page in Lemon's article as page 771, instead of 77.

[402]Porter, *Progress* (3 v., 1836-43), I (1836), 332.

[403]Sources and paginations are the same as those cited in note 395.

[404]*P.T. 1, P.P. 1833*, XLI, 90-91.

[405]Porter, *Progress* (3 v., 1836-43), I (1836), 332, and III (1843), 91-92.
In his 1851 edition (p. 578) Porter lists national output figures for 1801-48

112

Table 26

IMPORTS OF COPPER

Primary Sources

Government Documents	Books and Pamphlets

1786-1827: *P.P. 1828* (416), XIX, 276. *a*

1790-1798: "S.C. on the Copper Mines and Copper Trade (1800)," *Commons' Committees,* X, App. 37, p. 727. *b*

1806-1811: *J.H.C. 67,* 757-59; also in *P.P. 1812* (115), X, 30-33. *b,c,d*

1820-1831: *P.T. 1, P.P. 1833,* XLI, 90-91. *b,c,e*

1824-1846: *P.P. 1847* (637), LIX, 40-41. *b,c,e,f,g*

1827-1850: See Table 3. *a,c,e,g,h*

1786-1827: Marshall, *Digest* (1833), Part 3, p. 33. *a*

1826-1837: Lemon, "Statistics of Copper Mines," *J.S.S.L.,* I (1838), 83. *e,i*

Secondary Works

1790-1798: Hamilton, *English Brass and Copper Industries to 1800* (1926), App. 9, p. 364. *b*

1829-1850+: Mitchell and Deane, 165-66. *e,i*

Schumpeter: none.

Imports (by quantity, in cwts.) are into Great Britain unless otherwise noted.

a Unwrought copper only.

b Differentiates copper ore, unmanufactured copper, copper and brass manufactured, and copper in part manufactured.

c Series of re-exports also.

d Distinguishes imports into eighteen British ports.

e United Kingdom.

f Distinguishes a half dozen countries.

g Gives amounts retained for domestic consumption.

h Distinguishes two dozen countries.

i Copper ore only.

Table 27

EXPORTS OF COPPER

Primary Sources

Government Documents

1697-1707: *J.H.C. 16*, 106. *a,b,c*

1790-1798: "S.C. on the Copper Mines
and Copper Trade (1800)," *Commons'
Committees*, X, App. 33-34, pp. 720-
25. *b,c,d,e*

1806-1811: *J.H.C. 67*, 758-59; also in
P.P. 1812 (115), X, 32-33. *b,e,f,g*

1820-1831: *P.T. 1*, *P.P. 1833*, XLI,
90-91. *h,i*

1824-1846: *P.P. 1847* (637), LIX, 42-
43. *b,d,g,i,j*

1827-1850: See Table 4. *d,e,i,j*

Books and Pamphlets

1790-1799; Eden, *Eight Letters on
The Peace* (1802), 117. *b,c,d*

1796-1837; Lemon, "Statistics of
Copper Mines," *J.S.S.L.*, I
(1838), 83. *b,g*

1801-1840: Porter, *Progress* (3 v.,
1836-43), III (1843), 91-92. *b,g*

1805-1812: Porter, *Progress* (3 v.,
1836-43), I (1836), 297. *c,d,k*

1805-1827: Marshall, *Digest* (1833),
Part 3, p. 81. *c,d,k*

1805-1849: Porter, *Progress* (1851),
248. *d,k*

1814-1827: Marshall, *Digest* (1833),
Part 3, p. 81. *d,j,k*

1814-1834: Porter, *Progress* (3 v.,
1836-43), I (1836), 297. *d,j,k*

1814-1849: Porter, *Progress* (1851),
248. *d,j,k*

1820-1832: McCulloch, *Dictionary*
(1837), 399. *h*

Table 27
(Continued)

Secondary Works

1697-1808: Schumpeter, VII-IX, 19-28. b,c,d,g,l

1697-1850+: Mitchell and Deane, 164-66. b,d,m,n

1775-1808: Schumpeter, IX, 24-28. g,k,l

1790-1798: Hamilton, *English Brass and Copper Industries to 1800* (1926),
App. 10, p. 365.

Exports (by quantity, in tons) are from Great Britain unless otherwise noted.

[a] England and Wales only.

[b] Wrought copper.

[c] By official value as well as by quantity.

[d] Brass and copper manufactures.

[e] Distinguishes to two dozen countries.

[f] Distinguishes from eighteen British ports.

[g] Unwrought copper.

[h] Differentiates unwrought copper and coin, sheets-nails-miscellany, wire, and other wrought copper.

[i] United Kingdom.

[j] By declared value as well as by quantity.

[k] By quantity in cwts.

[l] 1697-1791, England and Wales; 1792-1808, Great Britain.

[m] 1697-1791, England and Wales; 1792-1811, Great Britain; 1816-1850+, United Kingdom.

[n] No valuation series in Mitchell and Deane.

Table 28

PRODUCTION OF COPPER ORE IN CORNWALL
(in tons)

Primary Sources

Government Documents	*Books and Pamphlets*
1820-1831: *P.T. 1, P.P. 1833,* XLI, 91. *a*	1726-1775: Pryce, *Mineralogia Cornubiensis* (1778), facing p. xiv.
	1726-1838: Courtenay, "Statistics of Cornwall," *Report of Royal Cornwall Polytechnic Society* (1838), 136-38. *a*
	1771-1786 Porter, *Progress* (3 v., 1796-1834 1836-43), I (1836), 322 [*a*]; reprinted in Salt, *Statistics and Calculations* (1845), 67 [*b*].
	1771-1789 *T.R.G.S.C.,* II (1822), 1794-1822 438-39. *a*
	1771-1789 *Geological Survey, Report* 1794-1838 (1839), 606. *a*
	1771-1837: Lemon, "Statistics of Copper Mines," *J.S.S.L.,* I (1838), 70. *a*
	1771-1838: Courtenay, J.S., "Statistics of Cornwall," *Report of Royal Cornwall Polytechnic Society* (1838), 136-38. *b*
	1771-1848: Porter, *Progress* (1851), 272.
	1800-1822: Tooke, *Thoughts and Details* (1824), App. 4, Part 5, p. 77.
	1800-1831: McCulloch, *Dictionary* (1837), 399. *a*

Table 28
(continued)

Government Documents   *Books and Pamphlets*

1800-1850: McCulloch, *Dictionary*
(2 v., 1854), I, 408. *a,c*

1820-1834: McCulloch, *Statistical
Account of British Empire* (2 v.,
1837), II, 15.

1828-1837: Salt, *Statistics and
Calculations* (1845), 66. *a*

1839-1846: Brownell, *Letter to . . .
Clarendon* (1847), 22.

Secondary Works

1726-1789   Mitchell and Deane, 156-59. *a*
1794-1850

1727-1850: Hunt, *British Mining* (1884), App. 12-14, pp. 891-92. *a*

1771-1786   Mitchell and Deane, 156-59. *b*
1796-1850

1801-1829: Rowe, *Cornwall in the Age of the Industrial Revolution* (1953),
App. 3, p. 331. *a*

All figures are for copper ore unless otherwise noted.

a Data for metallic copper as well as   *c* These figures are stated as being
copper ore.   for Cornwall and Devon together.

b Metallic copper only.

32.[406] By contrast, Mitchell and Deane offer national output statistics only from 1854 (when the official figures in *Mineral Statistics* begin) and no regional series outside Cornwall and Devon.[407]

(b) Tin

Ancient Britain was, with Spain, the chief supplier of tin to the Phoenicians and the Romans. In recent times, Britain's tin mines were worked only with moderate vigor until the eighteenth century. From 1700 to 1800, tin production increased by about 50 per cent as compared to an increase of 600 per cent in the copper industry; even by 1850 annual output was only 150 per cent greater than production in 1730. In the nineteenth century the greatest tin-producing areas of the world lay, not in England, but in the East Indies and Southeast Asia: Malay and Banca tin not only captured the Chinese markets but made inroads on the European continent as well.[408]

There are various types of prices of English tin. Courtenay gives us the annual average price paid to the tinner in Cornwall per hundredweight of tin from 1750 to 1837,[409] while Carne has a shorter but slightly earlier series from 1746 to 1788.[410]

and also offers data for domestic consumption levels (by subtracting exports from output) in this period.

[406]McCulloch, *Statistical Account of the British Empire* (2 v., 1837), II, 15; Salt, *Statistics and Calculations* (1845), 65. Rowe, *Cornwall* (1953), 128, produces decennial *totals* of the amount of fine copper (in tons) produced in Cornwall, the United Kingdom, and the world from 1801 to 1880.

[407]Their output figures before 1854 are for Cornwall and Devon *together* for 1726-89 and 1794-1860. For the production in Anglesea, they offer estimates at eight dates from 1778 to 1823/27. See Mitchell and Deane, 151, 156-59.

[408]McCulloch, *Dictionary* (2 v., 1854), II, 1311-12. The modern works include G. R. Lewis, *The Stannaries* (Cambridge, Mass., 1908), J. H. Jones, *The Tinplate Industry* (1914), W. E. Minchinton, *The British Tinplate Industry* (Oxford, 1957), and Denys Barton, *A History of Tin-mining and Smelting in Cornwall* (Truro, 1967). Minchinton's book has a valuable bibliography (pp. 263-69).

[409]J. S. Courtenay, "A Treatise on the Statistics of Cornwall," in *The Sixth Annual Report of the Royal Cornwall Polytechnic Society* (Falmouth, 1838), 134-35, bound in *Royal Cornwall Polytechnic Society, Reports, 1833-38*.

[410]Joseph Carne, "Statistics of the Tin Mines of Cornwall and of the Consumption of Tin in Great Britain," *J.S.S.L.*, II (1839), 262. Joseph Carne (1782-1858), the eldest son of a banker, was from 1810 to 1820 business manager of the Cornish Copper Company's smelting works at Hayle, Cornwall; afterwards, he moved to Penzance to be a partner in his father's bank. Geology was Carne's principal avocation. In 1814, he was one of the founding officers of the Royal Geological Society of Cornwall; from 1816 he contributed regularly to its *Transactions*. For many years he served as Treasurer of the Society. The Cambridge Philosophical Society made him an honorary member. Carne also had a lifelong interest in Wesleyanism and organized numerous Sunday schools. His articles on copper and tin for the Statistical Society of London, Robert Hunt, the statistician of mines (and author of his notice in the *D.N.B.*, III, 1045-46), described as "a most useful paper." Hunt, *British Mining* (1884), App. 5, p. 888, gives the price of tin per hundredweight, "exclusive of Prince's duty," for 1750-99.

Unwin provides a series of *quarterly* prices from 1750 to 1789.[411] A parliamentary paper sets out prices for 1783 to 1828; Marshall has prices for 1786-1830, as does McCulloch, for 1820-31.[412] Eden lists the prices of tin sold to the East India Company from 1792 to 1797, while Carne furnishes figures for common tin bought in London and tin refined in Wales for 1818-37.[413] Mitchell and Deane provide no tin price data, while Lewis, in his list covering six centuries, gives prices for twenty-one years after 1700.[414]

Printed statistics for the import of tin begin in 1812 and run continuously from 1814, the records for 1786-1811 and 1813 having been destroyed by fire.[415] In addition to the data in the sources in TABLE 29, there is information on tin importation into Holland from the East Indies.[416] A modern writer presents figures for British tinplate imports from Germany and Holland from 1698 to 1771.[417]

Statistics of the export of unwrought tin in blocks begin regularly from 1697. There are some earlier scattered figures for 1663, 1669, and 1686, as well as a decennial average for 1699-1710.[418] George Unwin, "Supervisor of the Exports of Tin beyond the Cape of Good Hope" (as he describes himself), has scattered figures for East India Company exports to China before 1789 and a full national export series for 1789-1809.[419] Schumpeter provides the geographical dimensions

Barton, *History of Tin-mining* (Truro, 1967), 47, has annual tin prices for 1800-49.

[411]George Unwin, *Letters . . . with a View to Open an Extensive Trade in . . . Tin* (1790), 28-29.

[412]Hohler's evidence in the "Select Committee on the Wool Trade," *P.P. 1828* (515), VIII, 727; Marshall, *Digest* (1833), Part 3, p. 33; McCulloch, *Dictionary* (1837), 1159. For Hunt's prices (1818-37), see note 432.

[413]Sir Frederick Morton Eden, *Eight Letters on the Peace* (1802), 100; Carne, "Statistics of the Tin Mines of Cornwall and of the Consumption of Tin in Great Britain," *J.S.S.L.*, II (1839), 265. Barton, *History of Tin-mining* (Truro, 1967), 28-29, gives the price of tin shipped from Cornwall by the East India Company from 1789 to 1813.

[414]Lewis, *The Stannaries* (Cambridge, Mass., 1908), App. U, pp. 275-78. Four-fifths of his prices are pre-1650. Minchinton, *British Tinplate Industry* (Oxford, 1957), App. D, p. 262, lists the monthly prices of tinplate (in shillings per box of 225 sheets, weighing 100 pounds) from 1827 to 1850.

[415]As stated in *P.P. 1828* (416), XIX, 277.

[416]See Unwin, *Letters . . . with a View to Open an Extensive Trade in . . . Tin* (1790), 30, or Carne, "Statistics of the Tin Mines of Cornwall and of the Consumption of Tin in Great Britain," *J.S.S.L.*, II (1839), 267.

[417]Minchinton, *British Tinplate Industry* (Oxford, 1957), App. D, p. 259. He cites P.R.O. Customs 3/1-70 as his source.

[418]A report of Davenant, cited by Joseph Massie, *Ways and Means for Raising the Extraordinary Supplies to Carry on the War, &c.* (1757), 69-70.

[419]Unwin, *Letters . . . with a View to Open an Extensive Trade in . . . Tin* (1790), 27, gives data for exports by the East India Company *from Cornwall only* to China in 1762, 1763, 1766, 1768, 1789, and 1790. Then, in his later work, *Observations upon the Export Trade of Tin and Copper to India* (Truro, 1811), 6, Unwin furnishes figures for English exports to China from 1789 to 1809. Robert Hunt, *British Mining* (1884), App. 10, p. 891, lists the amount of tin (in tons) supplied to the East India Company by Cornwall under the "stocking system" at twenty-seven dates from 1793 to 1822; he does not name his source. Barton, *His-*

of the eighteenth-century exportation by giving the quinquennial figures for exports to eight geographical areas.420 The sources for the more regular data appear in TABLE 30. Two modern writers provide us with figures for the export of tinplates (by value) for 1772-95 and 1815-50.421

Output data for the tin mines of Cornwall stretch back through the centuries. Scattered but full figures exist since 1199,422 but the modern series may be said to start in 1750. Unwin (1790) was the first to record "the number of blocks raised" in Cornwall from 1750 to 1789.423 The Royal Geological Society of Cornwall presents statistics for amounts of tin produced *quarterly* from 1817 until 1831,424 and an annual output series from 1750 to 1821.425 Porter offers figures for Cornish output (in tons) for 1750 to 1834.426 Courtenay gives statistics for 1750-1838; Carne has data for 1750-1837.427 A modern writer produces quinquennial averages of the tons of tin coined in Cornwall from 1720 to 1834.428 Mitchell and Deane print Cornish output figures from 1199, continuously from 1669 to 1837. From 1750 their figures are by value as well as quantity, though the sources which they cite list output by quantity only.429 No record of coining was kept by the Duchy of Cornwall after 1838, for in that year

tory of Tin-mining (Truro, 1967), 28-29, provides figures for the value and tonnage of tin exports from Cornwall by the East India Company from 1789 to 1813.

420Schumpeter, XXXI, 66.

421For 1772-95 (differentiating Europe, America, Asia, and Africa), see Minchinton, *British Tinplate Industry* (Oxford, 1957), App. D, p. 260 [source: P.R.O. 17/1-17]; for 1815-50+ (to 1912), see Jones, *Tinplate Industry* (1914), App. E, pp. 272-74.

422Actually, until 1838, the figures are for tin coined rather than produced. The period between mining and coining would result in a decrease in the actual output figure, due to some loss of ore and a certain amount of smuggling abroad of tin-stuff and smelted tin (Mitchell and Deane, 150).

423Unwin, *Letters . . . with a View to Open an Extensive Trade in . . . Tin* (1790), 28-29. The proportion was usually 6½ blocks to one ton (Hunt, *British Mining* [1884], App. 3, p. 887).

424See, for 1817-21, *T.R.G.S.C.*, II (1822), 424-25; for 1822-26, *T.R.G.S.C.*, III (1828), 339-41; for 1827-31, *T.R.G.S.C.*, IV (1832), 491. These series distinguish common from grain tin.

425*T.R.G.S.C.*, II (1822), 426-27. Over sixty years later, Hunt, *British Mining* (1884), App. 3, p. 887, printed a series for 1750 to 1817.

426Porter, *Progress* (3 v., 1836-43), I (1836), 329.

427Courtenay, "A Treatise on the Statistics of Cornwall," in *The Sixth Annual Report of the Royal Cornwall Polytechnic Society* (Falmouth, 1838), 134-35, bound in *Royal Cornwall Polytechnic Society, Reports, 1833-38.* The same series (1750-1838) is printed in Great Britain, *Geological Survey Memoirs: Report on the Geology of Cornwall, Devon, and West Somerset* (1839), 588-89. Carne, "Statistics of the Tin Mines of Cornwall and of the Consumption of Tin in Great Britain," *J.S.S.L.*, II (1839), 261; he also has figures for the production of grain tin, refined tin, and common tin from 1818 to 1837 (*ibid.*, 264).

428John Rowe, *Cornwall in the Age of the Industrial Revolution* (Liverpool, 1953), 58.

429Mitchell and Deane, 153-55; Lewis, *The Stannaries* (Cambridge, Mass., 1908), App. J, pp. 252-58.

Table 29

IMPORTS OF TIN

Primary Sources

Government Documents	*Books and Pamphlets*
1814-1827: *P.P. 1828* (416), XIX, 277.	1815-1838: Carne, "Statistics of Mines of Cornwall," *J.S.S.L.*, II (1839), 266. *a*
1820-1831: *P.T. 1, P.P. 1833*, XLI, 93. *a,b*	1820-1831: McCulloch, *Dictionary* (1837), 1159. *a,b*
1827-1850: See Table 3. *a,b,c*	1820-1835: Porter, *Progress* (3 v., 1836-43), I (1836), 330. *a,b*
1834-1841: *P.T. 11, P.P. 1843*, LVI, No. 104, p. 91. *a,b*	1820-1849: Porter, *Progress* (1851), 271. *a,b*

Secondary Works

1845-1850+:   Mitchell and Deane, 163. *b*

Imports (by quantity, in cwts.) are into Great Britain unless otherwise noted.

a Series of re-exports also.

b United Kingdom.

c Distinguishes from two dozen countries.

Table 30

EXPORTS OF TIN

Primary Sources

Government Documents[a]	*Books and Pamphlets*

Government Documents[a]

1796-1805: *J.H.C. 61, 786. b,c*

1820-1831: *P.T. 1, P.P. 1833*, XLI, 93. *d*

1827-1850: See Table 4. *d,e,f,g*

1834-1841: *P.T. 11, P.P. 1843*, LVI, No. 104, p. 91. *d*

Books and Pamphlets

1783-1817: J.S. Courtenay, "Statistics of Cornwall," *Report of Royal Cornwall Polytechnic Society* (1838), 134-35.

1783-1838: Carne, "Statistics of Mines of Cornwall," *J.S.S.L.*, II (1839), 265.

1789-1810: Unwin, *Observations upon the Export Trade of Tin* (1811), 5-6. *f*

1815-1834: Porter, *Progress* (3 v., 1836-43), I (1836), 331. *b,c*

1820-1832: McCulloch, *Dictionary* (1837), 1159.

1820-1835: Porter, *Progress* (3 v., 1836-43), I (1836), 331.

1820-1849: Porter, *Progress* (1851), 271. *d*

Secondary Works

1697-1808: Schumpeter, VII-IX, 19-28. *e,h,i*

1697-1850+: Mitchell and Deane, 161. *j,k*

1783-1799: Hunt, *British Mining* (1884), App. 5, p. 888. *l*

Table 30
(continued)

Exports (by quantity, in tons) are from Great Britain unless otherwise noted.

^a Numerous annual returns are in the *Index to the Parliamentary Papers, 1801-52* (1938), p. 982.

^b Tin plates only.

^c Declared value only.

^d United Kingdom.

^e Tin plates as well as unwrought tin.

^f Distinguishes to two dozen countries.

^g Declared value as well as quantity.

^h 1697-1791, England and Wales; 1792-1808, Great Britain.

ⁱ Official value as well as quantity.

^j 1697-1791, England and Wales; 1792-1844, Great Britain; 1845-50+, United Kingdom.

^k No series for tin plates until 1857.

^l Distinguishes to Europe, Africa, and America.

---

the coinage duty of £ 4 per ton was repealed.[430] Beginning in 1854, however, the Government began regular collection of mining figures, which appear in Mitchell and Deane.[431]

Statistics also exist for tin production in Devonshire. Porter in the first edition of his *Tables* (1833) provides figures not only for the amount of tin coined from 1820 to 1831 in Cornwall, but also for the amount (in blocks and hundredweights) coined in Devon from 1822 to 1831.[432] McCulloch has data for

[430]By 1 & 2 Vict., c. 120; as stated in *P.T. 11, P.P. 1843*, LVI, No. 104, p. 91. The duty produced a revenue of £ 16,000 to £ 20,000 a year, payable to the Duke of Cornwall. McCulloch, *Dictionary* (2 v., 1854), II, 1312, says the duty was "felt to be a serious grievance, not only from its amount, but from the vexatious regulations under which it was collected." The duty at least had the historical value of serving as a rough index of copper production in Cornwall.

[431]For a short critical note on Cornish tin statistics, see Rowe, *Cornwall in the Age of the Industrial Revolution* (Liverpool, 1953), 327-28.

[432]*P.T. 1, P.P. 1833*, XLI, 93. Barton, *History of Tin-mining* (Truro, 1967), 53, gives the number of blocks of common and grain tin coined at fifteen smelters in Cornwall from 1820 to 1830. In addition to output figures for Cornwall and Devon for 1818-37, Hunt, *British Mining* (1884), App. 4, p. 887, gives the price of refined tin in Wales and the price of common tin in Cornwall.

1820-31, distinguishing Cornwall from Devon.433 *Porter's Tables* of 1843 offer
data for 1834-38 (Cornwall and Devon).434 The *Transactions* of the Royal Geological Society of Cornwall furnish production statistics for Cornwall and Devon for 1832-49.435 Mitchell and Deane give no production figures for regions
other than Cornwall.436

A final note: one modern writer provides in a chart the location of the tinplate works in the ten leading counties in Britain in 1750, 1800, 1825, and 1850
(and at six later dates, to 1905).437

(c) Lead

Unlike the copper and tin mines, the lead mines were scattered across Britain, with the northern English counties and Wales producing the greatest a-
mounts; Scotland and Ireland produced only negligible quantities (one-thirteen-
th of the production of the British Isles in 1852). By a wide margin, Britain
was a net exporter of lead, shipping out of the country in the early nineteenth
century about twice as much as she imported.438

For lead prices various contemporary sources may be consulted. A parliamentary paper has prices for 1783-1828; Marshall has figures for 1786-1830, and
McCulloch, for 1800-32.439 Robert Hunt, the late nineteenth-century statistician of mines, provides various lead prices from 1780 to 1843.440 A modern
writer furnishes annual prices from 1780 to 1850.441

433McCulloch, *Dictionary* (1837), 1159.

434*P.T. 11, P.P. 1843*, LVI, No. 104, p. 91.

435See for 1832-46, *T.R.G.S.C.*, VI (1846), 358; for 1844-49, *T.R.G.S.C.*,
VII (1865), 112.

436Mitchell and Deane, 150.

437Jones, *Tinplate Industry* (1914), App. D, p. 270.

438McCulloch, *Dictionary* (2 v., 1854), II, 797-98. The modern work with tables is William J. Lewis, *Lead Mining in Wales* (Cardiff, 1967). Christopher
Hunt's *The Lead Miners of the Northern Pennines* (Manchester, 1970) and Arthur
Raistrick and Bernard Jennings' *A History of Lead Mining in the Pennines* (1965)
do not include tables of economic data.

439The evidence of Hohler, in "Select Committee on the Wool Trade, 1828,"
P.P. 1828 (515), VIII, 727; Marshall, *Digest* (1833), Part 3, p. 33; McCulloch,
Dictionary (1837), 750.

440Hunt's prices, like Hohler's, are per fodder for the period 1783-1828. (A
fodder averaged 2,200 pounds in weight at the mines and 2,000 pounds in London,
according to Hunt.) This particular time series is no more specific than Hohler's series of 1828; the type of lead and place of sale are in both series not
stated. Hunt also gives the price paid per ton of lead at the Smelting House
at Grassington from 1780 to 1843. See Hunt, *British Mining* (1884), App. 33-34,
pp. 903-04.

441William J. Lewis, *Lead Mining in Wales* (Cardiff, 1967), App. A, pp. 369-
70. Lewis also has prices at thirteen dates from 1205 to 1573, at twenty-four
dates from 1620 to 1699, and at thirty-seven dates from 1700 to 1779; he gives
the sources for each price listed. Hunt, *Lead Miners of the Northern Pennines*
(Manchester, 1970), 74, shows by line graph the average sale price of lead per
ton obtained by the firm of Blackett-Beaumonts in county Durham from 1755

The records of lead and lead ore imported from 1786 to 1815 have been destroyed,[442] but several government sources and McCulloch's *Dictionary* furnish import and re-export statistics for the period 1816-50.[443] Schumpeter does not provide figures for lead imports, but Mitchell and Deane do present a series beginning in 1824.[444]

For the export of lead and shot, both Schumpeter and Mitchell and Deane give figures from 1697 onwards.[445] In addition, Schumpeter provides figures quinquennially for exports to five parts of the world in the eighteenth century.[446] Eighteenth-century printed export data are scarce, but Massie (1757) has national totals for 1709-14 and a government paper has statistics for 1797-99.[447] For nineteenth-century sources, the series are continous from 1820 to 1850, based on parliamentary sources and McCulloch's *Dictionary*.[448]

There is no account of lead production in Britain before 1845. In 1884, Hunt published statistics of national production (in tons) of lead and lead ore for 1848-71;[449] he also differentiated the output in Cornwall, Durham, and Northumberland from 1845 to 1882.[450] A modern writer furnishes data on the production of lead ore (in tons) in each of the eleven counties of Wales from 1845 to 19-38.[451] Mitchell and Deane provide national but not county totals for the output of lead ore and metallic lead over the same long period.[452]

Finally, as a conclusion to this general section on mining, a most interesting table assembled by Hunt (1884) should be mentioned. His table sets forth the results of working eighty-eight tin, copper, and lead mines in the United Kingdom, from 1819 to 1855, detailing for each year and for each industry the number of mines both at work and closed, the total amount of capital invested, the amount of profits divided and reinvested, and the amount of capital returned from mines which were abandoned or sold.[453]

to 1828; he also graphs prices for 1829-55 from "Tooke" but cites no page references.

[442]As stated in *P.P. 1828* (416), XIX, 286.

[443]All sources differentiate pig lead, red and white lead, and lead ore, by quantity, in tons. For 1816-27, see *P.P. 1828* (559), XIX, 419-21 (official values also); for 1820-31, see *P.T. 1, P.P. 1833*, XLI, 92; for 1821-33, see McCulloch, *Dictionary* (1837), 749; for 1827-50, see above, Table 3.

[444]Mitchell and Deane, 170.

[445]Schumpeter, VII-IX, 19-28, by quantity and value, for 1697-1808; Mitchell and Deane, 169-71, for 1697-1850.

[446]Schumpeter, XXVII, 65.

[447]Massie, *Ways and Means* (1757), 67-68, and *J.H.C. 56*, 716, respectively. The figures in both sources are by quantity, not value.

[448]For 1820-26, see *P.P. 1826-27* (520), XVIII, 159, or *P.P. 1828* (344), XIX, 407-15; for 1820-31, see *P.T. 1, P.P. 1833*, XLI, 92; for 1821-33, see McCulloch, *Dictionary* (1837), 749; for 1827-50, see above, Table 4.

[449]Hunt, *British Mining* (1884), App. 24, p. 898.

[450]*Ibid.*, App. 25-26, pp. 898-99.

[451]Lewis, *Lead Mining in Wales* (Cardiff, 1967), App. E, folding table facing 379.

[452]Mitchell and Deane, 160.

[453]Hunt, *British Mining* (1884), 869.

(d) Coal

Since the sixteenth century, with the growing scarcity and resulting high price of timber, coal had been the primary commercial and domestic fuel used by Englishmen. But especially in the century after 1750 coal—— an essential ingredient in an age of iron and factories —— became a mineral of the utmost importance. No official records were kept of the production of coal until 1854, but we do know that the amount of coal consumed by Londoners alone trebled from 1750 to 1850. Since it required three and one-half tons of coal to produce one ton of iron, more than three times as much coal was being used in the smelting of iron as was consumed by Londoners. It has been estimated that in 1830 Britain, the homeland of the Industrial Revolution, produced some 25 million tons of coal, or 80 per cent of the total world production. Most of the island's coal lies in Northumberland and Durham, although Cumberland and the Midlands counties also have large amounts. Scotland has considerable beds of coal, while backward Ireland is deficient in this valuable mineral.[454] J. R. McCulloch was one of many observers who sensed the awesome importance and singular good fortune of Britain to be endowed with huge coal fields:

> [They are] vastly more precious to us
> than would have been mines of the precious
> metals, like those of Peru and Mexico; for
> coal, since it has been applied to the steam-
> engine, is really hoarded power, applicable
> to almost every purpose which human labour
> directed by ingenuity can accomplish. It
> is the possession of her coal mines which
> has rendered Britain, in relation to the whole
> world, what a city is to the rural district
> which surrounds it,——the producer and dispenser
> of the various products of art and industry.[455]

Price data for coal exist for the prices paid at the Northern collieries (especially at Newcastle and Sunderland) and at the coal markets in London. First, the Northern prices. A parliamentary committee report furnishes prices at various collieries in the Tyne area for 1803-29.[456] Porter sets out prices

[454]McCulloch, *Dictionary* (2 v., 1854), I, 301, 783; H. Hearder, *Europe in the Nineteenth Century 1830-1880* (New York, 1966), 83.

[455]McCulloch, *Dictionary* (2 v., 1854), I, 297. The leading works of statistical value on coal in Britain are John U. Nef, *The Rise of the British Coal Industry* (2 v., 1932), Thomas S. Ashton and J. Sykes, *The Coal Industry of the Eighteenth Century* (Manchester, 1929), and Paul M. Sweezy, *Monopoly and Competition in the English Coal Trade, 1550-1850* (Cambridge, Mass., 1938). H. Stanley Jevons' *The British Coal Trade* (1915) furnishes figures for the late nineteenth and early twentieth centuries, but none for earlier dates. Richard Meade's *The Coal and Iron Industries of the United Kingdom* (1882) and Robert L. Galloway's *History of Coal Mining in Great Britain* (1882) have no tables of coal statistics. A most useful 16-page bibliography for the coal industry has been compiled by Baron F. Duckham in the foreword to a reprint of Galloway's *History of Coal Mining in Great Britain* (1882; reprinted, Newton Abbot, Devon, 1969), no pag.

[456]"Select Committee on the Coal Trade, 1829 (Lords)," *P.P. 1830* (9), VIII, 412-13.

at Newcastle and Sunderland for 1801-45, as does Greg for 1801-41.[457] Dunn has prices at seven dates between 1800 and 1828.[458] Taylor offers price movements in (to use his phrase) a "singular diagram," a line graph of daily Newcastle prices between January 1 and May 18, 1846.[459] Two modern works present prices at various dates since the sixteenth century.[460]

TABLE 31 sets out the major sources for coal prices in London. In addition, two parliamentary works list the prices of Newcastle coal in London on *every day* of the year in 1773 and 1799.[461] A select committee report contains a graph of the *daily* price changes in the years 1831 and 1835.[462] One modern writer has graphed the prices of coal in London from 1807 to 1844.[463] Ashton and Sykes present London prices at thirty-eight dates from 1665 to 1800.[464]

There are also institutional records. For instance, we have prices paid for coal by the Foundling Hospital for 1791 and 1794-1800, and by Smith and Harrington's Corn Distillery in Old Brentford, Middlesex for 1788-1800.[465] The price records kept by the Westminster School (1585-1830) and the Greenwich Hospital (1716-1828) are reprinted in Mitchell and Deane.[466] A late nineteenth-century parliamentary source has prices for 1820-80.[467] For rates of entry duty in English ports and shipping costs, the appendices of various select committee reports may be consulted.[468]

[457]Porter, *Progress* (3 v., 1836-43), I (1836), 341; and *Progress* (1851), 277. J. R. Greg, *Observations on the Proposed Duties on the Exportation of Coals* (1842), No. 3, p. 26; he cites Porter as his source for 1801-35.

[458]Matthias Dunn, *An Historical, Geological, and Descriptive View of the Coal Trade of the North of England* (Newcastle, 1844), 73, for 1800-25 (quinquennially) and 1828. For the Felling colliery he has complete price data for 1803-20.

[459]T. John Taylor, *Observations, addressed to the Coal Owners of Northumberland and Durham on the Coal Trade of those Counties* (Newcastle, 1846), 32.

[460]John U. Nef, *The Rise of the British Coal Industry* (2 v., 1932), II, App. E, pp. 390-408, gives innumerable prices at pithead, retail, and wholesale, in England and Scotland, in London, for shipment from the Tyne and the Wear, at King's College, Cambridge, and "other" from the mid 16th to the early 18th century. T. S. Ashton and J. Sykes, *The Coal Industry of the Eighteenth Century* (Manchester, 1929), App. F, pp. 252-53, give prices at thirty-eight dates from 1665 to 1800.

[461]"Select Committee on the Coal Trade, 1800," *Commons' Committees*, X, Nos. 10-11, pp. 578-87, for each of thirteen types of coals.

[462]"Select Committee on the Coal Trade," *P.P. 1836* (522), XI, facing 452.

[463]Paul M. Sweezy, *Monopoly and Competition in the English Coal Trade, 1550-1850* (Cambridge, Mass., 1938), 155, 158. He presents the graphs but no tables of data.

[464]Ashton and Sykes, *Coal Industry of the Eighteenth Century* (Manchester, 1929), App. F, pp. 252-53.

[465]"Select Committee on the Coal Trade, 1800," *Commons' Committees*, X, Nos. 14, 16, pp. 588-89.

[466]Mitchell and Deane, 479-81. Sweezy, *Monopoly* (1938), 158, graphs the prices paid by Greenwich Hospital from 1765 to 1829.

[467]*P.P. 1881* (225), LXXXIII, 127. Figures for 1820-31 are per chaldron; for 1832-80, per ton.

[468]For entry duties for each port in the United Kingdom for 1826-28, see

Table 31

PRICES OF COAL IN THE LONDON MARKET

Primary Sources

Government Documents

1734-1743 "S.C. on Coal Trade
1769-1779 (1800)," *Commons'*
Committees, X, App. 13, p. 588. *a*

1788-1800[b] "S.C. on Coal Trade
1807-1829[c] (1830)," *P.P. 1830* (663),
VIII, 7-8.

1807-1829: "S.C. on Coal Trade
(Lords) (1829)," *P.P. 1830* (9),
VIII, App. 7, pp. 588-678. *d*

1813-1831: *P.T. 1, P.P. 1833*, XLI,
166. *e*

1819-1832: "S.C. on Bank of England
Charter," *P.P. 1831-32* (722), VI,
App. 92, pp. 92-93. *f*

1823-1836: "S.C. on Coal Trade
(1836)," *P.P. 1836* (522), XI, 278. *d*

Books and Pamphlets

1732-1793: Eden, *State of the*
Poor (3 v., 1797), III, appendix,
pp. lxxx-lxxxi. *g*

1808-1811[h] Dunn, *Historical . . .*
1822-1826[b] *View of Coal Trade* (1844),
68, 73.

1813-1835: Porter, *Progress* (3 v.,
1836-43), I (1836), 342. *i*

1813-1850: Porter, *Progress* (1851),
278. *i*

Secondary Works

1771-1781 Ashton and Sykes, *Coal Industry of the 18th Century* (1929),
1785-1800 App. F, pp. 252-53. *j*

1788-1850: Mitchell and Deane, 482-84. *b*

Table 31
(continued)

All prices are per London chaldron.

a From the estate books of the Earl of Thanet.

b Annual average price.

c Average price in May of each year.

d Price on the first market day of each month.

e Price in January and July of each year.

f Highest and lowest prices in every month of the year.

g Price on January 1 of each year.

h Prices at four dates in each year.

i Prices "in July" of each year.

j It is not stated whether these prices are annual averages or from particular dates in each year.

Statistics of coal imports are rare because Britain was the world's greatest producer.[469] But "imports" into London from the Tyne area began as early as the fourteenth century and were of large scale by the early seventeenth century. The increases from 1660 to 1850 were regular and sizable:[470]

Year	Chaldrons[471]
1660	200,000
1689	300,000
1750	500,000
1800	900,000
1854	1,700,000

"Select Committee on the Coal Trade, 1829 (Lords)," *P.P. 1830* (9), VIII, App. 5, pp. 546-79. For shipping charges and freight rates for 1818-36, see "Select Committee on the Coal Trade," *P.P. 1836* (522), XI, 265-66. For 1828-35, in greater detail by place and company, see *ibid.*, App. 34, pp. 417-21.

[469]For imports into the United Kingdom for 1819-28, giving each port of entry, see *P.P. 1830* (9), VIII, App. 2, pp. 532-42. For a microstatistic, the amount of coals imported from all countries into Yarmouth in 1734-44, see *J.H.C. 25*, 344.

[470]McCulloch, *Dictionary* (2 v., 1854), I, 300-01. McCulloch describes the use of coal in London in the later seventeenth century as "universal."

[471]These chaldrons and the chaldrons in Table 32 are "London chaldrons." A London chaldron would be 25½ hundredweight (Mitchell and Deane, 112) or 26 to 27 hundredweight (Nef, *Rise of the British Coal Industry* (2 v., 1932), II, App. C, pp. 367-70).

The major sources for coal brought coastwise to London are set out in TABLE 32 below. Hunter has some scattered eighteenth-century data,[472] as does Atcheson for the early years of the century.[473] An anonymous pamphlet calculates averages for five progressively shorter periods from 1767 to 1786.[474] The modern historian, John Nef, presents figures from 1580 which become annual after 1680; he also provides data on coal imports into ports other than London from the late sixteenth to the early seventeenth century.[475] Paul Sweezy has graphed the imports of coal into London from 1765 to 1837.[476] Frost and Atcheson print the totals of the several duties collected annually by the port of the City of London from 1728 to 1801.[477] The record of the number of ships carrying coal into London annually exists from 1817 onwards.[478] The bulk of London's coal was "sea-borne," but increasingly after 1840 it arrived by rail; finally in 1848, railways brought more coal to the capital than did ships.[479]

Because of the fragmentary and irregular returns of coal shipments from the North, Tables 33 and 34 are rather detailed and complicated, even after Newcastle and Sunderland are differentiated (as they must be, for coverage varies not only from each port but also by coastwise or overseas from each port). TABLE 33 indicates the sources for coal shipments from Newcastle coastwise, overseas, to Ireland, and to the British colonies. The standard of measurement

[472]William Hunter, *The Outport Collector and Comptroller's Guide, or a Complete View of the Method of Collecting the Duties on Coals, Culm, and Cinders* (1764), 184, has figures in "chalders" (chaldrons) for 1686-89, 1700-01, 1708, 1710, 1720, 1726, 1730, 1736, 1740, 1750, 1754-55.

[473]Nathaniel Atcheson, *Letter.., to Rowland Burdon on the Present State of the Carrying Part of the Coal Trade* (1802), Table 3, p. 33 ff., has data for 1700-01, 1708, and 1710 as well as the continuous series, from 1713 to 1801, as noted in Table 32.

[474]*The Late Measures of the Ship-owners in the Coal-Trade fully examined in a letter to the Rt. Hon. William Pitt* (1786), no pag.

[475]Nef, *Rise of the British Coal Industry* (2 v., 1932), II, App. D, pp. 381-85.

[476]Sweezy, *Monopoly* (1938), 160. Again, he prints no tables.

[477]John Frost, *Cheap Coals: or, a Countermine to the Minister and his Three City Members* (1792), appendix facing 70; for 1743-1801, see Atcheson, *Letter.. . . on . . . the Coal Trade* (1802), App. 4, p. 33 ff. For 1780-85 and 1790-99, see *A. & P. 1786* (139), X, and *A. & P. 1800* (1025), LII, respectively. For the duties paid at four dozen British ports in 1815-17, see *Tables and Facts relative to the Coal Duties* (1819), Table A, facing p. 2.

[478]For 1817-29, see "Select Committee on the Coal Trade," *P.P. 1830* (663), VIII, App. 5, p. 365; for 1828-35, see "Select Committee on the Coal Trade," *P.P. 1836* (522), XI, 305-06; for 1832-43, see Dunn, *View of the Coal Trade* (1844), 213.

[479]For coal brought by inland navigation for 1805-26, see *P.P. 1826-27* (495), XVIII, 13. For coal transported by canal and railroad for 1832-40, see *P.T. 20, P.P. 1852,* LII, No. 72, p. 86; for 1836-44, see *P.P. 1846* (70), XLIV, 407. The series of imports by rail in Mitchell and Deane, 113, begins in 1845. Richard Taylor, *Statistics of Coal* (Philadelphia, 1848), 296, sets out the amount of coal carried on the Liverpool and Manchester railroad from 1831 to 1837: it amounted to a tenfold increase.

Table 32

COAL IMPORTS COASTWISE INTO LONDON

Primary Sources

Government Documents

1780-1800: "S.C. on Coal Trade (1800)," *Commons' Committees*, X, App. 19, p. 591; App. 45, pp. 627-28.

1790-1799: *A.& P. 1799-1800* (979), XLIX.

1800-1826: *P.P. 1826-27* (495), XVIII, 13.

1801-1828: "S.C. on Coal Trade (1829) (Lords)," *P.P. 1830* (9), VIII, 505.

1817-1829: "S.C. on Coal Trade (1830)," *P.P. 1830* (663), VIII, App. 5, p. 365.

1820-1835: "S.C. on Coal Trade (1836)," *P.P. 1836* (522), XI, 267.

1826-1832: *P.P. 1833* (197), XXXIII, 205.

1836-1844: *P.P. 1846* (70), XLIV, 407.

Books and Pamphlets

1713-1801: Atcheson, *Letter . . . to R. Burdon* (1802), Tables 3-4, p. 33 ff.

1728-1792: Frost, *Cheap Coals* (1792), appendix, facing p. 70.

1770-1779: Anderson, *Origin of Commerce* (4 v., 1787-89), IV (1789), 321.

1780-1799: Macpherson, *Annals of Commerce* (4 v., 1805), IV, 54.

1801-1828: Salt, *Statistics and Calculations* (1845), 70.

1821-1842: Porter, *Progress* (3 v., 1836-43), III (1843), 95-96.

1832-1843: Dunn, *Historical . . . View of Coal Trade* (1844), 213.

Secondary Works

1680-1761: Nef, *Rise of British Coal Industry* (2 v., 1932), II, App. D, pp. 381-82.

1700-1800: Ashton and Sykes, *Coal Industry of the 18th Century* (1929), App. E, pp. 249-51.

1700-1850+: Mitchell and Deane, 112-13.

Imports are by quantity in London chaldrons.

Table 33

SHIPMENTS OF COAL FROM NEWCASTLE

Primary Sources

Government Documents

1790-1799: *J.H.C. 76*, 1072. *a*

1791-1799: "S.C. on Coal Trade (1800),"
Commons' Committees, X, App. 43, p.
614. *a,b*

1794-1832: *P.T. 3, P.P. 1835*, XLIX,
No. 369, p. 421. *a,b*

1819-1828: "S.C. on Coal Trade (1829)
(Lords)," *P.P. 1830* (9), VIII, App.
1, pp. 511-31. *a,b,c,d*

1830-1835: "S.C. on Coal Trade (1836),"
P.P. 1836 (522), XI, 286.

1840-1846: *P.P. 1847* (520), LX, 165-
273. *a,e*

1846-1847: *P.P. 1847-48* (335), LVIII,
317-22. *a,b*

Books and Pamphlets

1791-1799; Macpherson, *Annals of
Commerce* (4 v., 1805), IV, 512;
also in Dunn, *Historical . . .
View of Coal Trade* (1844), 70. *a,b*

1800-1828: Dunn, *Historical . . .
View of Coal Trade* (1844), 72. *a,b*

1801-1835: Porter, *Progress* (3 v.,
1836-43), I (1836), 338-39. *a,b*

1801-1849: Porter, *Progress* (1851),
275. *a,b*

1819-1835: Porter, *Progress* (3 v.,
1836-43), I (1836), 343. *a,b,c,d*

1833-1841: Greg, *Observations on
. . . the Exportation of Coals*
(1842), App. 4, p. 27. *a*

Secondary Works

1655-1710, 1733: Mitchell and Deane, 108-11 [omissions: 1656-57]. *b*

1665-1685: Nef, *Rise of British Coal Industry* (2 v., 1932), II, App. D,
facing p. 380 [omissions: 1668-72, 1681-83]. *a*

1665-1709: Nef, *Rise of British Coal Industry* (2 v., 1932), II, App. D,
facing p. 380 [omissions: 1691-93, 1699, 1701-04]. *b*

Table 33
(continued)

1700-1800: Ashton and Sykes, *Coal Industry of the 18th Century* (1929),
App. E, pp. 249-51 [omissions: 1711-22, 1768-69, 1771, 1773-75, 1777,
1779, 1788].

1723-1732   Mitchell and Deane, 108-11. [omissions: 1768-69, 1771, 1773-77,
1734-1793   1779].

1794-1832: Mitchell and Deane, 110-11. *a,b*

Figures refer to total shipments (in Newcastle chaldrons) with the differentiated shipments as noted.

a Shipment overseas.

b Shipment coastwise.

c Shipment to Ireland.

d Shipment to the British colonies.

e Newcastle is one of three dozen
ports in the United Kingdom
specified in this series.

---

in Tables 33 and 34 is the "Newcastle chaldron" which weighed 53 hundredweight.[480]
    Sunderland (see TABLE 34) was always a port of secondary importance to New-
castle, though its trade grew steadily. The proportion of Sunderland's to Newcastle's coal trade increased rather regularly: from one-fourth the size of
Newcastle's trade in 1690, to one-half in 1750, to two-thirds in the beginning
of the nineteenth century. In the overseas trade, however, Newcastle continued
to maintain a commanding lead, with Sunderland rarely exporting one-third as
much as Newcastle. In addition to statistics for the years listed in Table 34,
Mitchell and Deane have figures for shipments from Sunderland in 1658-61, 1667,
1674, 1676-80, 1685, and 1733.[481] They also print the *totals* of coal shipped
from Newcastle *and* Sunderland for the period 1749-67 and 1781-1832.[482]
    Substantially less coal was shipped from Hartley and Blythe than from Sunder-
land or Newcastle. Various sources furnish the figures for shipments from 1791

[480]Nef, *Rise of the British Coal Industry* (2 v., 1932), II, App. C, pp. 367-
70; Mitchell and Deane, 108. In 1421, this chaldron equalled 18 hundredweight;
its weight increased constantly over the centuries, but after 1687 it remained
at 53 hundredweight.
[481]Mitchell and Deane, 108-09.
[482]Mitchell and Deane, 108-11. With other totals at scattered dates: 1658-
60, 1674, 1676, 1678, 1685, 1733, 1770, 1772, and 1778.

Table 34

SHIPMENTS OF COAL FROM SUNDERLAND

Primary Sources

Government Documents	*Books and Pamphlets*

Government Documents

1772-1799: "S.C. on Coal Trade (1800)," *Commons' Committees*, X, App. 19, p. 591; App. 49, p. 630.

1788-1799: "S.C. on Coal Trade (1800)," *Commons' Committees*, X, App. 22, p. 592. *a*

1800-1828: "S.C. on Coal Trade (1829) (Lords)," *P.P. 1830* (9), VIII, 494. *a,b*

1819-1828: "S.C. on Coal Trade (1829) (Lords)," *P.P. 1830* (9), VIII, App. 1, pp. 511-31. *a,b,c,d*

1830-1835: "S.C. on Coal Trade (1836)," *P.P. 1836* (522), XI, 286.

1840-1846: *P.P. 1847* (520), LX, 165-273. *a,e*

1846-1847: *P.P. 1847-48* (335), LVIII, 317-22. *a,b*

Books and Pamphlets

1791-1799: Macpherson, *Annals of Commerce* (4 v., 1805), IV, 512; also in Dunn, *Historical . . . View of Coal Trade* (1844), 70. *a,b*

1800-1828: Dunn, *Historical . . . View of Coal Trade* (1844), 72. *a,b*

1801-1835: Porter, *Progress* (3 v., 1836-43), I (1836), 338-39. *a,b*

1801-1849: Porter, *Progress* (1851), 275. *a,b*

1819-1835: Porter, *Progress* (3 v., 1836-43), I (1836), 343. *a,b,c,d*

1833-1841: Greg, *Observations on . . . the Exportation of Coals* (1842), App. 4, p. 27. *a*

Secondary Works

1665-1685: Nef, *Rise of British Coal Industry* (2 v., 1932), II, App. D, facing p. 380 [omissions: 1668-72, 1681-83]. *a*

1673-1685: Nef, *Rise of British Coal Industry* (2 v., 1932), II, App. D, facing p. 380 [omissions: 1680-83]. *b*

1748-1788, 1800: Mitchell and Deane, 109-10.

Table 34
(continued)

1748-1800: Ashton and Sykes, *Coal Industry of the 18th Century* (1929), App.
E, pp. 249-51.

1789-1799   Mitchell and Deane, 110. *a,b*
1801-1828

1829-1832: Mitchell and Deane, 111.

Figures refer to total shipments (in Newcastle chaldrons) with the
differentiated shipments as noted.

a
Shipment overseas.

b
Shipment coastwise.

c
Shipment to Ireland.

d
Shipment to the British colonies.

e
Newcastle is one of three dozen
ports in the United Kingdom
specified in this series.

---

to 1799.[483] A select committee report provides statistics for 1819-28, while
Porter has figures for 1819-35.[484] Taylor presents export figures from Liverpool for the period 1833-45.[485] Mitchell and Deane print no figures for shipments from any of these towns. A modern writer shows by graph the coal ship-

[483]"Select Committee on the Coal Trade, 1800," *Commons' Committees*, X, No.
43, p. 614; Dunn, *View of the Coal Trade* (1844), 70; Macpherson, *Annals* (1805),
IV, 512. All figures are coastwise and for overseas.

[484]For 1819-28, see "Select Committee on the Coal Trade, 1829 (Lords)," *P.P.
1830* (9), VIII, App. 1, pp. 511-31; for 1819-35, see Porter, *Progress* (3 v.,
1836-43), I (1836), 343. All figures are coastwise, for overseas, to Ireland,
and to the colonies.

[485]Richard Taylor, *Statistics of Coal* (Philadelphia, 1848), 296. Richard
Cowling Taylor (1789-1851)—educated by William Smith, "the Father of British
Geology"—was by profession a land surveyor with the Ordnance Survey in Norfolk
and South Wales. In 1830 he emigrated to America where he surveyed the coal
fields of Pennsylvania; he died at Philadelphia in 1851. A member of both the
Geological Society of London and the American Philosophical Society, Taylor authored in addition to the work cited here: *On the Geology of Norfolk* (1827),
Statistics, History, and Description of Fossil Fuel (1841), and *The Coalfields
of Great Britain* (posthumously published, 1861). His compendious *Statistics of
Coal* (1848; 2nd ed., 1854) has data for over a dozen countries. On his life,
see the *D.N.B.*, XIX, 459.

ments (in tons) from "the Vend area" from 1765 to 1850.[486]

Miscellaneous series exist for exports from Scotland and Wales. A recent historian, A. H. John, has printed figures for the exports of coal from eight ports in Wales at nine dates from 1780 to 1853. There is also a series of exports from ports in Scotland from 1790 to 1799.[487]

Statistics of national exports of coal are plentiful, although there is a gap in the printed sources for 1809-15. A select committee report provides figures for 1790-99; other parliamentary papers take the record from 1819 to 1850, and Porter has statistics for 1819-49.[488] Greg presents data for 1833-41.[489] An extremely detailed series exists for 1840-46.[490] One of the longest series is that printed by Richard Taylor for 1828-47.[491] Schumpeter gives figures for coal exports from 1697 to 1808, including quinquennial figures for their geographical distribution to eight regions of the world.[492] Mitchell and Deane print figures for 1697-1808 and 1816-50.[493] The export of coal to France, a potential industrial rival, attracted attention at the time: Dunn provides figures for 1788-1842.[494]

Output consumption figures of coal were not officially recorded until 1854; even until 1873, Mitchell and Deane warn us, production figures must be "regarded with suspicion."[495] Some estimates were made before 1854. Hugh Taylor estimated

[486]Sweezy, *Monopoly* (1938), 160. Again, no tables.

[487]See A. H. John, *The Industrial Development of South Wales, 1750-1850* (Cardiff, 1950), App. E, p. 191; for exports from Swansea from 1780 to 1799, see "Select Committee on the Coal Trade, 1800," *Commons' Committees*, X, No. 47, p. 629; for the Scottish exports, see *ibid.*, No. 44, pp. 617-27.

[488]For 1790-99, see "Select Committee on the Coal Trade, 1800," *Commons' Committees*, X, No. 42, pp. 612-15. For 1819-28, see "Select Committee on the Coal Trade, 1829 (Lords)," *P.P. 1830* (9), VIII, App. 1, pp. 511-31; for 1827-50, see above, Table 4. Porter's figures are in *Progress* (3 v., 1836-43), I (1836), 343, and *Progress* (1851), 279.

[489]Greg, *Observations on the Proposed Duties on the Exportation of Coals* (1842), No. 4, pp. 27-28.

[490]*P.P. 1847* (520), LX, 165-272. The figures are for the number of ships and tons of coal leaving annually from each port in the United Kingdom for a specific destination.

[491]Taylor, *Statistics of Coal* (Philadelphia, 1848), 270.

[492]Schumpeter, VII-IX, 19-28; XX, 63.

[493]Mitchell and Deane, 120-21.

[494]Dunn, *View of the Coal Trade* (1844), 231. Greg, *Observation on the Proposed Duties on the Exportation of Coals* (1842), No. 5, p. 30, has an incomplete series (1788, 1821-38), but lists also Belgian, Prussian, and German exports of coal to France. Both Dunn (p. 230) and Greg (p. 30) provide official output figures for French coal mines from 1825 to 1839. Greg (p. 31) also gives Belgian output figures for 1831-37. Dunn (pp. 157-213) has a long discussion of French and Belgian mining.

[495]Mitchell and Deane, 106. Output data after 1854 may be found in *Mineral Statistics* and in Mitchell and Deane, 115-17. After 1854, the output is differentiated regionally by quantity and value. Until 1870, the figure for output by value is merely hypothetical, since it is derived from the constant attribution of five shillings' value per ton. Not until 1882 is the value figure reliable, as doubtful methods of calculation were used in the period 1870-81.

the output of the Durham and Northumberland coal fields in 1830.[496] Consumption levels, arrived at by deducting exports from output, were estimated for Great Britain in 1830,[497] as earlier guesses had been made for London in 1801-22.[498] The output estimates of the early nineteenth century are discussed in the Report of the Royal Commission on Coal Supply (*P.P. 1871*, XVIII, 880 ff.). Mitchell and Deane state that the figures for shipments from the Tyne and the Wear can be "regarded as indicators of total British output until the end of the eighteenth century, and as a rough guide for a few decades after that."[499] The modern authority, Clapham, felt sufficiently confident about contemporary estimates to graph the output of coal in Britain from 1770 to 1850.[500]

Finally, some gruesome yet very real and important statistics may be mentioned. These are the 1,566 deaths which occurred in 131 coal mine explosions from 1658 to 1835. The editor of the Newcastle *Courant* compiled a detailed list in the wake of the greatest mining disaster up to that time, the Wallsend explosion of June 18, 1835, in which 102 persons were killed.[501]

V. THE IRON INDUSTRY

Iron was, after cotton, the fastest growing industry in late eighteenth-century England. A nation which in 1700 had been a great net importer of iron was by 1800 exporting more than five times as much as she imported.[502] Innovations of earlier patented processes involving the use of coal instead of timber for the smelting of iron ore triggered the revolutionary increases in output,[503] so that in the century from 1750 to 1850 pig iron production roughly doubled every ten years. Reflecting the insatiable demand for iron in factories, ships, and, above all, railways, the levels of production by the mid-nineteenth century became enormous: 2,701,000 tons in 1852, compared to 243,000 tons in 1806![504]

Statistical recording, however, lagged considerably behind the incredible

[496]Quoted in J. R. McCulloch, *Remarks on the Coal Trade* (Newcastle, 1830), 21-23; also in McCulloch's *Observations on the Duty on sea-borne Coal* (1831), 47-49.

[497]J. R. McCulloch, *Observations on the Report from and Minutes of Evidence taken before the Select Committee of the House of Lords on the Coal Trade. From the Edinburgh Review for April 1830* (Newcastle, 1830), 15.

[498]Printed in Salt, *Statistics and Calculations* (1845), 70.

[499]Mitchell and Deane, 106.

[500]J. H. Clapham, *An Economic History of Modern Britain* (3 v., Cambridge, 1926), I, 431.

[501]John Sykes, *An Account of the Dreadful Explosion in Wallsend Colliery* (Newcastle, 1835), 29-30.

[502]T. S. Ashton, in Schumpeter, 12.

[503]Landes, *Unbound Prometheus* (Cambridge, 1969), 89-95.

[504]Landes, *Unbound Prometheus* (Cambridge, 1969), Table 1, p. 96; McCulloch, *Dictionary* (2 v., 1854), I, 782; Mitchell and Deane, 131. The important modern studies of iron are T. S. Ashton's *Iron and Steel in the Industrial Revolution* (Manchester, 1924), Howard G. Roepke's *Movements of the British Iron and Steel Industry, 1720 to 1951* (Urbana, Ill., 1956), and J. R. Schubert's *History of the*

growth of the industry. The first official iron statistics date from 1839, when the Treasury Department instructed the Museum of Practical Geology to begin keeping complete iron output records. This start was fitful, though, for it was only from 1854—when Robert Hunt, the statistician of mining, began publication of the annual *Mineral Statistics* for the Geological Survey—that output series were regularly maintained. Not until 1878 did the industry itself (as the British Iron Trade Federation, founded in 1875) begin to publish regular statistics. At length, in 1882, the Government created a Department of Mines which kept records for the Home Office.[505] While official recording does date only from the second half of the nineteenth century, many individuals did assemble useful statistical data in the first half of the century.

The first writer to present a price series for iron was Thomas Tooke (1824), who provides figures for English pig iron and Russian and Swedish bar iron from 1782 to 1822.[506] Porter has Midland pig iron and Liverpool merchant bar iron prices for 1801-49.[507] Harry Scrivenor, Secretary of the Liverpool Stock Exchange and owner of an ironworks in Monmouthshire,[508] in his valuable *History of the Iron Trade* (1841) sets out South Wales pit prices for bar and pig iron from 1803 to 1824.[509] An anonymous pamphlet gives us prices in Wales for 1824-31.[510] Scrivenor also furnishes iron prices in London markets from 1812 to 1840.[511] He also gives the price of Shropshire bar iron in Bristol from 1818

British Iron and Steel Industry, from c. 450 B.C. to A.D. 1775 (1957). Roepke produces thirty-nine valuable tables; Schubert has eighteen full tabular appendices.

[505]This paragraph is based on R. M. Shone, "The Iron and Steel Industry," in Maurice G. Kendall, ed., *The Sources and Nature of the Statistics of the United Kingdom* (1952), 151, and Mitchell and Deane, 126-28.

[506]Tooke, *Thoughts and Details* (1824), App. 4, No. 1, pp. 22-25. This book became a source for several later writers: see Hohler's evidence in the "Select Committee on the Wool Trade," *P.P.* 1828 (515), VIII, 727; and Harry Scrivenor, *A History of the Iron Trade* (1841), 405-06.

[507]Porter, *Progress* (1851), 577. Tooke, *History of Prices* (6 v., 1838-57), IV (1848), 428-29, has a series for bar and pig iron for 1840-47.

[508]Scrivenor, *History of the Iron Trade* (1841), title page and p. 126.

[509]Scrivenor, *History of the Iron Trade* (1841), 410. This work, in thirteen chapters, treats the industry in nine countries; four chapters are devoted to British iron. The book is studded with data and tables, and has the beginnings of a bibliographical essay (pp. vii-viii), a rare practice then. Citing many parliamentary papers, Scrivenor explains the ommission of many works by saying, "Many years had elapsed.before the idea of compiling and writing for publication originated." The 1854 edition has been reprinted by Frank Cass (1967) and A. M. Kelley (New York, 1968), although that edition is 120 pages shorter than the 1841 edition and lacks the valuable statistical appendices in the earlier edition. The 1854 edition does not print any statistics of iron beyond the year 1840.

[510]*The Manufacture of Iron* (1837), 104-05.

[511]Scrivenor, *History of the Iron Trade* (1841), 410; average monthly prices are given. See also *P.T. 1, P.P. 1833*, XLI, 166, which gives prices in January and July from 1813 to 1831. Scrivenor tells us that "the London price is 20 *s.* per ton above the prices at Cardiff and Newport, and 10 *s.* per ton higher than Liverpool" (p. 410).

to 1841 and of Staffordshire bar and pig iron from 1825 to 1841.[512] Barclay, an iron broker at Glasgow, provides us with prices at Glasgow for pig iron from 1830 to 1849 and for bar iron prices from 1813 to 1849,[513] while Porter has Glasgow pig iron prices for the period 1835-49.[514] There are also less useful (because the place is unidentified) sources for iron prices for 1819-35.[515] Mitchell and Deane furnish prices for Midland pig iron for 1801-30, for bar iron at Liverpool from 1806 to beyond 1850, and for Scottish (from 1846) and Cleveland (from 1865) pig iron.[516]

The level of imports of iron changed little in the eighteenth century but fell drastically after 1803. This of course makes the series no less important. Because of the high import duties, bar iron was sometimes brought in disguised as copper, on which duties were low, so that the figures are probably slightly less than the real number of imports. Scrivenor gives us the rates of duty per ton from 1782 to 1825.[517] He also has detailed data on imports from America for most of the period 1718-86.[518] TABLE 35 sets out the sources for iron imports into England from all countries since 1700.

The exports of iron are another story. In 1850 fifteen times as much iron was being exported as had been in 1815; eighty-seven times as much as in 1750. Sources for statistics of the exports of iron appear in TABLE 36. Schumpeter has constructed a table indicating the amount of iron exports quinquennially to eight regions of the world.[519] Clapham shows in a graph the exports of several types of iron from 1815 to 1850.[520] There is, finally, a short table of iron exports from Ireland for 1816-20, a series which is useful if only to delineate the contrast to the Industrial Revolution occurring across the Irish Sea.[521]

The earliest sources for the number of blast furnaces in Britain date from the seventeenth century. Dud Dudley (1665)—a relation of Edward, Lord Dudley, the inventor of the process of smelting iron by pit coal (instead of by timber)—

---

[512]Scrivenor, *History of the Iron Trade* (1841), 408-09.

[513]John Barclay, *Statistics of the Scotch Iron Trade* (Glasgow, 1850), Table 6, p. 20; Table 9, p. 21, respectively. The pig iron prices are monthly for 1844-49; the bar iron prices, monthly, for 1840-49.

[514]Porter, *Progress of the Nation* (3 v., 1836-43), III (1843), 90; see also p. 586 of the 1847 edition and p. 577 of the 1851 edition.

[515]See, for example, the highest and lowest prices per year from 1819 to 1832 for pig and bar iron, in "Select Committee on the Bank of England Charter," *P.P. 1831-32* (722), VI, App. 92, p. 92. See also the unspecified prices for 1824-35 in Salt, *Statistics and Calculations* (1845), 68. Marshall, *Digest* (1833), Part 3, p. 33, gives prices of "foreign iron" from 1786 to 1828.

[516]Mitchell and Deane, 492-93. Their data for Midland pig iron are from T. S. Ashton, *Iron and Steel in the Industrial Revolution* (Manchester, 1924), 156; Ashton comments that these prices are "a rough indication of industrial vicissitudes," though he notes that some individuals sold below the official price in harsh trade conditions.

[517]Scrivenor, *History of the Iron Trade* (1841), 127-28.

[518]Scrivenor, *History of the Iron Trade* (1841), 328, 331-33, 336-38, 340, 342-44.

[519]Schumpeter, XXV-XXVI, 64.

[520]J. H. Clapham, *An Economic History of Modern Britain* (3 v., Cambridge, 1926), I, 483.

[521]*J.H.C. 76*, 1118-24.

Table 35

IMPORTS OF BAR IRON

Primary Sources

| *Government Documents* | *Books and Pamphlets* |

1786-1827: *P.P. 1828* (416), XIX, 278-79. *a*

1800-1805: *J.H.C. 61*, 732-33. *b*

1805-1814: *J.H.C. 70*, 866-69; also in *P.P. 1814-15* (263,264), X, 430-37. *c,d,e*

1815-1820: *J.H.C. 76*, 1078-83; also in *P.P. 1821* (376), XVII, 175-78. *c,d,e*

1820-1831: *P.T. 1, P.P. 1833*, XLI, 90-91. *c,e,f*

1821-1824: *P.P. 1825* (191), XXI, 162-63. *c,d,e*

1827-1850: See Table 3. *d,e,f*

1711-1718; Scrivenor, *History of Iron Trade* (1841), 325-27. *d,g* [hereafter, cited as 'Scrivenor']

1729-1735: Scrivenor, 333-35. *d,g*

1750-1755: Scrivenor, 339. *d,g*

1761-1776: Scrivenor, 343-44. *d,g*

1786-1799: Scrivenor, 358. *d*

1786-1828: Marshall, *Digest* (1833), Part 3, p. 33. *d*

1800-1839: Scrivenor, 420, 422, 424. *a,c,d,e*

Secondary Works

1700-1808: Schumpeter, XV-XVII, 48-59. *b,c,h*

1700-1829: Mitchell and Deane, 287-88, 290. *i,j*

1700-1850+: Mitchell and Deane, 140-41. *e,k,l*

1799-1814: Ashton, *Iron and Steel in the Industrial Revolution* (1924), 147. *e*

Table 35
(continued)

Imports (by quantity, in tons) are into Great Britain unless otherwise noted.

[a] Series for pig iron also.

[b] By official value as well as by quantity.

[c] Distinguishes several types of iron including pig.

[d] Distinguishes from two dozen countries.

[e] Series of re-exports also.

[f] United Kingdom.

[g] England and Wales only.

[h] 1700-91, England and Wales; 1792-1808, Great Britain.

[i] By official value only.

[j] 1700-1791, England and Wales; 1792-1829, Great Britain.

[k] 1700-91, England and Wales; 1792-1815, Great Britain; 1815-1850+, United Kingdom.

[l] Series of re-exports only for the period 1815-50+.

---

quotes an estimate of Simon Sturtevant for the number of furnaces and forges in England in 1615. Dudley himself gives estimates and calculations for the 1660's.[522] Abraham Darby, who first used coke in his blast furnace at Coalbrookdale about 1709,[523] provides estimates of the number of furnaces and amount of iron production in eighteen British counties in 1740.[524] An anonymous work estimates the number of forges and furnaces for twenty-seven counties in 1756;[525] another has figures for twelve counties in 1788.[526] Scrivenor provides an estimate for the number of coke furnaces in 1790, but does not hazard a guess at

[522]Dud Dudley, *Metallum Martis: or, Iron made with Pit-coale, Seacoale, &c.* (1665; reprinted in 1851 by 'J.N.B.').
[523]For a discussion of Darby and the date of his work, see Landes, *Unbound Prometheus* (Cambridge, 1969), 89-90.
[524]Darby is discussed in Scrivenor, *History of the Iron Trade* (1841), 57. On forges and output in this period, see Ashton, *Iron and Steel in the Industrial Revolution* (Manchester, 1924), App. B, pp. 235-38.
[525]*The Interest of Great Britain in Supplying Herself with IRON: Impartially Consider'd* (1756?), table facing 26. The substance of this pamphlet, available at the Kress Library, is reprinted in Richard Meade, *The Coal and Iron Industries of the United Kingdom* (1882), 840-42.
[526]Scrivenor, *History of the Iron Trade* (1841), 86.

Table 36

EXPORTS OF IRON

Primary Sources

Government Documents

1796-1805: *J.H.C. 61*, 778-85. *a,b,c,d*

1800-1805: *J.H.C. 61*, 734. *b*

1805-1814: *J.H.C. 70*, 870-73; also in *P.P. 1814-15* (265), X, 440-45. *c,e*

1815-1820: *J.H.C. 76*, 1078-83; also in *P.P. 1821* (376), XVII, 168-74. *c,e*

1820-1831: *P.T. 1*, *P.P. 1833*, XLI, 90-91. *b,c,f*

1821-1824: *P.P. 1825* (191), XXI, 153-61, 164-202. *c,e*

1827-1850: See Table 4. *b,c,e,f*

Books and Pamphlets

1711-1718: Scrivenor, *History of the Iron Trade* (1841), 344-45. *c,d,g* [hereafter, cited as 'Scrivenor']

1729-1735: Scrivenor, 347-53. *c,e,g*

1796-1839: Scrivenor, 418-19, 421, 425. *c,e*

1801-1834: Porter, *Progress* (3 v., 1836-43), I (1836), 296. *c*

1801-1849: Porter, *Progress* (1851), 248. *c*

1805-1828: Marshall, *Digest* (1833), Part 3, pp. 34, 38-47. *b,c,e*

1815-1824: Powell, *Statistical Illustrations* (1825), 70-71. *a,b,c*

Secondary Works

1697-1808: Schumpeter, VII-IX, 19-28. *a,c,h*

1697-1829: Mitchell and Deane, 293-95. *i,j*

1697-1850+: Mitchell and Deane, 144-46. *k,l*

1814-1850+: Mitchell and Deane, 302-03. *m,n*

1829-1854: Meade, *Coal and Iron Industries* (1882), 839. *f,o*

Table 36
(continued)

Exports (by quantity, in tons) are from Great Britain unless otherwise noted.

[a] By official value as well as by quantity.

[b] By declared value as well as by quantity.

[c] Differentiates bar, bolt and rod, castings, and other types of iron.

[d] Distinguishes from several parts of the world.

[e] Distinguishes from two dozen countries.

[f] United Kingdom.

[g] England and Wales only.

[h] 1697-1791, England and Wales; 1792-1808, Great Britain.

[i] By official value only.

[j] 1697-1791, England and Wales; 1792-1829, Great Britain.

[k] Distinguishes for 1697-1808 bar iron and wrought iron; for 1805-50+, pig or puddled iron and bar iron.

[l] 1697-1791, England and Wales; 1792-1814, Great Britain; 1815-1850+, United Kingdom.

[m] By declared value only.

[n] 1814-29, Great Britain; 1826-50+, United Kingdom.

[o] Pig iron only.

---

their output.[527] *Porter's Tables* lists the number of iron furnaces in Great Britain in 1847-48.[528] Richard Taylor presents the longest series of the number of blast furnaces in England, and Scotland, at twenty dates from 1740 to 1846.[529] A modern authority lists the number of forges in each of six regions in England in 1574, 1600, 1630/40, 1653, 1664, 1717, and 1790; he also sets out the number of charcoal blast furnaces in England and Wales at twenty-one dates from 1490 to 1750 (at each place in each of six regions).[530] Another recent writer provides figures for the number of iron furnaces in South Wales in 1788, 1796, 1811, 1823,

[527]Scrivenor, *History of the Iron Trade* (1841), 359. He differentiates village and county, names of proprietors, occupiers, and the number and dates of the foundation of existing furnaces.
[528]*P.T. 18, P.P. 1850* [1159], LIV, No. 218, p. 198.
[529]Taylor, *Statistics of Coal* (Philadelphia, 1848), 330, 347.
[530]J. R. Schubert, *History of the British Iron and Steel Industry* (1957), 175; App. 4, pp. 346-52, respectively.

Table 37

OUTPUT OF PIG IRON IN GREAT BRITAIN
(in tons)

Source	Years
[a,b] *The Interest of Great Britain in Supplying Herself with IRON: Impartially Consider'd* (1756?), table facing 26	1750
[a] J. Marshall, *Digest* (1833), Part 3, 33	1825, 28
[a] G.R. Porter, *Progress of the Nation* (3 v., 1836-43), I (1836), 327-28	1740, 88, 96, 1802, 06, 23, 25, 28, 30
[a] J.R. McCulloch, *Dictionary of Commerce* (1837), 736	1750, [b]88, 96, 1806, 20, 23[b], 25[b], 28[b], 30
The Manufacture of Iron (1837), 107	1740[b], 88[b], 96[b], 1806, 20, 27[b]
[a,b] H. Scrivenor, *History of the Iron Trade* (1841), 57, 86, 93-97, 131-36, 139, 292	1740, 88, 96, 1806, 23-30 yearly, 39
[a] G.R. Porter, *Progress of the Nation* (3 v., 1836-43), III (1843), 85-87	1740, 88, 96, 1802, 06, 23, 25, 28, 30, 36, 40, 42
S. Salt, *Statistics and Calculations* (1845), 71	1806, 23, 25, 28, 35, 36, 40, 41
R. Taylor, *Statistics of Coal* (1848), 330	1740, 88, 96, 1802, 06, 18, 20, 23, 26, 30, 35, 36, 39-46 yearly
[a,b] J. Barclay, *Statistics of the Scotch Iron Trade* (1850), Table 1, pp. 11-12	1740, 88, 96, 1806, 20, 27, 30, 40, 45-49[f]

144

Table 37
(continued)

Source	Years
[a]R. Meade, *The Coal and Iron Industries of the United Kingdom* (1882), 829-37	1740, 88, 96, 1806, 23, 30, 39, 40, 43, 47, 52
[a,b]T.S. Ashton, *Iron and Steel in the Industrial Revolution* (1924), 98	1788, 96, 1806
[a,c]H.G. Roepke, *Movements of the British Iron and Steel Industry* (1956), 24, 28-29	1720[d], 37, 50, 57, 88, 96, 1802, 06, 20, 23, 25, 29, 30, 34, 40, 47, 52
J.R. Schubert, *History of the British Iron and Steel Industry* (1957), App. 4, pp. 346-52	1688-1718 (irregularly but fully)
[a,e]B.R. Mitchell and P. Deane, *Abstract of British Historical Statistics* (1962), 131	1720[d], 88, 96, 1806, 23, 30, 39, 40, 43, 47, 52
[e]D. Landes, *The Unbound Prometheus* (1969), 96	1740, 88, 96, 1806, 25, 30, 39, 48, 52

[a] In addition to national totals, the source has figures for Derbyshire, Durham, North Wales, Northumberland, Scotland, Shropshire, South Wales, Staffordshire, and Yorkshire.

[b] Lists also the number of furnaces.

[c] "Data from various [unnamed] sources."

[d] T.S. Ashton, *Iron and Steel in the Industrial Revolution* (Manchester, 1924), 235-38, has concluded that the estimate for 1740 really refers to 1720; Mitchell and Deane follow his conclusion. Contemporaries, however, believed the estimate pertained to 1740, so it is retained unaltered in this table.

[e] Cites several sources.

[f] For Scotland only.

1830, 1839, and 1848.[531] Barclay lists the number of furnaces in various villages in Scotland in 1788, 1796, 1823, 1830, and 1846-49.[532] Hulme has discussed the early eighteenth-century statistics of iron forges; Flinn's critical article is essential.[533]

There are several sources before 1854 for statistics of the output of iron. Several writers, contemporary and modern, provide regional and national summaries of iron output since 1740. A modern writer presents data for the output of blast furnaces at various dates since 1330, with figures for four regions at thirty-two dates between 1688 and 1718.[534] The historian, J. H. Clapham, provides by graph the output of iron in Britain from 1805 to 1855.[535] TABLE 37 sets out the principal sources for figures of iron production from 1740 to 1854.

Some very interesting series are ones provided by Scrivenor, showing the tons of manufactured iron which moved down the Monmouthshire canal (1802-40), the Glamorganshire canal (1817-40), and the Grand Junction canal (1814-40).[536]

Railways were linked to both the coal and iron industries. Many statistics may be found in Harry Scrivenor's 811-page *Railways of the United Kingdom Statistically Considered* (1849). Other important contemporary accounts are F. Wishaw's *Railways of Great Britain and Ireland* (1840) and J. Francis' *History of the English Railway, 1820-1845* (2 vols., 1851). G. R. Porter prints a variety of railway statistics.[537] There are scattered returns in the *Parliamentary Papers* and in three select committee reports.[538] The leading secondary works are W. T. Jackman's *The Development of Transportation in Modern England* (2 vols., Cambridge, 1916) and H. G. Lewin's *Early British Railways* (1925). Mitchell and Deane provide numerous statistics relating to railways.[539]

Sources for wages of iron workers in our period are scarce, but there is a series in *Porter's Tables* which covers the period 1840-49.[540]

[531]A. H. John, *The Industrial Development of South Wales, 1750-1850* (Cardiff, 1950), App. F, p. 192.

[532]Barclay, *Statistics of the Scotch Iron Trade* (Glasgow, 1850), Table 2, p. 13.

[533]E. W. Hulme, "A Statistical History of the Iron Trade of England and Wales, 1717-50," *Transactions of the Newcomen Society*, IX (1928-29), 12-35; M. W. Flinn, "The Growth of the English Iron Industry, 1660-1760," *Economic History Review*, 2nd ser., XI (1958), 144-53.

[534]Schubert, *History of the British Iron and Steel Industry* (1957), App. 4, pp. 346-52. The regions: Forest of Dean and vicinity, Lancashire, Sussex, and Midlands/Cheshire.

[535]Clapham, *An Economic History of Modern Britain* (2nd ed., 3 v., Cambridge, 1930), I, 425.

[536]Scrivenor, *History of the Iron Trade* (1841), 123, 293, for Monmouthshire; pp. 126, 294, for Glamorganshire; and p. 413 for the Grand Junction canal.

[537]Porter, *Progress* (3 v., 1836-43), II (1838), 62-77.

[538]"Select Committee on the State of Communication by Railway," *P.P. 1839* (222,517), X; "Select Committee on Railway Communication," *P.P. 1840* (50, 92, 299, 437, 474), XIII; "Select Committee on Railways," *P.P. 1844* (25), XI.

[539]Mitchell and Deane, 122, 216, 225-29, 373-74.

[540]For weekly wages, distinguishing thirteen kinds of labor in the iron industry in South Wales, see *P.T. 18*, *P.P. 1850* [1159], LIV, No. 211, p. 196; No. 215, p. 197. This source also has wage figures for ten types of iron work in North Wales and sixteen types of work in Staffordshire from 1844 to 1849 (*ibid.*, Nos. 212-13, pp. 196-97). Porter, *Progress* (1851), 447-51, reprints many of these statistical series.

Although Parliament controlled the national finances after the Revolution of 1688, statistics of banking and finance in the eighteenth century were not therefore systematically collected and published. Some scattered materials may be found in the *Journals of the House of Commons* and in parliamentary debates, but it was not until 1823—in a period of financial retrenchment following the Napoleonic wars—that complete annual accounts of Government revenue and expenditure were made available to either Parliament or the public. And it was only in 1857 that the Treasury—under the guidance of the Chief Clerk of the Exchequer, H. S. Chisholm—began the work of compiling from the eighteenth-century records long historical series of the national income and expenditure since 1688.[541]

Banking statistics are also rare. Despite the drastic monetary depreciation from 1797 to 1815 which led to the return to specie payments in 1819, Parliament did not until 1833 require country banks to submit annual figures of their note issue and circulation. Founded in 1694, the Bank of England had long been legally compelled to publish statistics about its current operations; before 1833, however, the Bank did not make public its activities except in times of crisis when Parliament demanded information (for example, in 1797, 1810, and 1819). Detailed accounts were not made public until 1844. For private banks, there were no public accounts apart from ones concerning note issue until the *Economist* in 1877 published estimates of total bank deposits; and these were incomplete until 1889.[542] While Government was slow in making public its records in finance and banking, there were individuals who culled much important information from the official records.

Bullion was the foundation of the whole economic system, and gold (especially after the return to the gold standard in 1821) was the strength of the foundation. The sources for the price of gold in England appear in TABLE 38.

Among the most regular of Government statistics are those for the amount of gold and silver coined at the Royal Mint; the figures date from 1273, and a regular series runs from 1662.[543] Two nineteenth-century writers present data at some thirty dates from 1066 to 1816, though only three of the dates are after 1666.[544] Davenant estimated the amount of coin in England at four dates between

---

[541]A gap in 1801-02 in the original sources led Chisholm to a serious mistake. Chisholm and the Government publishers (*P.P. 1868-69* [366], XXXV), in order to maintain the comparability of the figures since 1801 with those before that date, altered the contents of most of the eighteenth-century categories! The problem arose because before 1801 income was net total income, while after that date it was gross total income. The constituent items changed, too, for property and income taxes joined the pre-1801 categories of customs, excise, stamps, post office, and land and assessed taxes. The changes within the categories of expenditure changed even more. Mitchell and Deane, 382, 386-400, have published both series in their original unreconstructed form.

[542]The above two paragraphs are based on Mitchell and Deane, 381-82, 434-35.

[543]Printed in Sir John Craig's definitive work, *The Mint* (Cambridge, 1953), App. 1.

[544]Henry James, *Essays on Money, Exchanges, and Political Economy* (1820), App. 2, facing p. 216; Joseph Macardy, *Outlines of Banks, Banking and Currency* (Manchester, 1840), 228-29. James' table is reprinted in Pablo Pebrer, *Taxation, Re-*

Table 38

PRICE OF GOLD AND SILVER

Primary Sources

<table>
<tr><td>Government Documents</td><td>Books and Pamphlets</td></tr>
<tr><td>

1790-1818: "Lords' Report on Cash Payments," *P.P. 1819* (291), III, App. C-1. *a,b,c*

1796-1849: *P.P. 1850* (460), LII, 319. *a,d*

1797-1842: *P.P. 1842* (580-II), XXVI, 249. *a,d*

1819-1832: "S.C. on Bank of England Charter," *P.P. 1831-32* (722), VI, App. 96, pp. 98-109. *a,b,c*

1820-1831: *P.T. 1, P.P. 1833*, XLI, 169. *a,b,e*

1832-1840: "S.C. on Banks of Issue," *P.P. 1840* (602), IV, App. 13, pp. 96-103. *a,b,c*

</td><td>

1744-1816: Boucherett, *A Few Observations on Corn, Currency, &c.* (1840), table facing 22. *b,d*

1760-1810: Mushet, *Enquiry . . . on the National Currency* (1810), 91-100. *a,f*

1760-1819: Joplin, *Outlines of a System of Political Economy* (1823), App. 13, pp. 42-47. *a,f*

1780-1815: Wilson, *Enquiry into . . . the High Prices* (1815), Table 1, pp. 77-80. *a,g*

1789-1796: King, *Thoughts on the Restriction of Payments* (1803), 91-98. *b,c*

1790-1809: Chalmers, *Considerations on Commerce, Bullion, and Coin* (1811), App. 2, facing p. 213; or see his *Historical View of the Domestic Economy* (1812), table facing 463. *a,b,d*

1790-1830: Marshall, *Digest* (1833), Part 3, p. 53. *a,b,d*

1797-1820: Tooke, *Letter to Lord Grenville* (1829), App. 4, p. 132. *a,b,e*

</td></tr>
</table>

Table 38
(continued)

Government Documents	*Books and Pamphlets*
	1800-1821: McCulloch, *Historical Sketch of the Bank of England* (1831), App. B, p. 72; reprinted in his *Dictionary* (1837), 86. *a,d*
	1800-1821: Macardy, *Outlines of . . . Banking* (1840), 74. *a,d*
	1800-1840: Bischoff, *Comprehensive History* (2 v., 1842), II, App. 10. *a,d*
	1810-1819: Macleod, *Theory . . . of Banking* (2 v., 1855), II, 221. *a,g*
	1815-1825: Mushet, *An Attempt to Explain . . . the Issues of the Bank of England* (1826), App. 1, pp. 209-14. *a,h*
	1839-1847: Tooke, *History of Prices* (6 v., 1838-57), IV (1848), 451. *a,b,g*

Secondary Works

John Craig, *The Mint:* none.	Mitchell and Deane: none.

a Gold

b Silver

c Price on the first day of every week.

d Annual average price.

e Price on the last day in February and August of each year.

f Price on the first day of *every other* month.

g Price on the first (or last) day of each quarterly period (January, April, July, October).

h Price on the first day of *every* month.

Table 39

AMOUNT OF GOLD AND SILVER COINED AT THE ROYAL MINT

Primary Sources

Government Documents

1760-1796: "Lords' Committee of Secrecy relating to the Bank (1797)," reprinted in *P.P. 1810* (17), III, 366. *a,b,c*

1760-1819: "Lords' Report on Cash Payments," *P.P. 1819* (291), III, App. D1, D2, pp. 370-71. *a,b*

1790-1829: *P.P. 1833* (138), XXIII, 347. *a,b*

1816-1836: *P.T. 6*, *P.P. 1837-38* [137], XLVII, No. 157, p. 171. *a,b,d,e*

1816-1847: *P.P. 1847-48* (601), XXXIX, 289-93. *a,b,d,e*

1830-1835: *P.P. 1836* (189), VIII Part 1, p. 516. *a,b*

1840-1853: *P.P. 1854* [1743], XXXIX, 155. *a,b,d*

Books and Pamphlets

1760-1797: Allardyce, *Address to . . . the Bank of England* (3rd ed., 1798), App. 38, p. 66. *a,b,c*

1760-1797: Wheatley, *Essay on the Theory of Money* (1807), table facing 151. *a*

1760-1811: Chalmers, *Historical View of the Domestic Economy* (1812), tables facing 315, 463. *a,b*

1771-1824: Powell, *Statistical Illustrations* (1825), 47. *a*

1778-1829: Marshall, *Digest* (1833), Part 3, p. 170. *a*

1790-1841: McCulloch, *Dictionary* (2 v., 1854), I, 326. *a,b*

1792-1843: Alison, *England in 1815 and 1845* (1845), appendix facing 94. *f*

1801-1836: Porter, *Progress* (3 v., 1836-43), II (1838), 239-40. *a,b*

1801-1849: Porter, *Progress* (1851), 437. *a,b*

1809-1829: Jacob, *Historical Inquiry into . . . the Precious Metals* (2 v., 1831), II, App. C-2, pp. 384-86. *a,b*

Table 39
(continued)

Government Documents	*Books and Pamphlets*

Books and Pamphlets

1841-1856: Tooke, *History of Prices*
(6 v., 1838-57), VI (1857), App.
22, p. 699. *a*

Secondary Works

1273-1951 (*b*)
1344-1951 (*a*)
1729-54, 1762-63,
1770-75, 1821-92 (*d*): Craig, *The Mint* (1953), App. 1, pp. 410-22.

1662-1821: Mitchell and Deane, 439-40. *a,b*

All figures are by value unless otherwise noted.

a Gold

b Silver

c By pounds weight as well as by value.

d Copper

e By pounds weight and types of pieces of coin as well as by value.

f Figures are for gold and silver *together*.

1599 and 1675.[545] Andrew Hooke, who believed Davenant's estimate to be too low, estimated the amount of Coinage in 1600, 1660, 1688, and 1749, and then extrapolated to *annual* figures for 1600 to 1748; the latter are highly suspect processed data.[546] The sources for statistics of coinage since 1662 are set out in TABLE 39. The Government was sufficiently interested in the amounts of gold raised and coined in mid-nineteenth-century South America, Russia, and the United States to publish figures in *Porter's Tables*.[547]

Bullion exports were more important in the early eighteenth century than in later years, since English merchants, specifically those in the East India Company, purchased goods from India and China with bullion. From 1702 to 1714 bullion accounted for roughly 75 per cent of all payments to the East; by 1770 the proportion was reversed, with bullion accounting for 25 per cent and woolens and other manufactures for 75 per cent of the total payments.[548] In 1832 England imported more bullion from the East than she sent there, but from 1832 to 1850 the figures fluctuate with no trend in either direction being established.[549] David Macpherson (1812) and John MacGregor (1848) set out annual data for bullion exports from England to China and India for 1708 to 1811.[550] Jacob has figures for 1810 to 1829.[551] McCulloch (1854) furnishes statistics for 1843 to 1852.[552]

Figures for the export of bullion to all countries exist for 1698 to 1717 and from 1783 onwards.[553]

venue, Expenditure, Power, Statistics, and Debt of the Whole British Empire (1833), Part 1, Table 51, p. 163.

[545]Charles D'Avenant, *Discourses on the Publick Revenues and on Trade, Part 2* (2 v., 1698), II, 104.

[546]Andrew Hooke, *An Essay on the National Debt, and National Capital: or, The Account truly stated, debtor and creditor* (1750), 55-59. Foxwell notes overleaf: "A very valuable tract . . . he seems to overrate the amount of cash."

[547]*P.T. 5, P.P. 1837*, XLIX, No. 139, pp. 127-28, has gold and silver production and coinage figures for Mexico, 'Buenos Ayres,' 'Chili,' Peru, Russia, and the United States from 1790 to 1835, "as far as the same can be prepared from the returns made by H. M. Consuls in those Countries." See also *P.T. 6, P.P. 1837-38*, XLVII, No. 155, pp. 169-70.

[548]T. S. Ashton, in Schumpeter, 10-11.

[549]McCulloch, *Dictionary* (2 v., 1854), II, 1056. Mitchell and Deane have no series of bullion exports.

[550]David Macpherson, *History of the European Commerce with India* (1812), App. 7, pp. 419-20; John MacGregor, *Commercial Statistics* (4 v., 1847-48), IV (1848), 404-10. A shorter series for 1788-1809 appears in "Select Committee on the High Price of Bullion," *P.P. 1810* (349), III, App. 9, p. 163.

[551]William Jacob, *Historical Inquiry into the Production and Consumption of the Precious Metals* (2 v., 1831), II, App. C-14, p. 409.

[552]McCulloch, *Dictionary* (2 v., 1854), II, 1056.

[553]For the early eighteenth century, see for 1698-1715, *J.H.C. 18*, facing 674; for 1710-17, see *J.H.C. 18*, facing 682. For 1783-96, see "Select Committee on the Bank of England," *Reports [of the House of Commons] 1796-97* (134), XIX, App. 6-7, pp. 163-65. For 1790-96, see "Lords' Committee of Secrecy (1797), relating to the Bank," *P.P. 1810* (17), III, 363. For 1800-09, see *P.P. 1810* (349), III, App. 1, pp. 156-59 (from a half-dozen ports to two dozen countries). For 1814-18, see *J.H.C. 74*, 1119-20. For 1814-24, see John Yates, *Essays on Currency and Circulation and on the Influence of our Paper System on the Industry, Trade, and Revenue of Great*

The rate of exchange —— the value which one unit of currency of standard mint weight and value holds for one or more other currency units —— is very important in commercial transactions. Foreign debts and credits were not negotiated by payments through the mails. Rather, the London debtor's agent in Hamburg or Paris, for example, would arrange to pay the foreign creditor by buying a bill of exchange in that city's local Exchange. This bill would then be turned into cash by the creditor drawing on the agent's account; the agent would be reimbursed by his client in London or by buying a bill in the London market. The rates of exchange constantly varied, due to the intrinsic metallic worth of a country's unit of currency or to the volume of the bills of exchange drawn in any one country. The rates would change in favor of or against merchants in London, Hamburg, or Paris. Thus, a London businessman who owed money in Paris but found the Paris rate against him and the Hamburg rate in favor of London, would draw a bill on Hamburg and direct his agent to invest the proceeds in a bill on Paris, instead of discharging his debt directly at the Paris Exchange.[554] TABLE 40 presents the sources for the rates of exchange at London, Hamburg, and Paris. The rates were first published on a twice-weekly basis in 1698 by John Castaing, in his *Course of the Exchange*. Castaing, a Lombard Street broker, published until 1725; from 1725 until 1807 there were various publishers; from 1807 James Wetenhall, a broker in Throgmorton Street, published this twice-weekly journal.[555] Mitchell and Deane devote a paragraph to the rates but present no figures.[556]

Although Government did not publish until the middle of the nineteenth century an historical series of its own income and expenditure,[557] numerous private individuals had compiled fairly long series of public finance statistics. The great expenditures resulting from the War of the Spanish Succession led to some early-eighteenth-century compilations. Charles Davenant presents a table of annual government expenditures for 1702-09;[558] an anonymous pamphlet lists

Britain (Liverpool, 1827), App. G-1, p. 180. For 1830-53, see Tooke and Newmarch, *History of Prices* (6 v., 1838-57), VI (1857), 709. Mitchell and Deane present no data for bullion imports or exports.

[554]For a discussion of the system, see McCulloch, *Dictionary* (2 v., 1854), I, 577-84.

[555]*The Course of the Exchange* reflects the growth of industry in England. In the early eighteenth century the work published the rates of exchange in fifteen cities and the prices of Government Funds (Bank of England, East India Company, South Sea, and some other stocks); by the early nineteeth century, the journal was also publishing the prices of foreign stock, coal and wheat, the cost of shares in canals and docks, insurance companies, bridge and railway and gaslight companies, and waterworks, road, and mining concerns. The publishers in the period 1725-1807 were: 1725-29, Castaing and Edward Jackson; 1730-35, Jackson alone; 1735-64, Richard Shergold; 1764-79, Peter Smithson; 1780-84, not known; 1784-1803, Edward Wetenhall; 1803-07, Edward Wetenhall and Lord Sheffield. Of the series for 1698-1850, Kress Library has varying numbers of issues in all the years *except* for 1704, 1715, 1718, 1811-17, 1820-21, and 1837-38.

[556]Mitchell and Deane, 438.

[557]See *P.P. 1868-69* (366), XXXV.

[558]Charles D'Avenant, *New Dialogues upon the Present Posture of Affairs, the Species of Money, the National Debts, Publick Revenues, Bank and East-India Company, and the Trade now carried on between France and Holland* (2 v., 1710), II,

Table 40

RATES OF STERLING EXCHANGE AT VARIOUS EUROPEAN CITIES

Primary Sources

Government Documents	*Books and Pamphlets*

Government Documents

1790-1818: "Lords' Report on Cash Payments," *P.P. 1819* (291), III, App. C-1, pp. 350-54. *a,b,c,d*

1812-1818: "Lords' Report on Cash Payments," *P.P. 1819* (291), III, App. C-3, p. 357. *e,f,g*

1819-1832: "S.C. on Bank of England Charter," *P.P. 1831-32* (722), VI, App. 96, pp. 98-109. *a,b,c,d*

1832-1840: "S.C. on Banks of Issue," *P.P. 1840* (602), IV, App. 9, pp. 22-23; App. 13, pp. 96-103.

1844-1847: "Secret Committee on Commercial Distress," *P.P. 1847-48* (395), VIII Part 2, App. 6, pp. 16-21. *b,c,d,e*

Books and Pamphlets

1760-1809: Blake, *Observations on . . . the Course of Exchange* (1810), 123-32. *a,h*

1760-1809: Mushet, *Enquiry into . . . the National Currency* (1810), 91-100. *a,b,h*

1760-1819: Joplin, *Outlines of a System of Political Economy* (1823), App. 13, pp. 42-47. *a,h*

1770-1776: Chalmers, *Considerations on Commerce, Bullion, and Coin* (1811), p. 37 note. *a,i*

1776-1784: Atkinson, *Considerations on . . . the Bank of England* (1802), table facing 81. *a,e,h*

1780-1815: Wilson, *Enquiry into . . . the High Prices* (1815), Table 1, pp. 77-80. *a,j*

1789-1803: King, *Thoughts on the Restriction of Payments* (1803), 91-105. *a,b,d*

1790-1809: Chalmers, *Historical View of the Domestic Economy* (1812), table facing 463. *a,k*

1790-1829: Marshall, *Digest* (1833), Part 3, p. 53. *a,b,c,f,l*

154

Table 40
(continued)

Government Documents	*Books and Pamphlets*
	1797-1820: Tooke, *Letter to Lord Grenville* (1829), App. 4, p. 132. *a,b,m*
	1800-1819: *Cursory Observations on . . . Resuming Cash Payments* (1819), App. 16-19, pp. 152-56. *a,b,e,f,j*
	1815-1825: Mushet, *An Attempt to Explain . . . the Issues of the Bank of England* (1826), App. 1, pp. 209-14. *a,b,i*
	1819-1832: Quin, *The Trade of Banking* (1833), App. G, pp. xix-xx. *a,b,c,n*
	1833-1837: Porter, *Progress* (3 v., 1836-43), II (1838), 236-37; reprinted in his *Progress* (1851), 432. *a,b,i*
	1839-1847: Tooke, *History of Prices* (6 v., 1838-57), IV (1848), 451. *a,b,j*

Secondary Works

1700-1800: Ashton, *Economic History of England: the 18th Century* (1964), appendix, Table 15. *a,o*

Mitchell and Deane: none.

Table 40
(Continued)

[a] At Hamburg.	[i] Rate on the first day of *every month*.
[b] At Paris.	[j] Rate on the first (or last) day of each quarterly period (January, April, July, October).
[c] At Lisbon.	
[d] Weekly average rate.	[k] Annual average rate.
[e] At Amsterdam.	[l] In each year.
[f] Highest and lowest rates.	[m] Rate on the last day of February and August in each year.
[g] In each quarterly period.	
[h] Rate on the first day of *every other* month.	[n] At two dates in each year.
	[o] Rate on the first day in January in each year.

---

expenditures from 1702 to 1712;[559] and another pamphlet sets out in a folding table "the State of the Expence of the Late War," with annual expenditures for 1701-13, differentiating constituent parts in half a dozen columns.[560] Thirty years later, in the middle of the War of the Austrian Succession, Thomas Carte (1743) provides annual figures for Government expenditures on the Army and Navy from 1702 to 1742, distinguishing two dozen categories in each year.[561] An anonymous pamphlet, *A Survey of the National Debt* (1745), lists annual military expenditures for 1702-45.[562]

table facing 86.

[559]*A View of the Taxes, Funds, and Publick Revenues of England* (1712), no pag. Foxwell's note: *"Rare."*

[560]Charles D'Avenant, "A Report to the Honourable the Commissioners for putting in Execution the Act, intituled an Act for the taking, examining, and stating the Publick Accounts of the Kingdom (1711)," in *The Political and Commercial Works of that Celebrated Writer, Charles D'Avenant*, collected and revised by Sir Charles Whitworth (5 v., 1771), V, 353. A later writer, George Gordon, *The History of our National Debts and Taxes* (2nd ed., 1753), Part 3, table facing 144, also lists army and ordnance expenditures annually from 1702 to 1710.

[561]Thomas Carte, *A Full and Clear Vindication of the Full Answer to a Letter from a Bystander* (1743), no pag., appendix. The author gives his source as *The Journals of the House of Commons.*

[562]*A Survey of the National Debt* (1745), 72. The writer states that his sources were *A View of the Taxes* (1712), Carte's *Vindication* (1743), and *The Journals of*

By the middle of the century, contemporaries were tabulating total, rather than just military, expenditures; see TABLE 41. James Postlethwayt, Malachy's brother, presents statistics for Government expenditures from 1728 to 1751 and also for loans and Exchequer bills (calling them "Grants") over the same period, though he has no revenue figures.[563] Timothy Cunningham (1761), the historian of commerce, furnishes figures for "Grants" from 1688 to 1760 but no income or expenditure data.[564] Then, in 1763, Sir Charles Whitworth is the first to furnish income ("Ways and Means") as well as expenditure ("Supplies") statistics, presenting a long series for 1688 to 1762.[565] After 1763, many writers present statistical series. William Playfair, another compiler influenced by wartime spending, helps us to visualize, by means of a colored broken-line graph, the revenues of Britain and France from 1550 to 1795.[566] (The graph shows that after 1780 British revenues are closing the gap on her wealthier neighbor's lead in the absolute value of revenue collected; by 1800, the graph implies, Britain will be the leader.) There are several sources for the revenue of the Irish Government until 1817, at which time Ireland's fiscal system was merged with that of Great Britain.[567]

Taxation was of course one of the major sources of government revenue. The first historical series of considerable length was published by the Government only in 1869; it is this series on which Mitchell and Deane rely.[568] There were, however, earlier printed series. Four government documents of the 1780's print statistics for taxes collected from 1773 to 1787,[569] while *Porter's Tables* (1843)

the House of Commons. For 1702-42, his statistics differ slightly from Carte's.

[563]James Postlethwayt, *History of the Public Revenue* (1758), 205-08, 215-18, 234-35, and 326-37.

[564]Timothy Cunningham, *The History of our Customs, Aids, Subsidies, National Debts, and Taxes from the Time of William the Conqueror to the Present Year* (1761), Part 1, p. 85; Part 2, p. 92; Part 3, p. 96; Part 4, p. 145*. A second edition appeared in 1773. In the third edition (1778) Cunningham acknowledges Whitworth's *Collection of the Supplies* (1763) and presents his tables of revenue and expenditure in a fashion similar to Whitworth's (pp. 415*-417*). The occasionally starred pagination is peculiar to Cunningham.

[565]Sir Charles Whitworth, *A Collection of the Supplies, and Ways and Means, from the Revolution to the Present Time* (1763), folding table facing 183. The work was written for "my Brother Members [of Parliament]." The form of the book is mainly tabular; as Whitworth says in his preface, "There need [be] no Annotations to such a work as this, where Information and Facts are only necessary."

[566]William Playfair, *A Real Statement of the Finances and Resources of Great Britain* (1796), folding chart facing 8.

[567]For 1790-1817, see *J.H.C. 72*, 714; for 1800-16, see Powell, *Statistical Illustrations* (1827), Table 2, facing p. xx; for 1802-31, see Pebrer, *Taxation . . . of the British Empire* (1833), Part 1, pp. 155, 158-59. James Corry gives by colored line graph the revenues from 1700 to 1785 (in Playfair, *Commercial and Political Atlas* [1786], Plate 36, p. 153 ff.).

[568]*P.P. 1868-69* (366), XXXV; abstracts of this series are reprinted in Mitchell and Deane, 386-88, 392-93.

[569]For dozens of taxes, for 1773-82, see *A. & P. 1783* (42), IV; for 1775-85, see *A. & P. 1785* (120), IX; for 1786-87, see *A. & P. 1788* (566), XXII. Statistics for 1774-82 are set out in the report of the "Select Committee on Supply (1782)," in *Commons' Committees*, XI, No. 10, pp. 19-20.

Table 41

GOVERNMENT INCOME AND EXPENDITURE

Primary Sources

| *Government Documents* | *Books and Pamphlets* |

Government Documents

1786-1824: *J.H.C. 79*, 794.

1792-1831: *P.T. 1*, *P.P. 1833*, XLI,
1*-5*.

1797-1816: *J.H.C. 72*, 701-10.

1805-1821: *J.H.C. 77*, 901-10.

1822-1849: *P.P. 1850* (391), XXXIII,
158.

1828-1839: *P.P. 1840* (149), XXIX,
App. 7, pp. 193-210.

Books and Pamphlets

1688-1762: Whitworth, *Collection of
the Supplies* (1763), folding
table facing 183.

1688-1777: Cunningham, *History of
. . . National Debts and Taxes*
(3rd ed., 1778), 415-17.

1700-1800: McArthur, *Financial and
Political Facts* (1801), App. 4,
pp. 321-23.

1718-1752: J. Postlethwayt, *History
of the Public Revenue* (1758), 205-
07, 215-16, 234-35, 278-95, 326-29.

1760-1831: Pebrer, *Taxation . . . of
the Whole British Empire* (1833),
Part 1, pp. 152-57. *a*

1761-1812: Colquhoun, *Treatise on
the Wealth . . . of the British
Empire* (1814), 198-99. *b*

1792-1815: Congleton, *On Financial
Reform* (1830), App. 4, pp. xl-xli.

1792-1815: Macardy, *Outlines of . . .
Banking* (1840), table facing 13.

1792-1836: Porter, *Progress* (3 v.,
1836-43), II (1838), 290.

1792-1849: Porter, *Progress* (1851),
475.

Table 41
(continued)

a Expenditure from 1794 only.   *b* No figures for expenditure.

---

provides figures for 1815-41.[570] Various contemporary writers furnish statistics from 1792 to 1849.[571]

The failure of income to keep up with expenditure may be seen in the progress of the National Debt. The size of the unredeemed capital of the debt, by far

[570]*P.T. 11, P.P. 1843*, LVI, No. 6, p. 6. This series distinguishes customs, excise, stamp taxes, and assessed taxes as well as giving totals of taxation. For a slightly later series of the gross undifferentiated totals of taxation for 1827-66, see *P.P. 1866* (509), LXVI, 515.

[571]For 1792-1816, see Robert Hamilton, *An Inquiry concerning the Rise and Progress, Redemption and Present State, and Management of the National Debt of Great Britain and Ireland* (3rd ed., 1818), reprinted in J. R. McCulloch, ed., *Select Tracts on the National Debt* (1857), 578-79; for 1812-23, see Powell, *Statistical Illustrations* (1825), 29; for 1792-1832, see R. Montgomery Martin, *Taxation of the British Empire* (1833), 70-71; for 1798-1831, see Marshall, *Digest* (1833), Part 3, p. 48. For 1801-36, see Porter, *Progress* (3 v., 1836-43), II (1838), 305; for 1801-49, see Porter, *Progress* (1851), 485-86.

the largest component of the debt, doubled from 1750 to 1779, doubled again by 1796, doubled again by 1810, and increased by one-third by 1820. Thereafter, the secular trend was slightly downwards until the increases during World War I.[572] The net result was that the debt in 1820 was almost eleven times larger than it had been in 1750 and almost four times greater than the 1790 figure. That all of the large increases came during war years was little consolation to contemporaries who believed in strict balanced accounts. Richard Price, who believed population was declining, decried the size of the debt left by the Seven Years War and later by the American War.[573] William Morgan in the 1790's issued *An Appeal to the People of Great Britain* (which went through five editions in 1797) to rouse themselves before the coming catastrophe.[574] In the Napoleonic wars Sir John Sinclair,[575] J. J. Grellier,[576] and Robert Hamilton[577] felt moved to write on the progress of the debt. After 1820, with the huge debt somewhat stabilized and England hardly in financial ruins, contemporaries more or less learned to live with a large debt as a necessary evil and few writers were perturbed enough to write on the subject. TABLE 42 sets out the sources for figures on the debt. In addition to his continuous series, Hamilton provides figures for a dozen dates between 1688 and 1815,[578] with a view towards showing the effects of wars on the debt. James Corry has a colored graph for the national debt of Ireland from 1707 to 1784.[579]

[572]Wartime has always increased the debt. The Seven Years War, the American Revolution, the Napoleonic Wars, and most recently World Wars I and II all multiplied the debt to several times previous peacetime levels. For pre-World War II figures, see Mitchell and Deane, 401-03; for 1938-66, see Brian Mitchell and H. G. Jones, *Second Abstract of British Historical Statistics* (Cambridge, 1971), 162.

[573]See his *Appeal to the Public, on the Subject of the National Debt* (1772; 2nd ed., 1774) and *State of the Public Debts and Finances at the Signing of the Preliminary Articles of Peace in January* (1783).

[574]Full title: *An Appeal to the People of Great Britain on the Present Alarming State of the Public Finances and of Public Credit* (5 eds., 1797). See also Morgan's *Facts addressed to the Serious Attention of the People of Great Britain respecting the Expence of the War and the State of the National Debt* (4 eds., 1796) and his *Comparative View of the Public Finances from the Beginning to the Close of the late Administration* (1801). For an extensive bibliography of works on the debt on the eve of the French wars, see J. E. D. Binney, *British Public Finance and Administration, 1774-92* (Oxford, 1958), 291-306.

[575]*The History of the Public Revenue of the British Empire* (3rd ed., 3 v., 1803-04).

[576]*Terms of All the Loans which have been Raised for the Public Service during the Last Fifty Years* (1799; 3rd ed., 1805).

[577]*An Inquiry concerning the Rise and Progress, Redemption and Present State, and Management of the National Debt of Great Britain and Ireland* (1813; 2nd ed., 1814; 3rd ed., 1818).

[578]Hamilton, *Inquiry concerning the . . . National Debt* (3rd ed., 1818), in McCulloch, ed., *Select Tracts on the National Debt* (1857), 499-502. Thomas Joplin reprints Hamilton's figures in *Outlines of a System of Political Economy* (1823), App. 5, p. 29.

[579]Printed in Playfair, *Commercial and Political Atlas* (1786), Plate 39, p. 153 ff.

Table 42

THE NATIONAL DEBT

Primary Sources

Government Documents

1786-1819: *J.H.C. 74*, 791; or *J.H.C. 75*, 615-22; also in *P.P. 1819-20* (35), IV, 105.

1792-1831: *P.T. 1*, *P.P. 1833*, XLI, 1.

1796-1845: *P.P. 1846* (360), XLIV, 21.

1797-1842: *P.P. 1842* (580), XXVI, 244-45.

1819-1825: *J.H.C. 81*, 686-89.

1820-1831: *P.T. 1*, *P.P. 1833*, XLI, 6*.

1846-1848: *P.P. 1849* (54), XXX, 203.

Books and Pamphlets

1688-1800; Grellier, *History of the National Debt* (1810), *passim*.

1688-1801: Sinclair, *History of the Public Revenue* (3rd. ed., 3 v., 1803-04), I (1803), 474. *a*

1740-1744: *A Survey of the National Debt* (1745), 68.

1792-1799: Allardyce, *Second Address to the Proprietors* (1801), App. 10, p. 45.

1792-1816: Hamilton, *Inquiry concerning . . . the National Debt* (1818), 320-34.

1792-1843: Alison, *England in 1815 and 1845* (1845), appendix facing 94.

1805-1822: Fairman, *Account of the Public Funds* (1824), 204.

1817-1845: McCulloch, *Dictionary* (2 v., 1854), I, 608.

Secondary Works

1688-1850+: *P.P. 1868-69* (366), XXXV, p. 1 ff.

1688-1850+: Mitchell and Deane, 389-91, 396-97, 401-07.

1774-1792: Binney, *British Public Finance* (1958), App. 1, p. 283.

See the sources themselves for the numerous and complex details on the debt.

a For twelve years only in this period.

To redeem part of the debt George I instituted in 1717 the first Sinking Fund, whereby part of the revenue would be put aside as a credit. The Fund was kept up until 1729, when portions of the Fund began to be spent for different purposes; an act of 1748 at length ended this practice. The first really effective redemption of the debt, however, came only in 1786 with Pitt's reform of the Sinking Fund. The new practice was to purchase public stock with that part of the revenue set aside for the Sinking Fund; the dividends on all stocks in which Fund moneys were invested were also to be applied to the Fund. In 1792 it was further enacted that 1 per cent of the value of the capital of the stocks of the Consolidated Fund should be applied to the Sinking Fund.[580] The system had hardly begun operation before Pitt's successors borrowed from the Fund, gradually weakening its ability to reduce the debt; finally, in 1828, the mechanism of the Sinking Fund was irreparably damaged when a parliamentary committee declared that the Sinking Fund should operate only when a year's revenue exceeded its expenditure.[581]

The earliest writer to set out the statistics for redemption of the debt by the Sinking Fund was James Postlethwayt, who gives annual figures for 1718 to 1751.[582] Another tabular series, published in 1764, sets out figures for 1718-63.[583] Richard Price, the architect of Pitt's reform act of 1786, presents a table which demonstrates how a £ 50 million credit would have paid off the Debt, had the Fund been rigorously applied from 1717 to 1771.[584] He also provides figures for the amount actually paid off for 1770-74.[585] Sinclair has data for the Fund for 1762-82.[586] Lauderdale lists the amounts paid off at five periods: 1723-24, 1727-34, 1736-38, 1751-52, and 1765-75.[587] Hamilton gives scattered early figures and annual figures for 1775-80.[588] For the effects of the act of 1786, there are statistics for 1786 to 1811 compiled by Hamilton; for 1794 to 1816, by Pebrer; and for 1794 to 1823, by Fairman.[589] William Playfair, excited in 1801 by the three-

[580]A table which shows the effect of applying this provision in peacetime, may be found in an anonymous pamphlet, *Considerations on the Sinking Fund* (1819), App. A, pp. 121-25.

[581]See the account by an advocate of the Sinking Fund: Pebrer, *Taxation . . . of the British Empire* (1833), Part 2, pp. 173-74, 181-84, 235-38. Mitchell and Deane, 406, have figures for redemption of the debt by the 'Sinking Fund' after 1835 (irregularly) but give no earlier figures.

[582]Postlethwayt, *History of the Public Revenue* (1759), 240-49.

[583]*An Annual Abstract of the Sinking Fund from Michaelmas 1718, when it was first stated to Parliament, to the 10th of October, 1763, by a Member of Parliament, Many Years in the Treasury; collected for his own private Amusement, and now made publick* (1764). Attributed to Sir Archibald Grant. Foxwell notes on the copy at Kress Library: "rare & valuable: the best account we have for this period."

[584]Price, *Appeal to the Public* (1772), 69-71.

[585]Price, *Observations on the Nature of Civil Liberty* (1776), 120.

[586]Sir John Sinclair, *Hints: addressed to the Public calculated to dispel the gloomy ideas which have been lately entertained of the state of our finances* (17-83), 21.

[587]James Maitland, the 8th Earl of Lauderdale, *An Inquiry into the Nature and Origin of Public Wealth* (Edinburgh, 1804), 233 n. *.

[588]Hamilton, *Inquiry concerning the . . . National Debt* (3rd ed., 1818), in McCulloch, ed., *Select Tracts on the National Debt* (1857), 529.

[589]Hamilton, *Inquiry concerning the . . . National Debt* (1813), 215-23; Pebrer, *Taxation . . . of the British Empire* (1833), Part 1, Table 33, facing 154; and

fold increase of the Fund since 1794, projected on one of his colored copper-plate graphs the erasure of the National Debt by 1855.[590]

The rates of interest on the Government's perpetual annuities, at 5 per cent in 1717, fell to 4 per cent ten years later; by the 1750's, the rate dropped to 3 per cent. Pelham in 1757 merged several issues into one 'Consolidated Stock.'[591] The sources for these stock prices, or 'Consols' as they were familiarly known appear in TABLE 43. John Castaing published twice weekly the prices of Bank, East India Company, South Sea, and other stocks from 1698 onwards.[592] The first writer to present full data on the Consols in historical sequence was Sir John Sinclair. Historian of the public revenue and editor of the multi-volume statistical survey of Scotland, Sinclair presents over a seventy-year period monthly averages of the prices of Consols and other stocks. By far the most comprehensive compilation, however, is that of James Van Sommer, Secretary to the Managers of the London Stock Exchange. In over one hundred pages, using bar graphs rather than tables, Van Sommer sets forth the weekly prices of the Consols from 1789 to 1847. Next to the vertical price axis (the horizontal axis representing time in weeks), he lists the dates of important events and occurrences which might affect stock prices. Mitchell and Deane, who do not print the prices of the Consols, do have a table of the percentage yield on the Consols since 1756.[593] T. S. Ashton has published the percentage yield on the Three Per Cents. from 1731 to 1801.[594]

The Bank of England, founded in 1694, was the leading private bank in the country and enjoyed virtually an official connection with the Government, since it was its leading creditor and the principal note-issuing institution in the kingdom. John Francis' *History of the Bank of England* (2 vols., 1847) is the leading work on the Bank in our period, but many statistical series may be found in other works.

Few eighteenth-century sources exist for the accounts of the Bank, because its affairs were then kept quite private. But James Postlethwayt does present various figures relating to "the historical state" of the Bank from 1694 to 1758, while Sinclair has figures through 1788.[595] Francis furnishes a list of the Directors from 1694 to 1847.[596] Only in the early nineteenth century, however, do statistical series of the Bank's activities appear. TABLE 44 presents the sources for statistics of the circulation and deposits and the securities and bullion of the Bank of England. A modern writer has graphed the various data for the period 1720-1800.[597] A few sources present only the amount of bullion in the possession

William Fairman, *An Account of the Public Funds, transferrable at the Bank of England* (7th ed.), revised by Bernard Cohen, 1824), 226.

[590]Playfair, *Statistical Breviary* (1801), Plate XXI.

[591]T. S. Ashton, *The Industrial Revolution, 1760-1830* (2nd ed., Oxford, 1962), 8-9.

[592]John Castaing, *The Course of the Exchange* (1698 *et seq.*). For a discussion of this work, see note 555.

[593]Mitchell and Deane, 455. Their series is complete through 1956.

[594]T. S. Ashton, *Economic Fluctuations in England 1700-1800* (Oxford, 1959), 187.

[595]Postlethwayt, *History of the Public Revenue* (1759), 301-10; Sinclair, *History of the Public Revenue* (3rd ed., 3 v., 1803-04), III (1804), 19.

[596]John Francis, *History of the Bank of England* (2 v., 1847), II, 262-66.

[597]J. H. Clapham, *The Bank of England* (2 v., Cambridge, 1944), I, App. C, p. 298.

Table 43

PRICES OF THE 3 PER CENT CONSOLS

Primary Sources

Government Documents

1786-1823: *J.H.C. 79*, 797. *a,b*

1797-1832: "S.C. on Bank of England Charter," *P.P. 1831-32* (722), VI, App. 94, pp. 96-97. *c*

1797-1842: *P.P. 1842* (580), XXVI, 244-45. *c*

1822-1846: *P.P. 1847-48* (3), XXXIX, 625. *a,d*

1834-1843: *P.P. 1844* (453), XXXII, 799. *d*

Books and Pamphlets

1731-1802; Sinclair, *History of the Public Revenue* (3rd ed., 3 v., 1803-04), II (1803), App. 2, pp. 28-48. *b,e,f*

1731-1822: Joplin, *Outlines of a System of Political Economy* (1823), App. 4, pp. 17-28. *a,e*

1731-1825: *Illustration of Mr. Joplin's Views on Currency* (1825), App. 17-18, pp. 112-19. *e*

1731-1847: Francis, *Chronicles and Characters* (1849), 384-85. *e*

1760-1826: Cohen, *Supplement to the Seventh Edition of Fairman on the Funds* (1827), 42-46. *g*

1789-1847: Van Sommer, *Tables exhibiting the Various Fluctuations in the Three Per Cent Consols* (1848), 1-121, 147. *d,h*

1792-1811: Wilson, *Observations on the Depreciation of Money* (1811), Table 2, pp. 51-54. *i*

1797-1832: Pebrer, *Taxation . . . of the Whole British Empire* (1833), Part 2, p. 281. *c*

1799-1831: Marshall, *Digest* (1833), Part 3, p. 180. *a*

Table 43
(continued)

<table>
<tr><td>*Government Documents*</td><td>*Books and Pamphlets*</td></tr>
<tr><td></td><td>1820-1847: McCulloch, *Dictionary*
(2 v., 1854), I, 611. *a*</td></tr>
</table>

Secondary Works

1727-1800: Ashton, *Economic History of England: the 18th Century* (1964), Table 13, p. 251. *a,j*

Mitchell and Deane: none.

---

a Annual average price.

b Also prices for the 3½, 4, and 5 per cent stocks.

c Prices on February 28 and August 31 annually.

d Highest and lowest prices in each year.

e Monthly average price.

f Also prices for East India Company, Bank, and South Sea stock.

g Prices on the first Thursday in February, May, August, and November.

h Weekly average price.

i Prices on the first day of January, April, July, and October.

j Prices for Bank stock also.

---

of the Bank.[598] Of interest also is the work of John Danson who uses diagrams to chart the Bank crises of 1836 and 1839.[599] For 1815-32 there are several sources which have figures for the amount of *coined gold* (as opposed to bullion) in the Bank's possession.[600] Two sources present data for the amounts of bul-

[598]For 1790-96, see *Reports [of the House of Commons] 1796-97* (134), XIX, App. 1, p. 155. For 1815-28 (annually, on February 28), see "Select Committee on the Bank of England Charter," *P.P. 1831-32* (722), VI, App. 85, p. 86. For 1834-43 (at four dates in each year), see John Hubbard, baron Addington, *The Currency and the Country* (1843), facing 56.

[599]John T. Danson, *The Accounts of the Bank of England* (1847), facing 16, 18.

[600]For 1815-32, see "Select Committee on the Bank of England Charter," *P.P. 1831-32* (722), VI, App. 75, p. 71; see also Pebrer, *Taxation . . . of the British Empire* (1833), Part 2, Table 16, p. 270. For 1814-32, see Michael Quin, *The Trade of Banking in England* (1833), App. G, pp. xix-xx.

Table 44

CIRCULATION, DEPOSITS, SECURITIES,
AND BULLION OF THE BANK OF ENGLAND

Primary Sources

Government Documents

1778-1832: "S.C. on Bank of England Charter," *P.P. 1831-32* (722), VI, App. 5, pp. 13-25. *a*

1778-1847: "Secret Committee on Commercial Distress," *P.P. 1847-48* (395), VIII Part 2, App. 4, pp. 7-9. *a*

1797-1841: *P.T. 11, P.P. 1843,* LVI, No. 15, pp. 11-12. *a*

1797-1842: *P.P. 1842* (580), XXVI, 246-47. *a*

1832-1840: "S.C. on Banks of Issue," *P.P. 1840* (602), IV, App. 12, pp. 25-96, 106-251. *b*

1841-1847: "Secret Committee on Commercial Distress," *P.P. 1847-48* (395), VIII Part 2, App. 8, pp. 25-143. *b*

Books and Pamphlets

1778-1831; McCulloch, *Dictionary* (1837), 86-90. *a*

1778-1832: *History of . . . Banking* (1833), facing 474. *a*

1778-1832: Marshall, *Digest* (1833), Part 3, pp. 170-71. *a*

1778-1832: Pebrer, *Taxation . . . of the Whole British Empire* (1833), Part 2, Table 14, pp. 255-69; Table 30, facing p. 279. *a*

1778-1832: Quin, *Trade of Banking* (1833), App. G, pp. xvi-xvii, xix-xx. *a*

1778-1832: Gilbart, *History . . . of Banking* (1834), 71.

1778-1844: Francis, *History of Bank of England* (2 v., 1847), II, 277-80. *a*

1781-1840: Macardy, *Outlines of . . . Banking* (1840), 68-106. *a,c*

1797-1819: Tooke, *Letter to Lord Grenville* (1829), 46. *d*

1833-1837: Porter, *Progress* (3 v., 1836-43), II (1838), 236-37. *a*

1834-1856: Tooke and Newmarch, *History of Prices* (6 v., 1838-57), VI (1857), 545-57, 583. *a*

Table 44
(continued)

Government Documents   *Books and Pamphlets*

1840-1847: Tooke, *History of Prices*
(6 v., 1838-57), IV (1848), 436-
46. b

Secondary Works

1720-1797: Clapham, *Bank of England* (2 v., 1944), I, App. C, pp. 295-97. e

1720-1850+: Mitchell and Deane, 441-44. e

---

a On February 28 and August 31 in each
year.

b Weekly figures.

c For 1832-40 figures are for ten dates
in each year.

d Figures at two to four dates in
each year.

e On August 31 for 1720-64; on
February 28 for 1766-73; on February
28 and August 31 after 1773.

---

lion bought and sold by the Bank *monthly* from 1832 to 1847.[601]
Various sources have statistics of the circulation of Bank of England notes
(see TABLE 45), in addition to those sources which give a comprehensive state
of the Bank's activities (see Table 44). The earliest figures (from 1698) were
published by J. R. McCulloch, who commented that

> no previously published table of the
> circulation of the Bank of England
> extends further back than 1777; we are
> indebted to the Court of Directors [of
> the Bank] for being able to supply this
> striking defect, and to exhibit, for the
> first time, the circulation of the Bank from
> within four years of its establishment down
> to the present day.[602]

He was correct to the extent that the Government had published no figures before

[601]For 1832-40, see "Select Committee on Banks of Issue," *P.P. 1840* (602), IV,
App. 23, p. 260; for 1832-47, see "Secret Committee on Commercial Distress," *P.P.
1847-48* (395), VIII Part 2, App. 21, pp. 193-95.
[602]McCulloch, *Dictionary* (1837), 93.

Table 45

CIRCULATION OF BANK OF ENGLAND NOTES

Primary Sources

Government Documents

1782-1784: "Lords Committee of Secrecy (1797) relating to the Bank," *P.P. 1810* (17), III, 328. *a*

1787-1796: "Lords Committee of Secrecy (1797) relating to the Bank," *P.P. 1810* (17), III, 328. *b*

1790-1796: *Reports 1796-97* (134), XIX, App. 21, p. 233. *c*

1790-1819: "Lords' Report on Cash Payments," *P.P. 1819* (291), III, App. B, pp. 320-22. *c,d*

1792-1832: "S.C. on Bank of England Charter," *P.P. 1831-32* (722); VI, App. 82-83, pp. 74-85. *c,e*

1796-1820: *J.H.C. 76*, 1185. *f*

1820-1831: *P.T. 1, P.P. 1833*, XLI, 3. *d*

1840-1844: *P.P. 1844* (95), XXXII, 220-254. *e*

1841-1847: "Secret Committee on Commercial Distress," *P.P. 1847-48* (395, 584), VIII Part 2, App. 8, pp. 25-143. *e*

Books and Pamphlets

1698-1721: J, Taylor, *Catechism of Foreign Exchanges* (1835), 50. *g*

1698-1792: McCulloch, *Dictionary* (1837), 93. *f*

1778-1832: Marshall, *Digest* (1833), Part 3, pp. 170-71. *d*

1782-1792: Tooke, *Considerations on the State of the Currency* (2nd ed., 1826), Table 5, pp. 193-94. *c*

1783-1818: Rooke, *Inquiry into the Principles of National Wealth* (1824), 470. *b*

1787-1796: *History of . . . Banking* (1833), 472-73. *b*

1787-1828: *Address to the Proprietors of Bank Stock* (1828), App. 9, p. 53. *h*

1790-1796: Allardyce, *Address to . . . the Bank of England* (1798), 76. *c*

1790-1832: James, *State of the Nation* (1835), table facing 1. *b,d*

1792-1819: Joplin, *Outlines of a System of Political Economy* (1832), App. 6, pp. 30-31. *f*

1792-1819: *Address to the Proprietors of Bank Stock* (1828), App. 7, pp. 46-47. *d,f*

Table 45
(Continued)

Government Documents   *Books and Pamphlets*

1792-1822: *Illustrations of Mr. Joplin's Views on Currency* (1825), App. 1, pp. 95-96. *i*

1792-1830: McCulloch, *Historical Sketch of the Bank of England* (1831), App. F, pp. 76-77. *d,f*

1792-1832: Pebrer, *Taxation . . . of the Whole British Empire* (1833), Part 2, Table 10, pp. 250-52. *c,d*

1792-1833: McCulloch, *Dictionary* (1837), 94. *d,f*

1792-1843: Alison, *England in 1815 and 1845* (1845), appendix, facing p. 94. *h*

1793-1820: Tooke, *On the Currency* (1829), 8. *f*

1797-1815: Ricardo, *Proposals for an Economical and Secure Currency* (2nd ed., 1816), App. 4, p. 104. *b,d*

1797-1822: Tooke, *Letter to Lord Grenville* (1829), App. 3, p. 131. *d,f*

1798-1810: Ricardo, *Observations on . . . Paper Currency* (1811), 24. *b,d*

1833-1849: Porter, *Progress* (1851), 432-33. *c*

1841-1853: McCulloch, *Dictionary* (2 v., 1854), II, 1436-37. *j*

Table 45
(continued)

Secondary Works

1720-1764 (*g*)
1766-1773 (*b*)   Clapham, *The Bank of England* (2 v., 1944), I, App. C,
1775-1797 (*f*)   pp. 295-98.

1720-1843: Coppieters, *English Bank Note Circulation* (1955), appendix, Table
6, pp. 149-51. *d,g,k*

1720-1764 (*g*)
1766-1773 (*b*)   Mitchell and Deane, 441-44.
1775-1850+(*f*)

[a] On the first day of March, June, October, and December in each year.

[b] On the last day of February in each year.

[c] At the end of the quarterly period in each year.

[d] Differentiates the total value of notes above and below the denomination of £5.

[e] At the close of every business week.

[f] On the last day of February and August in each year.

[g] On the last day of August in each year.

[h] Annual average circulation.

[i] On the last day of June and December in each year.

[j] At a date once every four weeks.

[k] Rounded to the nearest tenth of a million pounds sterling.

1777, but Taylor (1835) had published series before that date (see Table 45), while Rooke (1824) provided figures at nine dates between 1718 and 1778.[603]

One of the important functions of the Bank was as creditor to the Government. Several sources furnish figures for the advances made to Government on Exchequer Bills from 1777 to 1828.[604]

For the prices of Bank of England stock, the leading compilers are Sinclair, who has monthly figures for 1731-1802 and Francis, who gives the highest and lowest price in each year from 1732 to 1846.[605] Two writers may be consulted for data on the annual profits of the Bank,[606] while several sources give scattered figures for the dividends paid on Bank of England stock before 1790, with complete series after that date.[607]

The Bank of Ireland was of little importance or interest to contemporary British statisticians. The longest series, provided by McCulloch, is for that Bank's note circulation for 1797-1819 and 1841-53.[608] Lauderdale lists monthly prices

[603]John Rooke, *An Inquiry into the Principles of National Wealth* (Edinburgh, 1824), 470.

[604]For 1777-1828, see *An Address to the Proprietors of Bank Stock, the London and Country Bankers and the Public in General, on the Affairs of the Bank of England* (1828), App. 5-6, 9, pp. 43-45, 53; for 1781-93, see Joseph Macardy, *Outlines of Banks, Banking, and Currency* (Manchester, 1840), 68; for 1792-1819, see Joplin, *Outlines of a System of Political Economy* (1823) App. 9, pp. 36-38; for 1797-1816, see *J.H.C. 71*, 978-82; and for 1819-25, see Quin, *Trade of Banking in England* (1833), App. G, p. xviii.

[605]Sir John Sinclair, *History of the Public Revenue* (3rd. ed., 3 v., 1803-04), II (1803), App. 2, pp. 28-48; John Francis, *History of the Bank of England* (2 v., 1847), II, 260-61. Other sources: for 1796-1809, see "Select Committee on the High Price of Bullion," *P.P. 1810* (349), III, App. 44, p. 194; for 1807-28, see *An Address to the Proprietors of Bank Stock . . .* (1828), App. 4, p. 42; for 1811-30, see Thomas Joplin, *The Advantages of the Proposed National Bank of England, both to the Public and its Proprietory, briefly explained* (1833), 20. T. S. Ashton, *An Economic History of England: the 18th Century* (1964 ed.), Table 13, p. 251, has Bank stock prices for 1700-1800.

[606]For 1779-1832, see James W. Gilbart, *The History and Principles of Banking* (1834), 75; for 1790-1831, see Quin, *Trade of Banking in England* (1833), App. E, pp. ix-xi.

[607]A. Allardyce, *An Address to the Proprietors of the Bank of England* (3rd ed., 1798), 129, has dividends at eighteen dates between 1694 and 1788. *An Address to the Proprietors of Bank Stock . . .* (1828), App. 2, p. 40, and Quin, *Trade of Banking in England* (1833), App. E, p.ix,both give dividends at thirteen dates from 1694 to 1788. For annual dividends between 1790 and 1831, see the "Select Committee on the Bank of England Charter," *P.P. 1831-32* (722), VI, App. 34, p. 42, or Quin, *Trade of Banking in England* (1833), App. E, pp. ix-xi. For 1811-30, see Joplin, *Advantages of the Proposed National Bank of England . . .* (1833), 20. Francis, *History of the Bank of England* (2 v., 1847), II, 267-76, sets out the annual dividends paid with the rate of discount from 1694 to 1847.

[608]For 1797-1819, see McCulloch, *Dictionary* (1837), 106; for 1841-53, see the 1854 edition of the above work, vol. 2, pp. 1436-37. Peter King, *Thoughts on the Restriction of Payments in Specie at the Banks of England and Ireland* (1803), 106, has quarterly figures for 1797 and 1801-03. Porter, *Progress* (1851), 434, has quarterly figures for 1842-49.

171

of Bank of Ireland stock for 1798-1804.[609] Macardy gives a very short statistical survey of the history of the Bank of Ireland.[610] The comparative neglect by
contemporaries has been remedied by a modern scholar, F. G. Hall, in a massive
work on *The Bank of Ireland, 1783-1946* (Dublin and Oxford, 1949).[611]
   Country banking had its great period of growth from 1780 to 1815. The definitive history is L. S. Pressnell's *Country Banking in the Industrial Revolution*
(Oxford, 1956), a thorough and critical study which interweaves text and statistics. Various *Directories* may be consulted as sources for the number of country
banks before the official recording of statistics began in 1809.[612] An act of
1808, 48 Geo.III,c. 149, required each office to take out a license from the Stamp
Office. But there are statistical snares in the procedures of registration.
Each office had to be licensed, but there was no distinction between branches and
central offices of the banks. Those offices, moreover, which existed before 1808
did not need a license. Non-issuing banks were not licensed until 1821, but there
were few of these outside Lancashire. Finally, it must be stressed that the figures do not reflect the reality of country *banking* for there were many unlicensed
agents and merchants who performed banking services.[613] Official figures from
1808 to 1818 appear in a select committee report.[614] An anonymous pamphlet of
1821 has figures for 1811-19, by county and the number of banks and partners, in
England, Wales, and Scotland.[615] A select committee report has statistics for
1808-32.[616] Gilbart and McCulloch each provide figures for 1809-32.[617] Finally,
a parliamentary paper has data from 1820 to 1842.[618] There is also more detailed
information for selected years: 1810, 1813, 1830.[619] Pressnell has assembled the

[609]James Maitland, the 8th Earl of Lauderdale, *Thoughts on the Alarming State
of the Circulation and on the Means of Redressing the Pecuniary Grievances in Ireland* (Edinburgh, 1805), App. 4, pp. 115-17.
   [610]Macardy, *Outlines of Banks, Banking, and Currency* (Manchester, 1840), 136-38.
   [611]For a series of Bank of Ireland note issues from 1783 to 1922, see Appendix
E, pp. 391-98, in Hall's work; the figures are *quarterly* for 1783-1844 (after 1802,
differentiating notes over and under £ 5) and annually for 1845-1922. See Appendix G, p. 399, in the same book for the dividends paid on Bank of Ireland stock
from 1783 to 1946, for a list of the Governors of the Bank from 1783, and for a
list of the branches of the Bank since 1825.
   [612]See L. S. Pressnell, *Country Banking in the Industrial Revolution* (Oxford,
1956), 4-9.
   [613]Pressnell, *Country Banking,* (Oxford, 1956), 9-11.
   [614]"Select Committee on the Resumption of Cash Payments," *P.P. 1819* (291), III,
App. F-9, pp. 416-19. The statistics are differentiated by county and number of
banks and partners in England and Scotland.
   [615]*A Review of the Banking System of Britain; with observations on the injurious effects of the Bank of England Charter, and the general benefits of unrestricted banking companies* (Edinburgh, 1821), table facing 248.
   [616]"Select Committee on the Bank of England Charter," *P.P. 1831-32* (722), VI,
App. 98, p. 111.
   [617]Gilbart, *History and Principles of Banking* (1834), 95; McCulloch, *Dictionary* (1837), 99.
   [618]*P.P. 1843* (85), LII, 9-20. The figures are for the number of private banks
for 1820-42; for the number of joint-stock banks, for 1826-42.
   [619]For detailed county and town figures for 1810, see George Chalmers, *Considerations on Commerce, Bullion and Coin, Circulation and Exchange* (2nd ed., 1811),

data in a table covering the periods 1784-98 (irregularly) and 1800-42; another modern writer, Emmanuel Coppieters, sets out statistics for the number of private and joint-stock banks from 1809 to 1842.[620]

There is a long (1780-1830) series of the number of commissions of bankruptcy issued against country bankers. First appearing in a select committee report,[621] the table was reprinted by Pebrer (1833), McCulloch (1837), and Macardy (1840).[622] Unfortunately, the figures are of limited usefulness. Because of the double-counting of firms receiving more than one commission of bankruptcy, the figures reflect only the number of commissions, not the number of actual bank failures.

Among the most abundant data relating to country banking are the figures of the amount of duties paid (beginning in 1804) to the Stamp Office by bankers in return for the right to issue private bank-notes: see TABLE 46. L. S. Pressnell, in a concise piece of demolition work, has disabused historians of the utility of the stampings for measuring note circulation. He has concluded that the 'life' of the bank notes was sometimes from five to nine years instead of the two or three that had been assumed, and that the amounts which the banks kept in reserve, once thought to be 10 per cent of total deposits, actually in times of depression (which were frequent in our period) approached 25 per cent. Further, un-stamped notes were commonly in circulation; notes were issued only to specified banking partners, so that whenever changes in ownership occurred new notes had to be issued, and any notes which had already been issued to a firm could not legally be used until the name of the erstwhile partner(s) had been removed from the notes. Changes of partners were, in fact, frequent and the law was probably, almost of necessity, irregularly observed— all of which merely further complicates interpretation of the statistics. Differing with Silberling and Clapham, Pressnell concludes that the wisest course is to avoid entirely 'guess-timates' of note circulation based on the stamp-duties figures: "To yield to the temptation to use faulty statistics because no others are available may lead only to faulty conclusions."[623]

The joint-stock banks were authorized in 1826.[624] Seven or more partners with varying amounts of capital might form a bank on the principle of limited liability. The joint-stock banks began a serious competition with the private banks, but both were hurt by the authorization of *branches* of the Bank of England anywhere in England and by restrictions in 1829 and 1844 on the note issue of pri-

App. 3, pp. 217-37; for 1813, see *List of Country Bankers* (1813), 1-88; for 1830, see *Twigg's Corrected List of the Country Bankers of England and Wales* (1830), 33-81, which includes a manuscript list of country bankers in Ireland and Scotland (p. 83 ff.).

[620]Pressnell, *Country Banking* (Oxford, 1956), Table 1, p. 11; Coppieters, *English Bank Note Circulation, 1694-1954* (Louvain, 1955), appendix, Table 8, p. 158.

[621]"Select Committee on the Bank of England Charter," *P.P.* 1831-32 (722), VI, App. 101, pp. 115-16. A series for 1816-26 is in *J.H.C. 81*, 722-25.

[622]Pebrer, *Taxation . . . of the British Empire* (1833), Part 2, Table 36, p. 284; McCulloch, *Dictionary* (1837), 95, has figures for 1809-30; Macardy, *Outlines of Banks, Banking, and Currency* (Manchester, 1840), 127, has statistics for 1805-30. Coppieters, *English Bank Note Circulation, 1694-1954* (Louvain, 1955), appendix, Table 8, p. 158, presents a bankruptcy series for 1809-30.

[623]Pressnell, *Country Banking* (Oxford, 1956), 189. The above criticisms are derived from Pressnell's work (pp. 180-89).

[624]7 Geo.IV, c. 26.

Table 46

TOTAL VALUE OF PRIVATE NOTES ON WHICH STAMP DUTIES WERE PAID

Primary Sources

Government Documents

1805-1818: "Lords' Report on Cash Payments," *P.P. 1819* (291), III, App. F-1, pp. 396-97. *a*

1805-1820: *J.H.C. 76,* 942. *a*

1819-1826: *P.P. 1826-27* (125), XVII, 34-35. *a,b*

1820-1824: *J.H.C. 80,* 931. *a*

1826-1832: *P.P. 1833* (456), XXIII, 328-29. *a,b*

Books and Pamphlets

1805-1825: Mushet, *An Attempt to Explain . . , the Issues of the Bank of England* (1826), App. 2, p, 215. *c*

1805-1831: Marshall, *Digest* (1833), Part 3, p. 172. *a*

1807-1825: McCulloch, *Dictionary* (1837), 100. *c*

1810-1825: *Illustration of Mr. Joplin's Views on Currency* (1825), p. xxii, and App. 4, p. 99.

1810-1825: Yates, *Essays on Currency and Circulation* (1827), App. C-2, p. 168.

1810-1825: Joplin, *Analysis . . . of the Currency Question* (1832), 89, 122-23.

1813-1822: Joplin, *Views on the Currency* (1828), 31.

1814-1826: Marshall, *Digest* (1833), Part 3, pp. 62-63.

1814-1842: Alison, *England in 1815 and 1845* (1845), appendix, facing p. 94.

1819-1828: *Address to the Proprietors of Bank Stock* (1828), App. 14, p. 91. *a*

Table 46
(continued)

Government Documents	*Books and Pamphlets*
	1820-1825: Wade, *Digest of Facts* (1826), App. 3, pp. 109-10. *a*
	1820-1831: Gilbart, *History and Principles of Banking* (1834), 96. *a*

Secondary Works

1805-1825: Pressnell, *Country Banking in the Industrial Revolution* (1956), Table 16, p. 188. *d,e*

1807-1825: Coppieters, *English Bank Note Circulation* (1955), App. 7, pp. 154-56. *e*

Figures are for the amounts annually stamped unless otherwise noted.

a Differentiates six categories of note denominations from £1 to £100.

b Amounts in each quarterly period of the year.

c Gives the annual percentage increase or decrease as well as absolute amounts.

d Differentiates amounts for notes of denominations above and below £2, 2 s.

e Rounded to the nearest tenth of a million pounds sterling.

---

vate banks. A select committee of 1836 lists the eighty joint-stock banks created since 1826,[625] and other sources carry the figures through 1846.[626] The

[625]"Select Committee on the Joint-Stock Banks," *P.P. 1836* (591), IX, App. 65, pp. 660-61.

[626]For the number of registered private and joint-stock banks from 1826-42, see *P.P. 1843* (85), LII, 9. Several writers present statistics. For 1826-36, see Porter, *Progress* (3 v., 1836-43), II (1838), 218-21; for 1827-36, see McCulloch, *Dictionary* (1837), 99, and *ibid.*, "Supplement," 11-15; for 1826-37, see Macardy, *Outlines of Banks, Banking, and Currency* (Manchester, 1840), 122-26. McCulloch, *Dictionary* (2 v., 1854), I, 107-10, lists the existing banks in England in 1846 with their dates of founding. For Irish private and joint-stock banks, see Macardy, *Outlines of Banks, Banking, and Currency* (Manchester, 1840), 204.

Table 47

CIRCULATION OF PRIVATE AND JOINT STOCK BANK NOTES

Primary Sources

Government Documents

1833-1839: "S.C. on Banks of Issue," *P.P. 1840* (602), IV, App. 2, p. 3 (*a*); App. 29, pp. 265-70 (*b*)

1834-1856: "S.C. on Bank Acts," *P.P. 1857* (220-I-Sess. 2), X Part 2, App. 15-16, pp. 148-81. *c,d*

1844-1847: "Secret Committee on Commercial Distress," *P.P. 1847-48* (395,584), VIII Part 2, App. 24, pp. 201-03. *b*

Books and Pamphlets

1833-1840: Macardy, *Outlines of . . . Banking* (1840), 200-01. *c*

1833-1841: Page, *Banks and Bankers* (2nd ed., 1843), 321-24. *c*

1834-1837: Porter, *Progress* (3 v., 1836-43), II (1838), 236-37. *a*

1834-1854: Tooke and Newmarch, *History of Prices* (6 v., 1838-57), VI (1857), 583. *e*

1838-1849: Porter, *Progress* (1851), 432-33. *a*

1840-1847: Tooke, *History of Prices* (6 v., 1838-57), IV (1848), 447-48. *c*

1841-1853: McCulloch, *Dictionary* (2 v., 1854), II, 1436-37. *c*

Secondary Works

1833-1875: Coppieters, *English Bank Note Circulation* (1955), App. 7, pp. 154-56. *f*

1833-1920: Mitchell and Deane, 450-51. *g*

1834-1857: Pressnell, *Country Banking in the Industrial Revolution* (1956), Table 10, p. 160. *f,h*

176

Table 47
(continued)

^{a} At the end of the quarterly period in each year.

^{b} On the last day of every week in each year.

^{c} On a date once every four weeks.

^{d} For 1844-56 aggregate *daily* circulation.

^{e} Annual average circulation.

^{f} Rounded to the nearest tenth of a million pounds sterling.

^{g} Totals for country banks generally; no differentiation of private and joint-stock banks.

^{h} Average circulation for January in each year.

---

circulation of bank notes, distinguishing private from joint-stock banks, is set out in TABLE 47. William Leatham, a Quaker banker in Wakefield, furnishes a most interesting chart of twenty-six occupations of the 188 shareholders of 5,000 shares in a joint-stock bank in Yorkshire in 1838.[627]

Savings banks were established in 1817 to make it possible for working men to deposit small sums of money (a maximum of £ 150 was allowed) which would earn a small rate of interest. H. Oliver Horne, the modern authority, sets out statistics of the number of depositors and total balances in all savings banks, annually from 1829.[628] The contemporary statistician, G. R. Porter, published data for the number of banks, the number of depositors and amount of deposits, and the balances of accounts from 1830 to 1849.[629]

Bills of exchange were of great importance at the heart of the Industrial Revolution in Lancashire. The larger transactions assumed this form, and it was not uncommon for some bills — say, for £ 10 — to bear sixty or more signatures. Estimates for the circulation of the bills of exchange are based on

[627]William Leatham, *Letters on the Currency* (1840), 70.

[628]H. Oliver Horne, *A History of Savings Banks* (Oxford, 1947), App. 2, pp. 386-91; a series for 1817-1934 is reprinted in Mitchell and Deane, 453-54. Horne also lists the dates at which savings banks were established from 1812 to beyond 1850 (Appendix 1, pp. 379-85).

[629]G. R. Porter, "Sketch of the Progress and Present Extent of Savings Banks in the United Kingdom," *J.S.S.L.*, IX (1846), 3-4. Porter, *Progress* (3 v., 1836-43), III (1843), 143-46, gives figures for 1830-41 (in the same volume, p. 148, he lists the occupations of depositors in banks in the Manchester environs in 1842). In a later edition of *Progress* (1851), 612-13, Porter provides data for 1830-49. Neil Smelser, *Social Change in the Industrial Revolution* (Chicago, 1959), 374, distinguishes ten occupational classes among the depositors in the Manchester and Salford Savings Bank in the period 1821-39.

177

Table 48

NUMBER OF COMMISSIONS OF BANKRUPTCY

Primary Sources

Government Documents	*Books and Pamphlets*

Government Documents

1780-1830: "S.C. on the Bank of England Charter," *P.P. 1831-32* (722), VI, App. 101, pp. 115-16.

1790-1818: "Lords' Report on Cash Payments," *P.P. 1819* (291), III, App. G-3, p. 426.

1834-1840: "S.C. on Banks of Issue," *P.P. 1841* (366), V, App. 30, p. 318.

Books and Pamphlets

1700-1798: Chalmers, *Estimate* (1794), p. xlii.

1700-1797: Doubleday, *A Financial . . . History of England* (1847), 130.

1748-1797: Sinclair, *History of the Public Revenue* (3 v., 1803-04), II (1803), App. 6, p. 62.

1780-1830: Taylor, "Currency Fallacies," in Taylor, *Currency Investigated* (1844), appendix, p. 83.

1790-1818: Joplin, *Essay . . . on Banking* (1823), p. 6, note.

1790-1823: Tooke, *Thoughts and Details* (1824), App. 1, No. 7, p. 14; also in Powell, *Statistical Illustrations* (1825), 61.

1790-1826: Wade, *Digest of Facts* (1826), App. 7, p. 114.

1791-1840: Bischoff, *Comprehensive History* (2 v., 1842), II, appendix, Table 10.

1807-1821: Rooke, *Inquiry into . . . Wealth* (1824), 472.

Secondary Works

1710-1825: Pressnell, *Country Banking in the Industrial Revolution* (1956), 74, and App. 20, pp. 536-38.

All figures are for national totals.

stamp duties; the statistical problems which arise in using the duties to determine country bank note circulation fortunately do not exist for the bills. Wade furnishes figures for 1805-25, while Tooke has data for the circulation in 1830-53.[630] William Leatham, on whom Pressnell relies, presents estimates at nine dates from 1815 to 1839.[631] Mitchell and Deane give no figures.

Bankruptcy statistics date from 1710, with the keeping of the docket books of the High Court of Justice in Bankruptcy. Most printed sources, however, have figures only after 1780, with the exception of Chalmers (1794), Sinclair (1803), and Doubleday (1847), as TABLE 48 indicates. There are two main problems in the bankruptcy statistics. First, the figures may in some cases be for dockets drawn up in court, not for the issuing of commissions or the actual failure of banks. Many dockets were drawn up which did not result in commissions. Secondly, there is the problem of double-counting. Commissions were issued against partners and branches of a firm, not against the bank itself, so there is an inevitable inflation in the bankruptcy figures. Pressnell has figured that in one list the difference is on the order of 20 per cent.[632]

One final set of statistics might be mentioned. Data for the forgeries of bank notes may be of more interest to the social than to the economic historian. Figures exist for the number of persons convicted and capitally convicted for having in their possession forged Bank of England notes. A parliamentary paper of 1821 has statistics for 1790 to 1820,[633] and McCulloch prints figures for 1791-1829.[634] A modern writer, Emmanuel Coppieters, lists by thirteen categories of pound notes (up to £ 500 in value) the total number of forged notes presented at the Bank in the periods, 1806-10, 1811-20, 1821, 1821-30, 1831-40, and 1841-50.[635]

[630]John Wade, *Digest of Facts and Principles on Banking and Commerce* (1826), App. 6, p. 113 (foreign and inland bills differentiated); Tooke and Newmarch, *History of Prices* (6 v., 1838-57), VI (1857), App. 11, pp. 584-608.

[631]William Leatham, *Letters on the Currency* (1840), 67-68. Reprinted in Pressnell, *Country Banking* (Oxford, 1956), 172.

[632]Pressnell, *Country Banking* (Oxford, 1956), 447. The source to which he refers is the "Select Committee on the Bank of England Charter," *P.P. 1831-32* (722), VI, App. 101, pp. 115-16. The 407 commissions of bankruptcy issued between 1780 and 1830 refer to 321 banking firms, according to Pressnell (*Country Banking* [Oxford, 1956], 443-48). See also Pressnell's revised table of bankruptcies (from 1710 to 1825) which allows for double-counting (Appendix 20, pp. 536-38) and his graph of the number of *bankruptcies* and of bankrupt country *banks* from 1775 to 1830 (Appendix 27, p. 545).

[633]*P.P. 1821* (264), XVI, 187. For shorter series, see for 1812-16, *J.H.C. 71*, 983; for 1816-18, *J.H.C. 73*, 762. See *J.H.C. 73*, 762-64, for the expenditures of the Bank of England at various places for the prosecution of persons charged with forgery between 1797 and 1818.

[634]J. R. McCulloch, *Historical Sketch of the Bank of England* (1831), App. A, 69-71. Reprinted in his *Dictionary* (1837), 85.

[635]Coppieters, *English Bank Note Circulation, 1694-1954* (Louvain, 1955), appendix, Table 5, p. 148.

Because of the specific and precise nature of this guide to the sources of economic statistics—its purpose being that of a compendium or handbook—it is difficult to draw meaningful general conclusions. Some, however, do come to mind. One seems to be the inordinate importance of Scottish writers. Like economic theory, which was represented by Adam Smith and James Mill, economic statistics was the domain of Scotsmen. The pre-eminence of men like George Chalmers, David Macpherson, William Playfair, Patrick Colquhoun, Andrew Ure, and John Ramsay McCulloch is surprising given the size of their native land; in our period Scotland, three-fifths as large as England, was only one-sixth as populous. Of course Englishmen did make contributions: Charles Whitworth, Edward Baines, James Postlethwayt, George Richardson Porter, and others may be recalled. Yet, on balance, the high proportion of Scotsmen is surprising. Why this is the case —whether because of the religious training or strong morality, the strenuous work-ethic or the educational system, in Scotland—is a question beyond the purposes of this essay.

Another general observation would appear to be that the statisticians, while revolutionary in their tabular economic presentations, were conservative and patriotic in politics. The tabulators of the output of the Industrial Revolution were uniformly hostile to the American and French Revolutions and to radicalism at home. Perhaps this should not be surprising; economic output depends upon order, continuity, and subordination among the working classes. For whatever reasons, the contrast of the statisticians' revolutionary methodology and their political and social conservatism is striking.

The development of economic statistics paralleled the growth of the economy. The first economic statisticians—Whitworth, Chalmers, and Playfair—were writing at the time of the 'take-off' of the Industrial Revolution in the late 1770's and the 1780's. Later writers, from Macpherson during the war years to Porter in the 1840's, set out in tabular form the statistics which reflected that unprecedented growth in output and trade which constituted the English economic revolution. The use of tables (and, by Playfair, of graphs) simply made clearer and more indelible the impression of England's unquestioned economic supremacy. The science of economic statistics was therefore a kind of self-congratulation which could not be controverted since it rested solidly on 'the facts.' This revolutionary insistence on 'hard data' is a legacy which is today very much present in the workshops of economists, sociologists, and historians.

The purpose of this essay has been merely to point out for the use of today's economic historians those tables or bodies of data on various subjects which writers before 1850 assembled for their own purposes. The biases and shortcomings in some of the statistics have been mentioned, but it has not been the purpose of this compendium to stress this aspect of the figures. Many of the authors of the works mentioned in this bibliography point out the statistical problems and emphasize the delicacy with which some figures must be treated.

In the end, quantitative precision is of course important only insofar as it

relates to our understanding of the qualitative aspects of the age. While Quanti-
fication should not be made the new religion, neither should it be rejected out-
right. For men—however vehemently some may protest—must deal with numbers.
The world of numbers and the world of ideas are not discrete universes: matters
of quantitative preponderance have a way of effecting qualitative changes. The
Malachy Postlethwayts and their more number-conscious brothers, the James Postlethwayts, are more closely related than they would appear. We may perhaps believe
with the artisans who formed the first London Statistical Society that not only
are "exhibitions of well-arranged statistical facts" helpful to "promote the wel-
fare of society," they also "exemplify the way of God to man."[636]

[636]John Powell, *Statistical Illustrations* (1827), dedication.

BIBLIOGRAPHY

Individual government publications are not listed here, but may be found throughout the essay. The different kinds of official sources (used by the author in the Documents Division of Widener Library, Harvard University), and the key to short-title references, are listed below:

A. & P.	Accounts and papers, in the collection of papers printed, at the request of Speaker Abbot, by order of the House of Commons, from 1731 to 1800. 1807; reprinted, 1954
Commons' Committees	First Series, or reports from committees of the House of Commons, 1715-1801, forming a series of 15 volumes of reports. 1803; reprinted, 1953
J.H.C.	*Journals [of the Proceedings] of the House of Commons*, 89 vols., 1699-1834
P.P.	*Parliamentary Papers*, being the accounts and papers and select committee reports of the Houses of Commons and Lords, 1801-52
P.T.	*Porter's Tables*, being a comprehensive annual statistical return (Nos. 1-18, from 1833 to 1850) in the *Parliamentary Papers*
Rep.	Reports, in the collection of papers printed, at the request of Speaker Abbot, by order of the House of Commons, from 1731 to 1800. 1807; reprinted, 1954.

And for private publications:

D.N.B.	*The Dictionary of National Biography*, 22 vols., Oxford, 1885-1901; reprinted, 1963-64
J.S.S.L.	*Journal of the Statistical Society of London*, later the Royal Statistical Society; vols. 1-13 (1838-50)
T.R.G.S.C.	*Transactions of the Royal Geological Society of Cornwall*, vols. 1-7 (1818-65)

183

The following list includes those primary and secondary works which contain statistical data cited in the present essay. For each entry, *the place of publication is London, unless otherwise noted.*

PRIMARY SOURCES

Addington, 1st Baron, John Gellibrand Hubbard. *The Currency and the Country.* 1843.
An Address to the Proprietors of Bank Stock, the London and Country Bankers and the Public in General, on the Affairs of the Bank of England. 1828.
Alison, Archibald. *England in 1815 and 1845: or, a sufficient and a contracted currency.* Edinburgh and London, 1845.
Allardyce, A. *An Address to the Proprietors of the Bank of England.* 3rd ed., 1798.
—— *A Second Address to the Proprietors of Bank of England Stock.* 1801.
Anderson, Adam. *An Historical and Chronological Deduction of the Origin of Commerce from the earliest accounts to the present time, containing an History of the great Commercial Interests of the British Empire. To which is prefixed an Introduction exhibiting a View of the ancient and modern State of Europe; of the Importance of our Colonies; and of the Commerce, Shipping, Manufactures, Fisheries, &c., of Great Britain and Ireland, and their Influence on the Landed Interest, with an Appendix containing the Modern Politico-Commercial Geography of the several Countries of Europe.* 2 v., 1764; 2nd ed., 4 v., 1787-89.
An Annual Abstract of the Sinking Fund from Michaelmas 1718, when it was first stated to Parliament, to the 10th of October, 1763, by a Member of Parliament, Many Years in the Treasury; collected for his own private Amusement, and now made publick. 1764.
Atcheson, Nathaniel. *A Letter addressed to Rowland Burdon on the Present State of the Carrying Part of the Coal Trade. With Tables of Several of the Duties on Coals received by the Corporation of the City of London.* 1802.
Atkinson, Jasper. *Considerations on the Propriety of the Bank of England Resuming its Payments in Specie at the Period prescribed by the Act 37th, George III.* 1802.

Badcock, Benjamin. *Tables Exhibiting the Prices of Wheat, from the Year 1100 to 1830; also the Prices of Beans, Barley, and Oats from 1790 to 1830.* 1832.
Baines, Edward. *A History of the Cotton Manufactures in Great Britain.* 1835.
Banks, Sir Joseph. *The Propriety of Allowing a Qualified Exportation of Wool.* 1782.
Barclay, John. *Statistics of the Scotch Iron Trade.* Glasgow, 1850.
Beeke, Henry. *Observations on the Produce of the Income Tax and its Proportion to the whole Income of Great Britain.* 1800.
Bischoff, James. *A Comprehensive History of the Woollen and Worsted Manufactures.* 2 v., 1842.

Blake, William. *Observations on the Principles which Regulate the Course of Exchange; and on the Present Depreciated State of the Currency.* 1810.

Boucherett, Ayscoghe. *A Few Observations on Corn, Currency, &c. with a Plan for Promoting the Interests of Agriculture and Manufactures.* 1840.

Brownell, Charles. *A Letter to the Right Honourable the Earl of Clarendon, President of the Board of Trade, on the Copper Ore Duties, in reply to the Letter of Sir Charles Lemon, Bart.* 1847.

The Builder's Price Book. 1788.

Burn, Richard. *Statistics of the Cotton Trade arranged in a Tabular Form; also a Chronological History of its Various Inventions, Improvements, etc., etc.* 1847.

Carne, Joseph. "Statistics of the Tin Mines of Cornwall and of the Consumption of Tin in Great Britain," *Journal of the Statistical Society of London,* II (1839), 260-67.

Carte, Thomas. *A Full and Clear Vindication of the Full Answer to a Letter from a Bystander.* 1743.

Castaing, John. *The Course of the Exchange.* 1698, and annually thereafter.

Cayley, Edward S. *On Commercial Economy, in Six Essays; viz., Machinery, Accumulation of Capital, Production, Consumption, Currency, and Free Trade.* 1830.

Chalmers, George. *Considerations on Commerce, Bullion and Coin, Circulation and Exchanges; with a View to our Present Circumstances.* 2nd ed., 1811.

——— *An Estimate of the Comparative Strength of Britain during the Present and Four Preceding Reigns; and of the Losses of Her Trade from every War since the Revolution.* 1782; 2nd ed., 1794; 3rd ed., 1802; 4th ed., 1804; 5th ed., 1810. Beginning with the 1794 edition, the title is slightly changed to, ". . . of Great-Britain . . ."; with the 1810 edition, to ". . . of Great Britain . . .".

——— *An Historical View of the Domestic Economy of Great Britain and Ireland,* Edinburgh, 1812.

Chronology of Public Events and Remarkable Occurrences within the last Fifty Years; or, from 1771 to 1821. 1821.

Clarke, Thomas B. *A Survey of the Strength and Opulence of Great Britain.* 1801.

Cohen, Bernard. *Supplement to the Seventh Edition of [William] Fairman on the Funds.* 1827.

Colquhoun, Patrick. *A Treatise on the Wealth, Power, and Resources of the British Empire.* 1814; 2nd ed., 1815.

Congleton, 1st Baron, Sir Henry Brooke Parnell. *On Financial Reform.* 1830.

Considerations on the Sinking Fund. 1819.

Considerations relative to a Plan of Relief for the Cotton Manufactury. 1788.

Courtenay, J. S. "A Treatise on the Statistics of Cornwall," *The Sixth Annual Report of the Royal Cornwall Polytechnic Society* (Falmouth, 1838), pp. 81-153, in *Royal Cornwall Polytechnic Society Reports, 1833-1838.*

Courtenay, Thomas Peregrine. *Observations upon the Present State of the Finances of Great Britain; suggested by Mr. Morgan's Supplement to his 'Comparative View,' and by Mr. Addington's Financial Measures.* 1803.

Cunningham, Timothy. *The History of our Customs, Aids, Subsidies, National Debts and Taxes from William the Conqueror to the Present Year.* 1761; 2nd ed., 1773; 3rd ed., revised by Sir Charles Whitworth, 1778.
Cursory Observations on some parts of the evidence before the Committees of both Houses of Parliament, on the expediency of resuming cash-payments at the Bank of England. 1819.

Danson, John Towne. *The Accounts of the Bank of England.* 1847.
Davenant, Charles. *Discourses on the Publick Revenues, and on the Trade of England, Part 2.* 2 v., 1698.
—— *New Dialogues upon the Present Posture of Affairs, the Species of Money, the National Debts, Publick Revenues, Bank and East-India Company, and the Trade now carried on between France and Holland.* 2 v., 1710.
—— *The Political and Commercial Works of that Celebrated Writer, Charles D'Avenant.* Collected and revised by Sir Charles Whitworth. 5 v., 1771.
—— *A Report to the Honourable the Commissioners for putting in Execution the Act, intituled an Act for the taking, examining, and stating the Publick Accounts of the Kingdom.* 1711.
—— *A Second Report to the Honourable the Commissioners for putting in Execution the Act, intituled an Act for the taking, examining, and stating the Publick Accounts of the Kingdom.* 1712.
Doubleday, Thomas. *A Financial, Monetary and Statistical History of England from the Revolution of 1688 to the Present Time.* 1847.
Dudley, Dud. *Metallum Martis: or, Iron made with Pit-coale, Sea-coale, &c.* 1665. Reprinted in 1851 by 'J.N.B.'
Dunn, Matthias. *An Historical, Geological and Descriptive View of the Coal Trade of the North of England.* Newcastle, 1844.
Dymock, James. *The Manufacturer's Assistant; showing the Nett Cost of the Pound and Spyndle of Cotton Yarn, at any Discount from one and a fourth to Sixty per cent., by Two and a half, and at every Number from Five to Two Hundred and Twenty.* Glasgow, 1798.

Eden, Sir Frederick Morton. *Eight Letters on the Peace; and on the Commerce and Manufactures of Great Britain and Ireland.* 1802.
—— *The State of the Poor.* 3 v., 1797.
Ellison, Thomas. *Handbook of the Cotton Trade.* 1858.

Fairman, William. *An Account of the Public Funds transferrable at the Bank of England, and of the Stocks of some of the Principal Public Companies in London.* 7th ed., revised by Bernard Cohen, 1824.
Fitton, W. *National Regeneration.* 1834.
Fleetwood, William. *Chronicon Preciosum: or, an Account of English Gold and Silver Money; the Price of Corn and other Commodities.* 1707; reprinted, 1745.
Francis, John. *Chronicles and Characters of the Stock Exchange.* 1849.

———— *History of the Bank of England, its times and traditions.* 2 v., 1847.

Frost, John. *Cheap Coals: or, a Countermine to the Minister and his Three City Members.* 1792.

[Great Britain] *Geological Survey Memoirs. Report on the Geology of Cornwall, Devon, and West Somerset* [by Sir Henry Thomas de la Bêche]. 1839.

Gilbart, James William. *The History and Principles of Banking.* 1834.

Glover, Richard. *The Substance of the Evidence delivered to a Committee of the Honourable House of Commons by the Merchants and Traders of London, concerned in the Trade to Germany and Holland, and of the Dealers in Foreign Linens, as summed up by Mr. Glover.* 1774.

Gordon, George, *The History of our National Debts and Taxes, from the Year MDCLXXXVIII to the Year MDCLI [sic].* 2nd ed., 1753.

Greg, J. R. *Observations on the Proposed Duties on the Exportation of Coals; with Tables and Statements, from Parliamentary Returns and other Authentic Sources.* 1842.

Grellier, J. J. *A History of the National Debt, from the Revolution in 1688 to the Beginning of the Year 1800.* 1810.

———— *Terms of All the Loans which have been Raised for the Public Service during the Last Fifty Years.* 1799; 3rd ed., 1805.

Hamilton, Robert. *An Inquiry concerning the Rise and Progress, Redemption and Present State, and Management of the National Debt of Great Britain and Ireland.* 1813; 3rd ed., Edinburgh, 1818, reprinted in J. R. McCulloch, ed., *Select Tracts on the National Debt* (1857), 427-688.

Hely-Hutchinson, John. *The Commercial Restraints of Ireland Considered.* Dublin, 1779.

Henwood, W. J. "Statistical Notices of the Mines in Cornwall and Devon," *Transactions of The Royal Geological Society of Cornwall,* V (London and Penzance, 1843), 461-82.

History of the Rise, Progress, and Present State of Banking in All Parts of the World. 1833.

Hooke, Andrew. *An Essay on the National Debt, and National Capital: or, The Account truly stated, debtor and creditor.* 1750.

Hopkins, Thomas. *Great Britain for the last Forty Years; being an Historical and Analytical Account of its Finances, Economy, & General Condition, during that Period.* 1834.

Hunter, William. *The Outport Collector and Comptroller's Guide, or a Complete View of the Method of Collecting the Duties on Coals, Culm, and Cinders.* 1764.

An Illustration of Mr. Joplin's Views on Currency, and Plan for its Improvement; together with Observations applicable to the Present State of the Money Market; in a series of Letters. 1825.

An Important Crisis, in the Callico and Muslin Manufactory in Great Britain, Explained. 1788.

PRIMARY SOURCES

The Interest of Great Britain in Supplying Herself with IRON: Impartially Consider'd. 1756?

Ireland. Trustees of the Linen and Hempen Manufactures. *To the Right Honourable and Honourable The Trustees of the Linen Board, The Report of John Arbuthnot, Esq., Inspector-General for the Provinces of Leinster, Munster and Connaught.* Dublin, 1783.

Jacob, William. *An Historical Inquiry into the Production and Consumption of the Precious Metals.* 2 v., 1831.

James, Henry. *Essays on Money, Exchanges, and Political Economy.* 1820.

———— *State of the Nation. The Causes and Effects of the Rise and Fall in Value of Property and Commodities from the year 1790 to the present time.* 1835.

James, John. *History of the Worsted Manufacture in England.* 1857.

Joplin, Thomas. *The Advantages of the Proposed National Bank of England, both to the Public and its Proprietory, briefly explained.* 1833.

———— *An Analysis and History of the Currency Question.* 1832.

———— *Outlines of a System of Political Economy.* 1823.

———— *Views on the Currency: in which the Connexion between Corn and Currency is shown; the nature of our System of Currency explained; and the Merits of the Corn Bill, the Branch Banks, the Extension of the Bank Charter, and the Small Note Act Examined.* 1828.

Kelly, Patrick. *The Universal Cambist and Commercial Instructor.* 1811.

King, 7th Baron, Peter. *Thoughts on the Restriction of Payments in Specie at the Banks of England and Ireland.* 1803.

The Late Measures of the Ship-owners in the Coal-Trade fully examined in a letter to the Rt. Hon. William Pitt. 1786.

Lauderdale, 8th Earl of, James Maitland. *An Inquiry into the Nature and Origin of Public Wealth, and into the Means and Causes of its Increase.* Edinburgh, 1804.

———— *Thoughts on the Alarming State of the Circulation and on the Means of Redressing the Pecuniary Grievances in Ireland.* Edinburgh, 1805.

Laybourne, Henry. *Tracts upon our Wool, and Woollen Trade.* 1744.

Leatham, William. *Letters on the Currency.* 1840.

Lemon, Sir Charles. "Statistics of the Copper Mines of Cornwall," *Journal of the Statistical Society of London,* I (1838), 65-84.

A Letter to the Honourable A————r M————re, Com————ner of Trade and Plantation. 1714.

List of Country Bankers. 1813.

London, John. *Some Considerations on the Importance of the Woollen Manufactures.* 1740.

Lowe, Joseph. *The Present State of England.* 1822.

Luccock, John. *The Nature and Properties of Wool.* Leeds, 1805.

188

Macardy, Joseph. *Outlines of Banks, Banking, and Currency.* Manchester, 1840.
McArthur, John. *Financial and Political Facts of the Eighteenth and the Present Century; with comparative estimates of the revenue, expediture, debts, manufactures, and commerce of Great Britain.* 3rd. ed., 1801.
McCulloch, John Ramsay. *A Dictionary, Practical, Theoretical and Historical, of Commerce and Commercial Navigation.* 1832; 3rd ed., 1837; 8th ed., 2 v., 1854.
———— *Historical Sketch of the Bank of England.* 1831.
———— *The Literature of Political Economy: a classified catalogue of select publications in the different departments of that science, with historical, critical, and biographical notices.* 1845.
———— *Observations on the Duty on Sea-Borne Coal.* 1380.
———— *Observations on the Report from and Minutes of Evidence taken before the Select Committee of the House of Lords on The Coal Trade. From The Edinburgh Review for April 1830.* Newcastle, 1830.
———— *Remarks on the Coal Trade; and on the various duties and charges on coal, in the Port of London, &c.* Newcastle, 1830.
———— ed., *Select Tracts on the National Debt.* 1857.
———— *A Statistical Account of the British Empire: exhibiting its extent, physical capacities, population, industry, and civil and religious institutions.* 2 v., 1837.
MacGregor, John. *Commercial Statistics. A Digest of the Productive Resources, Commercial Legislation, Customs Tariffs, Navigation, Port and Quarantine Laws, and Charges, Shipping, Imports and Exports, and the Monies, Weights, and Measures of all Nations.* 4 v., 1847-48.
Macleod, Henry Dunning. *The Theory and Practice of Banking: with the elementary principles of Currency, Prices, Credit, and Exchanges.* 2 v., 1855.
Macpherson, David. *Annals of Commerce, Manufactures, Fisheries, and Navigation, with brief notices of the arts and sciences connected with them. Containing the commercial transactions of the British Empire and other countries, from the earliest accounts to the Meeting of the Union Parliament in January, 1801; and comprehending the most valuable part of the late Mr. Anderson's History of Commerce.* 4 v., 1805.
———— *The History of the European Commerce with India.* 1812.
The Manufacture of Iron. 1837.
Marshall, John. *Digest of all the Accounts relating to the Population, Productions, Revenues, Financial Operations, Manufactures, Shipping, Colonies, Commerce, &c. &c. of the United Kingdom of Great Britain and Ireland, diffused through more than 600 volumes of Journals, Reports and Papers presented to Parliament during the last thirty-five years.* 1833.
Martin, R. Montgomery. *Taxation of the British Empire.* 1833.
Massie, Joseph. *Ways and Means for Raising the Extraordinary Supplies to Carry On the War, &c.* 1757.
Morgan, William. *An Appeal to the People of Great Britain, on the Present Alarming State of the Public Finances, and of Public Credit.* 5 eds., 1797.
Mushet, Robert. *An Attempt to Explain from Facts the Effect of the Issues of the Bank of England, upon its own Interests, Public Credit, and Country Banks.* 1826.

————— *An Enquiry into the Effects produced on the National Currency and Rates of Exchange, by the Bank Restriction Bill.* 1810.

Oddy, J. Jepson. *European Commerce.* 1805.

Page, Richard. *Banks and Bankers.* 2nd ed., 1843.

Pebrer, Pablo. *Taxation, Revenue, Expenditure, Power, Statistics, and Debt of the Whole British Empire.* 1833.

Playfair, William. *The Commerical and Political Atlas, representing, by means of stained copper-plate charts, the exports, imports, and general trade of England; the national debt, and other public accounts; with observations and remarks. To which are added charts of the revenue and debts of Ireland, done in the same manner by James Corry, Esq.* 1786; 2nd ed., 1787; 3rd ed., 1801.

————— *A Letter on our Agricultural Distresses, their causes and remedies: accompanied with tables and copper-plate charts, shewing and comparing the prices of wheat and labour, from 1565 to 1821, addressed to the Lords and Commons.* 1821; 2nd and 3rd eds., 1822.

————— *A Real Statement of the Finances and Resources of Great Britain; illustrated by two Copper-Plate Charts. For the Use of the Enemies of England.* 1796.

————— *The Statistical Breviary.* 1801.

Porter, George R. *The Progress of the Nation, in its Various Social and Economical Relations, from the Beginning of the Nineteenth Century to the Present Day.* 3 v., 1836-43; 2nd ed., 1846; 3rd ed., 1851.

————— A "Sketch of the Progress and Present Extent of Savings Banks in the United Kingdom," *Journal of the Statistical Society of London,* IX (1846), 1-13.

Postlethwayt, James. *A History of the Public Revenue.* 1758.

Powell, John [attributed to]. *The Assize and Price of Bread.* 1808.

Powell, John. *The Causes of the Present Crisis Explained. First part of an analytical exposition of the erroneous principles and ruinous consequences of the commercial system of Great Britain, Illustrative of its influence on the physical, social, and moral condition of the people.* 1825.

————— *Statistical Illustrations of the Territorial Extent and Population; Commerce, Taxation, Consumption, Insolvency, Pauperism and Crime of the British Empire.* 1825; 3rd ed., 1827.

Price, Richard. *An Appeal to the Public, on the Subject of the National Debt.* 1772; 2nd ed., 1774.

————— *Observations on the Nature of Civil Liberty.* 1776.

————— *State of the Public Debts and Finances at the Signing of the Preliminary Articles of Peace in January.* 1783.

Pryce, W. *Mineralogia Cornubiensis; a treatise on minerals, mines and mining.* 1778.

Quin, Michael Joseph. *The Trade of Banking in England: embracing the substance of the evidence taken before the Secret Committee of the House of Commons, digested and arranged under appropriate heads.* 1833.

A Review of the Banking System of Britain; with observations on the injurious effects of the Bank of England Charter, and the general benefits of unrestricted banking companies. Edinburgh, 1821.

Ricardo, David. *Observations on some Passages in an Article in the Edinburgh Review, on the Depreciation of Paper Currency.* 1811.

——— *Proposals for an Economical and Secure Currency; with Observations on the Profits of the Bank of England, as they regard the Public and the Proprietors of Bank Stock.* 2nd ed., 1816.

Roberts, Lewes. *The Treasure of Trafficke.* 1641.

Rooke, John. *An Inquiry into the Principles of National Wealth.* Edinburgh, 1824.

Rose, George. *A Brief Examination into the Increase of the Revenue, Commerce, and Manufactures of Great Britain from 1792 to 1799.* 5th ed., 1799.

Salt, Samuel. *Statistics and Calculations.* 1845.

Savary des Bruslons, Jacques. *The Universal Dictionary of Trade and Commerce.* Translated, with large additions and "improvements," by Malachy Postlethwayt. 2 v., 1751-55.

Scrivenor, Harry. *A History of the Iron Trade, from the Earliest Records to the Present Period.* 1841; 2nd ed., 1854.

——— *The Railroads of the United Kingdom Statistically Considered, in relation to their Extent, Capital, Amalgamations...concisely arranged from solely authentic documents.* 1849.

Sheffield, 1st Earl of, John Baker Holroyd. *Observations on the Manufactures, Trade, and Present State of Ireland.* 2nd ed., 1785.

——— *Remarks on the Deficiency of Grain, occasioned by the Bad Harvest of 1799.* 1800.

A Short Essay upon Trade in General. By "A Lover of His Country." 1741.

Sinclair, Sir John. *Hints; addressed to the Public calculated to dispel the gloomy ideas which have been lately entertained of the state of our finances.* 1783.

——— *The History of the Public Revenue of the British Empire.* 3rd ed., 3 v., 1803-04.

Smith, Adam. *An Enquiry into the Wealth of Nations.* 2 v. 1776.

Smith, John. *Memoirs of Wool.* 2 v., 1747; 2nd ed., 1757.

Some Further Observations on the Treaty of Navigation and Commerce, between Great-Britain and France. 1713.

State of the Facts Relating to the Linen-Manufacture of Great Britain and Ireland. 1750?

Stephenson, Robert. *An Inquiry into the State and Progress of the Linen Manufacture of Ireland.* Dublin, 1757.

A Survey of the National Debt, 1745.

Sykes, John. *An Account of the Dreadful Explosion in Wallsend Colliery.* Newcastle, 1835.

Tables and Facts Relative to the Coal Duties. 1819.

Taylor, John. *A Catechism of Foreign Exchanges, and the Effects of an Abasement of Bullion.* 1835.

———— *Currency Investigated, with a View to its Scientific Principles. In a series of essays, published between the years 1832 and 1845.* 1845.

Taylor, Richard Cowling. *Statistics of Coal.* Philadelphia, 1848.

Taylor, T. John. *Observations, addressed to the Coal Owners of Northumberland and Durham on the Coal Trade of those Counties.* Newcastle, 1846.

Temple, William. *A Refutation of one of the Principal Arguments in the Reverend Mr. Smith's Memoirs of Wool.* 1750.

Tooke, Thomas. *Considerations on the State of the Currency.* 1826.

———— *A History of Prices and of the State of the Circulation from 1793 to 1837.* 6 v., 1838-57. Vols. 5 and 6 (1857) with the collaboration of William Newmarch.

———— *A Letter to Lord Grenville on the Effects ascribed to the Resumption of Cash Payments on the Value of the Currency.* 1829.

———— *On the Currency in connexion with the Corn Trade; and on the Corn Laws.* 1829.

———— *Thoughts and Details on the High and Low Prices of the Thirty Years from 1793 to 1822.* 1824.

Twigg's Corrected List of the Country Bankers of England and Wales. [Assembled by T. Twigg.] 1830.

Unwin, George. *Letters, Remarks, &c. with a View to Open an Extensive Trade in the Article of Tin, from the County of Cornwall to India, Persia and China.* 1790.

———— *Observations upon the Export Trade of Tin and Copper to India, with reference to the expected renewal of the Honourable East India Company's Charter; and also upon the present state of the tin trade with Europe and its colonies, Africa, and America.* Truro, 1811.

Ure, Andrew. *The Cotton Manufacture of Great Britain.* 2 v., 1836.

Vansittart, Nicholas. *An Inquiry into the State of the Finances of Great Britain; in answer to Mr. Morgan's facts.* 1796.

Van Sommer, James. *Tables exhibiting the Various Fluctuations in Three Per Cent Consols, in every month during each year, from 1789 to 1847 inclusive.* 1848.

Vaughan, William. "On Wet Docks, Quays, and Warehouses, for the Port of London; with hints respecting trade" (1793), in Vaughan, *Tracts on Docks and Commerce.* 1839.

A View of the Taxes, Funds, and Publick Revenues of England. 1712.

Wade, John. *Digest of Facts and Principles, on Banking and Commerce, with a Plan for preventing future re-actions.* 1826.

PRIMARY SOURCES

Waterston, William. *Cyclopaedia of Commerce.* 1843.

Wheatley, John. *An Essay on the Theory of Money and Principles of Commerce.* 1807.

———— *Remarks on Currency and Commerce.* 1803.

Whitworth, Sir Charles. *A Collection of the Supplies, and Ways and Means, from the Revolution to the Present Time.* 1763; 2nd ed., 1765.

———— *The State of the Trade of Great Britain in its Imports and Exports, progressively from the Year 1697: also of the Trade to each particular Country, during the above period, distinguishing each year.* 1776.

Wilson, Robert. *An Enquiry into the Causes of the High Prices of Corn and Labour.* Edinburgh, 1811.

———— *Observations on the Depreciation of Money and the State of our Currency.* Edinburgh, 1811.

Yates, John Ashton. *Essays on Currency and Circulation and on the Influence of our Paper System on the Industry, Trade, and Revenue of Great Britain.* Liverpool, 1827.

———— *A Letter on the Distresses of the Country.* 2nd ed., 1817.

Young, Arthur. *An Enquiry into the Progressive Value of Money in England, as marked by the price of agricultural products, with observations upon Sir G. Shuckburgh's table of appreciation: the whole deduced from a great variety of authorities, not before collected.* 1812.

———— *Political Arithmetic. Containing observations on the present state of Great Britain; and the principles of her policy in the encouragement of agriculture. Addressed to the oeconomical societies established in Europe.* 1774.

SECONDARY SOURCES

Andrews, J. H. "Two Problems in the Interpretation of the Port Books," *Economic History Review,* 2nd series, IX (1956), 119-22.

Annals of the Royal Statistical Society, 1834-1934. [By Henry W. Macrosty, with a contribution by J. Bonar.] 1934.

Ashton, Thomas Southcliffe. *Economic Fluctuations in England 1700-1800.* Oxford, 1959.

SECONDARY SOURCES

———— *An Economic History of England: the 18th Century.* 1964.
———— *Iron and Steel in the Industrial Revolution.* Manchester and London, 1924.
———— and Joseph Sykes. *The Coal Industry of the Eighteenth Century.* Manchester, 1929.

Barton, Denys B. *A History of Tin Mining and Smelting in Cornwall.* Truro [1967].
Beveridge, Sir William H., and others. *Prices and Wages in England from the Twelfth to the Nineteenth Century.* Vol. 1. 1939.
Binney, John E. D. *British Public Finance and Administration, 1774-92.* Oxford, 1958.
Black, Robert Denis Collison. *A Catalogue of Pamphlets on Economic Subjects Published between 1750 and 1900 and Now Housed in Irish Libraries.* New York, 1969.
Bowley, A. L. *Wages in the United Kingdom in the Nineteenth Century.* 1900.

Carus-Wilson, Eleanora M., and Olive Coleman. *England's Export Trade, 1275-1547.* Oxford, 1963.
Chapman, Sir Sydney J. *The Lancashire Cotton Industry: a Study in Economic Development.* Manchester, 1904.
Clapham, John H. *The Bank of England.* 2 v., Cambridge, 1944.
———— *An Economic History of Modern Britian.* 3 v., Cambridge, 1926-38; 2nd ed. of vol. 1, 1930.
Clark, George Norman. *Guide to English Commercial Statistics, 1696-1782.* 1938.
Cockroft, Grace Amelia. *The Public Life of George Chalmers.* New York, 1939.
Cole, W. A. "Trends in Eighteenth-Century Smuggling," *Economic History Review,* 2nd series, X (1958), 395-410.
Collier, Frances. *The Family Economy of the Working Classes in the Cotton Industry, 1784-1833.* Manchester, 1965.
Coppieters, Emmanuel. *English Bank Note Circulation, 1694-1954.* Louvain, 1955.
Craig, Sir John. *The Mint: a History of the London Mint from A.D. 287 to 1948.* Cambridge, 1953.

Davis, Ralph. "English Foreign Trade, 1660-1700," *Economic History Review,* 2nd series, VII (1954), 150-66.
———— "Merchant Shipping in the Economy of the Late Seventeenth Century," *Economic History Review,* 2nd series, IX (1956), 59-73.
Deane, Phyllis. "The Output of the British Woolen Industry in the Eighteenth Century," *Journal of Economic History,* XVII (1957), 207-23.
———— and W. A. Cole. *British Economic Growth, 1688-1959.* Cambridge, 1962; 2nd ed., 1967.
Edwards, Michael M. *The Growth of the British Cotton Trade, 1780-1815.* Manchester, 1967.

194

Ellison, Thomas. *The Cotton Trade of Great Britain.* 1886.
Flinn, M. W. "The Growth of the English Iron Industry, 1660-1760," *Economic History Review,* 2nd series, XI (1958), 144-53.
Funkhouser, H. G. "The Historical Development of the Graphical Representation of Statistical Data," *Osiris,* III (1937), 269-397.
Fussell, G. E., and Constance Goodman, "Eighteenth Century Estimates of British Sheep and Wool Production," *Agricultural History,* IV (1930), 131-51.

Gayer, Arthur D., W. W. Rostow, and Anna J. Schwartz. *The Growth and Fluctuation of the British Economy, 1790-1850.* 2 v., Oxford, 1953.
Gill, Conrad. *The Rise of the Irish Linen Industry.* Oxford, 1925.

Hall, Frederick George. *The Bank of Ireland, 1783-1946.* Dublin, 1949.
Hamilton, Henry. *The English Brass and Copper Industries to 1800.* 1926.
Harvard University. Graduate School of Business. Baker Library. Kress Library of Business and Economics. *Catalogue.* 4 v., Boston, Mass., 1940-67.
Horne, H. Oliver. *A History of Savings Banks.* 1947.
Horner, John. *The Linen Trade of Europe during the Spinning-wheel Period.* Belfast, 1920.
Hulme, E. W. "A Statistical History of the Iron Trade of England and Wales, 1717-50," *Transactions of the Newcomen Society,* IX (1928-29), 12-35.
Hunt, Christopher J. *The Lead Miners of the Northern Pennines.* Manchester, 1970.
Hunt, Robert. *British Mining: a treatise on the history, discovery, practical development and future prospects of metalliferous mines in the United Kingdom.* 1884.

Imlah, Albert H. *Economic Elements in the Pax Britannica: Studies in British Foreign Trade in the Nineteenth Century.* Cambridge, Mass., 1958.

John, Arthur H. *The Industrial Development of South Wales, 1750-1850.* Cardiff, 1950.
Jones, John Harry. *The Tinplate Industry.* 1914.

Kendall, Maurice George, ed. *The Sources and Nature of the Statistics of the United Kingdom.* 2 v., 1952-57.

Landes, David S. *The Unbound Prometheus: Technological Change and Industrial Development in Western Europe from 1750 to the Present.* 1969.
Lewis, George Randall. *The Stannaries: a Study of the English Tin Miner.* Boston and New York, 1908.
Lewis, William John. *Lead Mining in Wales.* Cardiff, 1967.

London, University [of]. Goldsmiths' Company's Library of Economic Literature. *Catalogue of the Goldsmiths' Library of Economic Literature*. Compiled by Margaret Canney and David Knott. Vol. I. Cambridge, 1970.

Mantoux, Paul J. *The Industrial Revolution in the Eighteenth Century*. 1961.
Meade, Richard. *The Coal and Iron Industries of the United Kingdom*. 1882.
Minchinton, W. E. *The British Tinplate Industry, a History*. Oxford, 1957.
Mitchell, Brian R., with the collaboration of Phyllis Deane. *Abstract of British Historical Statistics*. Cambridge, 1962.
———— and H. G. Jones. *Second Abstract of British Historical Statistics*. Cambridge, 1971.
Mouat, Frederick J. *A History of the Statistical Society of London*. 1885.

Nef, John U. *The Rise of the British Coal Industry*. 2 v., 1932.

Pressnell, Leslie Sedden. *Country Banking in the Industrial Revolution*. Oxford, 1956.
Price, Jacob M. "Notes on Some London Price-Currents, 1667-1715," *Economic History Review*, 2nd series, VII (1954), 240-50.

Rive, Alfred. "A Short History of Tobacco Smuggling," *Economic History*, I (1929), 554-69.
Robson, Robert. *The Cotton Industry in Britain*. 1957.
Roepke, Howard G. *Movements of the British Iron and Steel Industry, 1720 to 1951*. Urbana, Illinois, 1956.
Rogers, James E. T. *A History of Agriculture and Prices in England, from the Year after the Oxford Parliament (1259) to the Commencement of the Continental War (1793)*. 7 v., Oxford, 1866-1902.
Rowe, John. *Cornwall in the Age of the Industrial Revolution*. Liverpool, 1953.

Schubert, John R. T. *History of the British Iron and Steel Industry from c. 450 B.C. to A.D. 1775*. 1957.
Schumpeter, Elizabeth Boody. *English Overseas Trade Statistics, 1697-1808* [with an introduction by T. S. Ashton]. Oxford, 1960.
———— "English Prices and Public Finance, 1660-1822," *Review of Economic Statistics*, XX (1938), 21-37.
Silberling, Norman J. "British Prices and Business Cycles, 1779-1850," *Review of Economic Statistics*, V (1923), Supplement 2, 219-62.
Smelser, Neil J. *Social Change in the Industrial Revolution, an Application of Theory to the British cotton industry*. Chicago and London, 1959.
Stone, Lawrence. "Elizabethan Overseas Trade," *Economic History Review*, 2nd series, II (1949), 30-58.
———— "State Control in Sixteenth-Century England," *Economic History Review*, XVII (1947), 103-20.

Sweezy, Paul M. *Monopoly and Competition in the English Coal Trade, 1550-1850.*
Cambridge, Mass., 1938.

Taylor, A. J. "Concentration and Specialization in the Lancashire Cotton Industry, 1825-1850," *Economic History Review,* 2nd series, I (1949), 114-22.

Wadsworth, Alfred P., and Julia D. Mann. *The Cotton Trade and Industrial
Lancashire, 1600-1780.* Manchester, 1931.
Willan, Thomas S. *The English Coasting Trade, 1600-1750.* Manchester, 1938.
Williams, Judith B. *A Guide to the Printed Materials for English Social and
Economic History, 1750-1850.* 2 v., New York, 1926.
Wood, George Henry. *The History of Wages in the Cotton Trade during the Past
Hundred Years.* 1910.